Environmental Networks and Social Movement Theory

SU
COL

Environmental Networks and Social Movement Theory

Clare Saunders

B L O O M S B U R Y
LONDON • NEW DELHI • NEW YORK • SYDNEY

Bloomsbury Academic

An imprint of Bloomsbury Publishing Plc

50 Bedford Square	1385 Broadway
London	New York
WC1B 3DP	NY 10018
UK	USA

www.bloomsbury.com

Bloomsbury is a registered trade mark of Bloomsbury Publishing Plc

First published 2013
Paperback edition first published 2014

© Clare Saunders, 2013

British Library Cataloguing-in-Publication Data
A catalogue record for this book is available from the British Library.

ISBN: HB:	978-1-8496-6052-5
PB:	978-1-4725-8971-2
ePub:	978-1-8496-6053-2
ePDF:	978-1-8496-6487-5

Library of Congress Cataloging-in-Publication Data
A catalog record for this book is available from the Library of Congress.

Typeset by Newgen Imaging Systems Pvt Ltd, Chennai, India
Printed and bound by CPI Group (UK) Ltd, Croydon, CR0 4YY

I dedicate this book to all the good people who are working hard to protect Mother Earth.

Contents

List of Tables

List of Figures

Acknowledgements

This book would not have happened without the support of many people to whom I am very grateful. Thanks to Graham Smith who sparked my interest in environmental politics. He also carefully read more than one draft and offered comments that have immensely improved the book. Christopher Rootes, Christopher Pickvance, Brian Doherty, Stephan Price, Silke Roth and David Owen have each helped shape my work. Thanks also to Cristiana Olcese for keeping the Caught in the Act project work ticking along while I've been preoccupied with this book project. *Sociological Research Online* and the *British Journal of Sociology* have allowed me to reproduce versions of papers that have been published in their journals (Chapter 5 [Saunders 2009a] and Chapter 7 [Saunders 2008]). Special thanks to Caroline Wintersgill from Bloomsbury for commissioning this book, and for her patience for the final manuscript.

My nearest and dearest also deserve their fair share of accolades. Special thanks to my dear husband, Ian, who has taken more than his fair share of turns at cleaning out our pet rabbits' hutches to buy me time to finish this book. Those cups of tea delivered to my desk on rainy days – when he has been unable to go out and do his gardening work – are worth more than he can know. Thanks also to my family, particularly to Mum who inspired me by repeating (countless times), 'Have you finished that book yet? Come on, Clare!'

I am very grateful for the opportunity to have been a part of the late Local Groups Department at Friends of the Earth (now the Capacity Building Team), the Environmental Direct Action Group, and Chiswick Wildlife Group. Participation in these groups allowed me to develop, first-hand, a broad understanding of different types of environmental action.

This book is based on research conducted throughout my academic career, but which began during my time as a Research Assistant on an EC Framework Programme 7 project called the Transformation of Environmental Activism (ENV4-CT97_0514), directed by Christopher Rootes. I extended this research with my PhD thesis, 'Collaboration, Competition and Conflict: Social movement and interaction dynamics in London's environmental movement', which was funded by the Economic and Social Research Council (award number R42200134447). I thank the ESRC for funding my doctoral research.

1 Introduction

ONDON, 1 APRIL 2009. 'Fossil Fools Day'. On this day activists from a number of different environmental and social justice organizations took to the streets for two days of action to call an end to 'climate chaos, economic meltdown and repossessions'. These actions were planned to coincide with a meeting of the leaders of the world's 20 richest countries: the G20. Their meeting was designed to negotiate a rescue package for the flailing world economy. There were three main protest actions, organized by different wings of what has been termed the environmental movement. The Campaign Against Climate Change, armed with a rapidly melting 'iceberg' (a large chunk of ice), held a 'climate emergency' demonstration and rally at the Excel Centre; around 4,000 Climate Campers pitched tents outside the Climate Exchange and shut it down; and there was a 'G20 Meltdown' street party outside the Bank of England.

After much deliberation, my husband and I decided that the Campaign Against Climate Change's legally approved demonstration outside the Excel Centre was the most approachable; it would, we believed, land us in the least trouble. Since it was billed to last from 12.30 p.m. to 7.30 p.m., we were disappointed to find only around 40 people there for the lunchtime photo opportunity, with numbers dwindling rapidly to single figures by 2 p.m. Although there was a small rally in the evening, it seemed fruitless to wait all afternoon so we set off to visit the Climate Camp. But, before we had returned to the train station, we were stopped by police officers and searched under terrorism legislation on suspicion of intent to conduct criminal damage. If the police were behaving like that near a legally approved demonstration, what would they be like in the vicinity of the Climate Camp? Concerned about heavy-handed policing, we were put off from attending other events and returned home, instead.

Our experience in London that day is illustrative of several issues discussed in depth in this book. Why did only around 40 people attend a legal demonstration on what is, arguably, the most important issue facing humanity and all the species with which we share the planet? In particular, where were the Friends of the Earth and Greenpeace supporters? And why did the Climate Camp hold a separate demonstration rather than collaborate with the Campaign Against Climate Change?

Phil Thornhill, coordinator of the Campaign Against Climate Change, responded to the first question stating, 'Well, this is fairly typical of a Wednesday lunchtime demonstration' (personal correspondence, 1 April 2009). However, this could not account for the presence of thousands of people congregating elsewhere in central London at the same point in time. A better explanation, particularly to the second and third questions, stems from the fact that environmental organizations each have different strategies, degrees of reputability with decision-makers, organizational identities and resource constraints. The Campaign Against Climate Change's approach was a media-friendly stunt. Others might interpret it as a form of lobbying – attempting to politely persuade the G20 leaders to take climate change seriously. This is part of the Campaign Against Climate Change's broader goal to build a mass movement by attracting wide-ranging public support for demands for strong national climate change legislation and a robust international climate policy framework. In contrast, Climate Campers and G20 Meltdown participants, generally adverse to what they deem ineffectual lobbying, attempted to directly close down the institutions they considered responsible for causing climate change. Unlike the Campaign Against Climate Change and Friends of the Earth, Climate Camp and G20 Meltdown are fluid networks of activists, without formal organizational structures. Consequently, they are immune from some of the constraints faced by formal organizations. Formal organizations have to engage in organizational maintenance; it is necessary for them to maintain their memberships to keep themselves financially afloat and they have responsibilities towards their staff. The need for organizational maintenance is arguably a key reason why Friends of the Earth, conspicuously absent from events on Fossil Fools Day, had instead participated in the 'Put People First' march and rally the previous Saturday. This mainstream and legally authorized demonstration, organized by a coalition of over 100 environmental, social justice and labour organizations was a safer bet for an organization with a reputation to uphold. In the event, around 35,000 people marched against poverty, inequality and the threat of climate chaos. Unlike the Climate Camp and G20 meltdown, the Put People First march was non-confrontational and remained peaceful throughout, leaving Friends of the Earth's reputation and public image untarnished.

The choices for collaboration that are made by environmental organizations are, to a large extent, determined by these strategic, identity and resource differences. In this book, I consider the extent to which social movement theory can help us understand how and why these differences occur and why they have such a profound affect on the shape and form of networking between environmental organizations. The rest of this introductory chapter outlines the central aims of the book; provides a rationale for studying the environmental networks from a social movement theory perspective; introduces the theoretical and methodological approach and gives a flavour of the chapters that follow.

Aims

This book has three central aims. The first is to evaluate and contextualize, in relation to British environmentalism, key strands of social movement theory. The second is to identify and account for interaction between environmental organizations[1] within environmental networks. The third is to make a theoretical contribution by introducing and applying an analytical framework that has potential to explain the nature of inter-organizational interactions in a range of social movement fields.

I use the term 'environmental networks' to avoid 'environmental movement', which I suggest is less analytically useful. The concept of a social movement is explored in more depth in Chapter 2, but suffice it for now to point out that the concept of 'social movement' does not comfortably sit with the broad range of environmental organizations commonly thought to be part of the environmental movement. To be too prescriptive about which organizations are in or out of a movement would preclude examination of interesting interactions between a wide range of organizations – across the networks' spatial dimensions (national, regional and local) *and* ideological strands (conservationists, political ecologists/reformists and radical environmentalists). As I have illustrated in my previous work, the concept of social movement is rather sketchy on the amount of networking required to create a social movement dynamic (Saunders 2007a, 2011). Without getting fixated on the question of whether the networking is sufficient to constitute a movement, I examine interaction mostly in terms of collaboration in campaigns, with some reference to the sharing of information. The central question then becomes not whether a movement exists, but how one might explain the patterns of interaction found.

In order to make generalizations about social movements it may be considered necessary to look beyond environmental networks. Yet there are also good reasons for restricting the study to a single field of contention. I focus specifically on environmentalism in order to give the social movement theories discussed a decent airing in relation to one particular field of contention. This helps avoid accusations of cherry-picking case studies that fit the theories, or being charged with theory bashing (a term coined by Lofland 1983, described below). Equally, there are important reasons for focusing on the British case: it is one of the most active and well-developed environmental movements in the world. In many ways it has had a similar trajectory to the equally well developed environmental movement in Germany (Rucht and Roose 2007). The most striking difference between the British and German cases is that resistance to nuclear power has been stronger in Germany, historically linking environmentalism with left-wing movements – something that has not occurred to the same extent in Britain (Rootes 1992). Despite this, the British environmental movement is not drastically different from many of its European counterparts: conservationist, reformist and radical environmental groups coexist in many Western European democracies (Rootes 2007). At the same time, the British case is illuminating because environmentalism in Britain is not torn by such dramatic divisions as it is in the United States. There, anthropes and misanthropes and preservationists and conservationists are in separate camps and are sometimes overtly hostile towards one another.

The research conducted for this book took place in London. The emphasis on London is justified because it has the highest concentration of environmental organizations in Britain (Rootes and Miller 2000). Of the 203 national environmental organizations listed in The Environment Council's *Who's Who in the Environment* (1999), 73 were located in London, as well as numerous regional groups such as the London Wildlife Trust and the Sustainable London Trust. London has also spawned vibrant local environmental networks (Rootes, et al. 2001). The abundance of different types of environmental organizations and networks provides plenty of scope for analysing interaction between and among environmental organizations working in different ways at multiple levels.

Why research networking among environmental organizations?

The most obvious reason for focusing on networking among environmental organizations is to address a gap in the literature. The three dominant phases of research on environmental movements have tended to overlook networking. The three phases are: new values, institutionalization, and radical conflicts/local oppositions (della Porta and Rucht 2002). The first suggested that environmentalism was spawned by new post-material values. The provision of economic security was considered to have made it more likely that people shift their attention to new non-material goals like securing a healthy environment (Inglehart 1971, 1987, 1990). The second phase noted how many environmental organizations had become increasingly tame as they became institutionalized – that is to say, as they grew in size, they developed formal organizational structures, gained access to policymakers and consequently lost their radical edge. The third looked at how radicals and locals crafted campaigns to supplement or supplant those of the increasingly tame national organizations.

While our understanding of environmentalism has benefited from many illuminating studies within these phases, there are some limitations in extant scholarship.

The commonly used approaches have tended to result in either broad-brush descriptions of environmentalism – which sometimes mistakenly assume ideological and tactical homogeneity – and analysis of individual organizations and/or specific conflicts. The focus on environmental networks deployed in this book extends work on environmentalism beyond broad-brush approaches and case studies. It finds heterogeneity rather than homogeneity and looks at groups campaigning on a wide range of issues, despite a special focus on campaigns against aviation and climate change. It also has the advantage deploying a multilevel approach, firmly placing frequently overlooked regional (by which I mean organizations working across London) and local organizations in the picture. And it allows us to explore interactions between different types of organizations that a focus on movements might have prevented. According to some scholars, for example, organizations that do not challenge the social order should not be included as part of a social movement (see Doherty's [2002] book on what he calls 'the green movement'). A focus on the system-challenging green movement (Doherty 2002) would prevent us from looking at conservation groups, local residents associations and not in my back yard (NIMBY) groups, each of which plays an important role in looking after the environment in one way or another (see Chapter 3).

Although an account made at the turn of the millennium stated that local environmentalism is 'very lively' and 'appears to be expanding in Britain' (Diani and Donati 1999 : 24–5), environmentalism in Britain has generally, with the exception of Lowe and Goyder's seminal work (1983), been interpreted through national organizations (e.g. Rawcliffe 1998). An exception is Doherty et al.'s (2007) work on local radical environmental networks in Oxford, Manchester and North Wales. By and large, though, when local environmental campaigns and organizations have been researched, findings often materialize as useful, but in some ways limited discussions of particular cases of contention (Seel 1997; North 1998; Barcena and Ibarra 2001; Fillieule 2002). To date, there has been little if any research on the relationship between local, regional and national environmental organizations in Britain, except for my own work (see Saunders 2007b).

The most extensive survey of local environmental activism to be undertaken was in a US context (Kempton et al. 2001: 578). The authors claim: 'We know of no census of local environmental groups previously reported in the literature'. They compared two sites of local environmental activism and concluded that case studies underplay their diversity. Their research also notes the general importance of local environmental groups: 'Local environmental groups are not pale, less influential versions of large national organizations, but are significant in their own right' (557). Drawing on Kempton et al., Lhotka et al. (2008) studied the extent to which local environmental groups exchanged information with one another in Alabama. Parisi et al. (2004) similarly note the importance of local activism, but all three sets of scholars fail to locate local groups within broader environmental networks and none of them have considered environmentalism in Britain.

In addition to there being a lacuna in the literature, it is important to study environmental networks because they are a pervasive component of citizen politics in Britain (Carter 2001: 131). Formal environmental organizations, which are significant players in environmental networks, have a greater total membership than political parties. According to the Database of Archives of Non-Governmental Organizations (2010), 5–8 million people are members of environmental organizations[2] in Britain. Besides actual membership support, the British are generally favourable towards environmental issues. Between 1996–7 and 2006–7, recycling rates rose from 7 per cent to 31 per cent, and over half of the British public claim to be considering doing more of the following: reducing water use, reducing gas and electricity use, wasting less food and recycling more (Randall 2008: 149–51). The environment clearly matters to people. But why is interaction in environmental networks important?

The importance of interaction and networks

In both environmental and social movement studies more broadly, organizational interaction *within* movements has been under-studied (see Zald and Ash 1966; Ash-Garner and Zald 1987). Where intra-social movement networks have been researched, disproportionate emphasis has been given to the role of individuals' social networks in the mobilization process (e.g. Gould 2000; Passy 2003; Mische 2003).[3]

Even though there is little consensus as to what constitutes a social movement, most theorists agree that social movements can be conceived of as *networks of interaction* between individuals and organizations engaging in collective action aimed at achieving or resisting social change (Diani 1992a). This conceptualization is growing in popularity (Diani and Eyerman 1992: 7–10; della Porta and Diani 1999).[4] Considering the abundant use of the term 'network' in social movement theory and its centrality in the concept of a social movement, it is somewhat ironic that systematic studies of intra-movement interaction are largely absent from the literature on environmental movements (note that Diani's work is an obvious and welcome exception, 1992 and with Rambaldo 2007).

The focus on networks also addresses Melucci's (1985: 799) concern over the inadequacy of the term movement. As he states, instead of using the term social movements, 'I prefer to speak of *movement networks* or *movement areas* as the network of groups and individuals sharing a conflictual culture and a collective identity' (emphasis added). While the possibility of a *broad* network of groups *sharing* a conflictual culture and collective identity is debateable (Chapter 7), the emphasis on networks is well placed. One might go so far as to argue that to understand a social movement properly requires due consideration of interaction, otherwise research becomes over-focused on mobilization processes and organizational characteristics (Diani 1992b). Little wonder, then, that Ash-Garner and Zald (1987: 179) claim that 'inter-social movement organization relations are a central dynamic of any social movement'. Further, a focus on networks makes it possible to overcome the 'myopia of the visible' that Melucci (1989: 44) cautioned against. Research subject to the 'myopia of the visible' would involve focusing exclusively on the most visible aspects of social movements, such as active protest events. Consequently, it might miss underlying ideologies, collective identity formation and networking. Networks are important because they allow movements to be sustained during periods of latency. They also provide solidarity and reinforcement crucial for campaign success (Melucci 1985). Thus, some have argued that networks are nothing less than the glue holding movements together (Gerlach 1983: 145). Networks also bring organizations into contact with other allies (including political parties). Consequently, they make organizations difficult to repress, increase their recruitment bases, and encourage innovation and adaptability.

Despite the centrality of the concept of networks in social movement research, Jasper (1997: 61) has been critical of what he calls 'the network approach'. He suggests that networks are overemphasized and only show the expected. This criticism stems mostly from his tendency to equate the use of networks with an approach that constitutes a single paradigm. For him, the network paradigm seeks to explain collective action solely on the basis of the extent to which actors are embedded in existing systems of social relations, ignoring other attributes of actors – such as organizational size, ideology and strategy. Part of his critique is directed towards Diani (1995), who found relatively few ties between environmental organizations in Milan, and apparently overrated their significance. Jasper (1997: 61) suggests that 'we need to push beyond the network metaphor . . . to see what resources, rules, cultural schemas and patterns of interaction lie behind it'. My retort would be that this is *exactly* what this book does – it uses theoretical insights from social movement theories to explore networking. In this book, I look at resources through the lens of resource mobilization theory (Chapter 4), opportunities and constraints through political process theory (Chapter 5) and cultural schemas via new social movement theory (Chapters 6 and 7). My primary research has the additional advantage that London's environment network appears much more vibrant than Milan's, with 149 groups surveyed, contrasting with the 42 that Diani (1995) surveyed.

Doherty (2002: 18) also questions the significance of placing strong emphasis on network links, especially as a key determinant of the existence of a movement. He suggests that focussing on networks as an indicator of social movement membership prevents us from distinguishing between radical groups, reformist groups and those with conservationist orientations. It also makes Greenpeace appear a more marginal player than it really is. However, as this book will demonstrate, it is possible to look at networks while simultaneously distinguishing between different types of environmental organizations. Organizational attributes *and* network properties can be analysed in tandem. Indeed, my synthetic analytical framework (Chapter 8), which recognizes the importance of interactions between and among each of individuals, organizations, campaign targets *and* the polity necessitates that both be analysed together.

Theoretical approach

The theoretical approach I adopt in this book is embedded in a broad range of literature known as social movement theory. This body of theory is drawn from traditions across political science, sociology and social psychology. Social movement theory generally serves *predictive* or *explanatory* functions (or both). While I give most attention to resource mobilization (Chapter 4), political opportunity/process (Chapter 5), new social movement (Chapter 6), identity-oriented (Chapter 7) theories and the *Dynamics of Contention* approach (McAdam et al. 2001) (Chapter 8), I do not entirely dismiss other theoretical approaches that complement these. Thus, the chapter on resource mobilization draws on organizational ecology; my account of political opportunity/process theory is enhanced with pressure group theory and the discussion of new social movements looks more broadly at elements of subcultural theory.

It is important to draw on this broad range of theories in the light of related studies on coalition building *across* different social movements. Like studies on intra-movement networks, coalition building has been given scant academic attention (Van Dyke and McCammon 2010). Yet it is possible to draw upon the few studies that do exist, particularly those that focus on the possibilities for collaboration among disparate groups (Pharr 1996; Ferree and Roth 1998; Rose 2000). This body of research has found that the social movement theories explored in this book each have something to contribute to an explanation of the chances of successful coalition formation. With regard to resources (Chapter 4), money is considered crucial for generating allies, particularly across national borders (Bandy and Smith 2005). In relation to political opportunities (Chapter 5), unfavourable policies and links with the elite can stimulate cooperation; unfavourable policies can bring people together when they feel threatened (McCammon and Campbell 2002); and links with elites provide an avenue contenders will readily coalesce around. On the issue of identity (Chapters 6 and 7), exclusive identities and strict ideologies have been found to restrict the chances of cooperation across movements (Ferree and Roth 1998), whereas flexible and multiple ones are facilitative (Barvoso-Carter 2001; della Porta 2005). And the role of individual movers and shakers who share connections from previous waves of mobilization is regarded as important in bridging different types of organizations (Rose 2000; Corrigal Brown and Meyer 2010). Van Dyke and McCammon (2010) found that the presence of political threats and common ideologies are sufficient conditions to explain coalition formation, and that social connections are an important add-on.

Given that elements of each of the theories work together to explain organizations' choices of allies across social movements, my intention is not to pit one theory against another to explain interaction within environmental networks, but to extract what is useful from each. I argue in Chapter 8 that the approaches are actually quite complementary. Thus, I avoid what might be viewed as a fashion among social movement scholars to engage in what Lofland (1993, 1996: 372) terms 'theory bashing'. This involves scholars attacking the work of their predecessors, sometimes unfairly, in order to carve out a theoretical niche for themselves. A quote from Killian (1983: 4) is reproduced here at length because it eloquently encapsulates strategies used by theory bashers. He suggests that 'theory bashing' is analogous to the means politicians use to oust opponents:

> quote the opponent selectively and out of context, carefully deleting statements of his which do not sustain the caricature. In particular, studiously ignore refutations of charges which have been levelled before you, or others – just repeat the charges. Quote from the opponent's political speeches regardless of the date they were made – never concede that minds do change. At the same time, do not hesitate to borrow freely from the opponents' ideas without acknowledging that despite party differences there is indeed a great deal of overlap in the platforms. Give the ideas you borrow new labels so the voters won't recognise them. Finally, use guilt by association by putting the opponent in the same bag with the others of which you're sure your opponents will disapprove and then quote what they say as if he agrees with it. Vague labels such as 'right-wing', 'liberal' and the like are particularly useful in smearing your opponent. The overall message is an old, familiar theme – turn the rascals out!

In the study of social movements, new paradigms have emerged as old ones have tired. In the process, useful insights from earlier schools of thought have sometimes been too easily dismissed.[5] Collective behaviour theory, which was seen – not entirely accurately – to belittle the rationality of activists, was replaced with resource mobilization in the United States, and with new social movement theory in Europe. The two newer schools of thought developed independently with little exchange until relatively recently. Resource mobilization theorists emphasized rationality and organizational aspects (Chapter 4), whereas new social movement theorists (Chapters 6 and 7) focused on cultural aspects. Yet, despite it being routinely dismissed in the 1980s, elements of collective behaviour theory have continued to pervade the social movement literature without direct reference to it. By 1983, Jenkins' overview of social movement theories in *Annual Review of Sociology*, made no mention of collective behaviour theories, despite their prominence a decade earlier (see also Buechler 2004, especially 51). This suggests that collective behaviour theory had been thoroughly and perhaps inappropriately theory-bashed. I give collective behaviour theory the attention it deserves to avoid contributing to the routine – and unfair – dismissal of the foundations of social movement theory.

To avoid 'theory bashing', one could go so far as to suggest that separate theories do not really exist – they are just a way of categorizing the 'sprawling, diffuse and inchoate' social movements' literature (Lofland 1993: 48). To cut my way through the complexity of the literature, it is necessary that I discuss each theory in a separate chapter. However, in Chapter 8, I apply an analytical framework that enables the different theories to talk to one another. I do this on the premise that environmental organizations operating within environmental networks act both strategically and normatively, and with knowledge that a static and/or state-focused approach can do little to explain the dynamism of environmental networks.

The roots of social movement theory

It is necessary at this juncture to visit the roots of social movement theory. In so doing, I have two objectives: (1) To redeem what is salvageable from collective behaviour theory to avoid theory bashing; (2) To begin to illustrate why a middle-range theory (Merton 1968) as developed in the penultimate chapter of the book, might be more useful than a grand-theoretical account like collective behaviour in understanding interaction in environmental networks.

The stereotypical interpretation of the collective behaviour approach wrongly and unhelpfully conflates it with a particular sub-branch of collective behaviour theory based on relative deprivation (Gurr 1970) often in tandem with the spurious frustration-aggression link (Davies 1969; Neff Gurney and Tierney 1982: 35–9).[6] Roughly put, the frustration-aggression thesis argues that protesters respond to their deprivation by forming crowds and, when in a crowd, lose their ability to behave rationally. At the extreme, the approach regards social movement protest as politically and/or psychologically deviant. A quote from Le Bon's (1969: 22–3) classic book on *The Crowd* is illustrative:

> Whoever be the individuals that compose it, however like or unlike their mode of life, their occupations, their intelligence, the fact that they have transformed into a crowd puts them in possession of a sort of collective mind which makes them feel, think and act in a manner quite differently from that in which each individual would . . . ordinarily behave.

Mass behaviour theories that focus on the crowd might, at first glance, be considered irrelevant to social movements and to the focus on environmental networks in particular. Yet there is something about crowds that *does*, without doubt, encourage people to behave differently from the norm. Just think of the student demonstrations that took place in London in November 2010. A critical mass of thousands of students was necessary to transform a section of what was a peaceful demonstration into a riot in which serious property damage to the Conservative Party Campaign Headquarters occurred to the tune of over a million pounds. It was certainly the case that many participants were, as a *Daily Mail* reporter so aptly puts it, 'caught up in the dizzying excitement of civil disobedience' (Harper 2010). Yet, without the coordinated mobilization efforts of student unions throughout the country, the crowd would not have materialized. To routinely dismiss this as mindless violence also precludes consideration of the social and political context that generated discontent.

Although extensive property damage is rare in environmental protests (Rootes 2007), the comfort of being part of large crowd has undoubtedly encouraged environmental activists to behave differently from how they might have done if acting individually. For example, the 1,500–5,000 strong crowd (depending on which sources you consult) at the Twyford Down mass trespass in July 1994 gave individual activists more confidence to engage in illicit behaviour, making it easier for a number of them to violate the injunctions that legally prevented them from entering the site of that particular roads protest. Many of these activists were dissatisfied, even angry, as some strands of collective behaviour theory would predict. But to claim that they were atomized is way off the mark. Those activists were, and other environmental activists continue to be, mobilized through organized efforts, whether via specific organizations or direct action networks. Indeed, all of the campaigns and actions I focus on in this book (see Chapter 3), whether large-scale protests or small affinity group actions, were carefully planned by networks of individuals and/ or organizations. Many collective behaviour theorists recognize the importance of such interaction within social movements, although this virtuous side of the story is rarely told.

Unfortunately, a number of scholars appear guilty of conflating the collective behaviour approach solely with the stereotypical interpretation. Hannigan (1985: 436), for example, suggests that collective behaviour theorists view social movements negatively – as disorganized, non-institutional, irrational, spontaneous and amorphous conglomerations of isolated individuals. Similarly, Jasper (1997: 20) places collective behaviour under the title of 'the myth of the maddening crowd' (McPhail 1991). Even Gamson, who was famous for popularizing study of the rational and institutional aspects of protest in the first edition of his famous – or, for collective behaviour theorists, infamous – *Strategy of Social Protest* (1975), lumped together Le Bon, Hoffer, Kornhauser and Smelser under the umbrella of mass theory and relative deprivation theories. After recognizing his mistake, in the second edition of that same book, Gamson (1990: 148) makes a worthy apology for making a 'too sweeping rejection of collective behaviour theory'. Gamson had realized that the stereotypical view of collective behaviour theory differs markedly from the much richer symbolic interactionist perspectives put forward by a small number of collective behaviour theorists who looked beyond the crowd towards protest dynamics, such as Park and Burgess, Blumer, Turner and Killian, and Smelser.[7]

Park and Burgess (1924: 226–9) claimed protests were a rational response to social situations, emerging due to structural changes in the difficult transition from primitive communities to the state of global interdependence. Blumer (1986) added to these ideas, regarding social movements as 'collective enterprises [seeking] to establish a new order of life' (8), resulting from 'cultural drifts'. Cultural drifts are not social-psychological, they are the gradual but significant changes in the way a society or group sees the world, incorporating such changes as the emergence of free education for all, universal franchise and emancipation of children (9). He even suggested that members of collective enterprises acquire a 'we-consciousness'. This can be viewed as an early conception of collective identity (Chapter 7), which took the class dimension out of earlier Marxist-inspired notions of identity/consciousness. Drawing on Weber, Blumer (1986) argued that this 'we-consciousness' developed through an esprit de corps, where members feel a sense of belonging, rapport and solidarity with comrades through being together and participating in ritualistic behaviour such as sentimental symbols, slogans, songs and expressive gestures. Collective behaviour, he argued, did *not* emerge through a group of atomized individuals converging, but instead through *interactions* among participants.

Turner and Killian (1957) appended further useful concepts, most notably that of 'emergent norms', which were conceived as new ways of viewing the world developed through discursive practices and *interactions* between those engaged in collective behaviour, known as 'milling'. According to their approach, a precipitating event – such as an environmental disaster – leads to a normative crisis, encouraging people to rally together and engage in collective action to challenge the norms deemed responsible for causing the precipitating factor. Extraordinary social situations, brought into sharp relief through precipitating factors, they argued, lead people to jointly come to view collective action as timely, useful, appropriate and even as a moral obligation. Via 'milling', participants come to define and redefine the social situation, test out alternatives and abandon previous behaviours. Turner and Killian (1957) also coined the term 'participation oriented movements' for social movements in which satisfaction stems mostly from participation. These were, much later, reconceived in a branch of new social movement theory as expressive groups (Hetherington 1998). It seems that new social movement theorists – including Melucci (1989), Touraine (1981, 1984) and Habermas (1981, 1984) (see Chapters 6 and 7) – failed to build upon these useful concepts.

Smelser's (1962) seminal work on collective behaviour is perhaps the most significant contribution to collective behaviour theory. It is regarded by Crossley (2002: 40) to be 'one of the most persuasive and important' in the field. Smelser bravely attempted to produce a rounded predictive model for the emergence of a variety of forms of collective behaviour. His 'value-added approach' argued that the more simple forms of collective behaviour – like the panic and the craze – have ingredients that are components of more complex forms – like social movements. In his own words 'value' is added as: 'earlier stages must combine *according to a certain pattern* before the next stage can contribute its particular value to the finished product' (19).

The most complex form of collective behaviour that Smelser referred to was the value-oriented social movement. Such a movement, he claimed, seeks a more satisfying culture, and is preoccupied with seeking the highest possible moral standards and abolishing sources of perceived evil. Examples include political and religious revolutions, sects and nationalist movements. But it also seems to suit the Green movement (the system challenging aspect of the environmental movement that Doherty [2002] focuses on), which had barely emerged when Smelser was writing.

Collective behaviour, he suggested, is based on 'generalized beliefs', which 'restructure an ambiguous situation in a short-circuited way' (Smelser 1962: 82). Smelser is vague about the meaning of short-circuiting, but it seems safe to assume he believed those engaged in collective behaviour simplify who or what is to blame for perceived injustice. The collective is then thought to 'create a "common culture" within which leadership, mobilization and concerted action can take place' (Smelser 1962: 82). He argued that, among other conditions, generalized beliefs would need to challenge the values of society for a value-oriented movement to occur, and to seek reform of societal norms for a norm-oriented movement to emerge. Less complex forms of generalized beliefs were thought to be part of the recipes for simpler forms of collective behaviour (like riots and lynch mobs). Similar to Park he argued that such generalized beliefs emerge from a structural strain, which provides a source of tension. For generalized beliefs to result in collective behaviour a precipitating factor – an event that brings a social strain into view – is required. At this point, mobilization occurs as communication *networks* emerge, sometimes under the direction of leaders. The shape and form of collective behaviour depend also upon structural conduciveness and social control. Smelser (1962: 15) defined structural conduciveness as the extent to which a state is 'permissive of a given type of collective behaviour', and social control as the methods the state uses to contain an episode of collective behaviour.

Smelser (1962: 72) has been accused of overgeneralizing because he had a tendency to view what he purported to be rational collective behaviour as 'clumsy or primitive in character'. In fact, social movements are qualitatively different from other types of collective behaviour as they have positive solidarity, ideology, organizations and strategies – making them, in reality more careful and sophisticated than Smelser implied (Traugott 1978). But the difficulty here is in squaring *episodes* of behaviour with movements. Although Smelser used the term 'social movement', he always emphasized *episodes* of behaviour rather than movements or networks as such. This was partly a result of how the field of social movement theorizing was scoped by previous scholars. We should not, therefore, be too surprised that the complexity and sophistication of movements and the relationships between different episodes of protest within movements seem underplayed. The emphasis on creating a general law-type theory for the emergence of forms of collective behaviour meant that a focus on the organizational level, in particular, was missing. It carried with it an assumption that protesters are a homogenous group. Weller and Quarantelli (1973), for example, criticize the concept of generalized beliefs, which they say implies a 'unitary outlook of collective action', which does not exist in social movements. In fact, as I show in this book, different environmental organizations engage in a wide variety of actions. Not all organizations in environmental networks, for example, will respond in the same way to situational factors, mobilization, values and norms, despite the importance of these concepts.

Regardless of these criticisms, Smelser and other collective behaviour theorists did recognize that collective behaviour is complex, is nested in the social order and has at least an element of legitimacy, even if it was sometimes wrongly branded as deviance. Smelser identified important determinants of collective behaviour, which have reappeared in more recent social movement theories. Structural strain, structural conduciveness, precipitating factors, and social control are concepts closely related to political process theory (Chapter 5). The concept of 'situational factors' – actors' awareness of opportunities – is also useful. It took political opportunity theorists until the mid-1990s to overcome their preoccupation with objective 'structures' and realize that the perception and evaluation of opportunities by activists are just as important in spurring on the emergence of a movement, and shaping movement form, tactics and goals (Suh 2001) as anything objectively measurable. Developed in the late 1980s, the framing approach, among other things, stressed the importance of problematizing a social or political issue and apportioning blame (Snow and Benford 1988). In some ways, its function is similar to that of a 'generalized belief' theorized by Smelser. The concept of generalized beliefs can be useful so long as it is not assumed that all activists within a movement have the same beliefs. To say that activists are homogenous in their positions and that these come from 'short-circuiting' is to take a step too far. Many environmental campaigns, for example, are based on rigorous scientific research, sometimes resulting in more sophisticated analyses than the research policymakers themselves draw upon.

Smelser also foreshadowed political opportunity structure theory by suggesting that differentiated societies – those with avenues for political participation (which political opportunity structure theorists later called 'open') – lead to norm-oriented movements, while non-differentiated societies – those with strong social control (termed 'closed' in the political opportunity structure literature) – lead to more broadly challenging value-oriented movements. Thus, it was a step ahead of broad-brush approaches to political opportunity structure theories, which wrongly assumed that all movement organizations within a given nation state would behave similarly to one another as a function of the political environment (Chapter 5). In line with the resource mobilization approach, collective behaviour theorists did note that some degree of organization – even if just restricted to 'milling' between individuals – *is* necessary to sustain a movement (Turner 1981: 8).

There are also links with new social movement theory. Laraña (1996: 1–13), writing on theoretical convergence between new social movement and collective behaviour approaches notes three main similarities. First, both view social movements as agents for positive, revolutionary or utopian change. The social movement theories examined in Chapter 6 discuss 'cultural drifts' in a similar fashion to Blumer (1986). Second, they share a focus on collective/shared identity and lifestyles of movement participants, and finally, they both define social movements inclusively as agents working through a variety of non-state focused media to promote or resist social change.

Although often subject to much disparagement, collective behaviour theory has been deemed the closest that theorists have come to generating a 'master theory' for explaining social movements. It 'has proved difficult to develop an alternative conceptualization of similar explanatory potential' (Eyerman and Jamison 1991: 14). But this should not detract from its biggest weakness: it has simply tried to do too much. In proposing general laws about a host of forms of collective behaviour, the peculiarities of particular forms of collective behaviour – like social movements – are downplayed, not to mention the peculiarities of particular organizations *within* movements. Arguably, the emergence of episodes of collective behaviour is not at the whims of such general social laws. Environmental networks, in particular, are not homogenous – they include a variety of different organizations with varying objectives and strategies (Chapter 3).

Methodological approach

I end the book with an illustration of the application of a synthetic analytical approach to social movement theory. This synthetic approach draws upon Bunge's mechanismic systemism (1997, 2004). While I do not seek to derive mechanisms as such, I draw on Bunge's concept of 'systemism', which fills the structure-agency gap by looking for feedbacks between the macro- and micro-level. Adopting this element of his approach allows me to avoid the individualism-holism divide, which has plagued social sciences – and especially social movement research – for centuries (Pickel 2004: 175). More specifically, it provides potential for uniting macro- and micro-level social movement theories. However, I modify Bunge's approach, which focuses just on individuals and structures, adding the organizational level and campaign targets in addition to the state to complete the picture. It is necessary to include the organizational level for two related reasons. First, the book's focus on interaction between environmental organizations makes it essential to factor the organizational level into my analytical framework. Second, the organizational level – whether the organizations are formal or informal – is crucial for understanding contention around environmental issues. Only within a group dynamic can grievances shared by individuals become public issues deemed worthy of collective action (Ferree and Miller 1985: 46).

To be a little clearer: the synthetic approach I adopt presupposes that organizations choose their allies as a result of the way in which they interact with individuals, campaign targets, the polity, society and their previous relations with other environmental organizations – whether strategic or normative (Habermas 1981). The overarching task then becomes to identify how organizations' interactions with each of these sets of actors shape their choices of allies.

Although explanation is also the central aim of mechanismic research (Gerring 2007: 178), I elect to not use mechanisms based research to avoid charges of overstating generalizability *and* of conceptual confusion. Mahoney (2001), for example, identified 24 different definitions of mechanisms by 21 different authors![8] Furthermore, the mechanismic approach is sometimes used as a form of cover for rational actor theory (see, e.g. Elster 2002). I do not wish to entirely distance myself from this approach, but I believe that overemphasis on rationality confines explanation to the realm of strategic action. This has been a key weakness of the resource mobilization school of thought (Chapter 4). While environmental organizations can sometimes behave rationally, such an approach puts strategic action in the spotlight at the expense of the normative, underplaying important lessons we can learn from cultural approaches to social movements (see Chapters 4 and 8). Nevertheless, I do draw on useful elements of the mechanismic approach and seek to capitalize on some of its advantages.

As with mechanismic research, my theoretical and methodological approach makes it possible to find a compromise between grand theories – like collective behaviour – on the one hand, and interpretivist 'storytelling', on the other (Hedström and Swedburg 1996: 281). Interpretivism can be criticized for collecting 'disjointed anecdotal material', which 'enshrines mysteries instead of turning them into research problems' (Bunge 1997: 421–2). Grand theory, on the other hand has been criticized for overgeneralization (Merton 1968) and even of emptiness (Hedström and Swedburg 1996: 299). As illustrated above, the grand theory of collective behaviour is clearly too general to explain the complex dynamics of interaction in environmental networks, even if a charge of emptiness is too harsh. Moreover, to explain interaction requires moving beyond compiling anecdotal material.

My approach also helps avoid a problem apparent in less sophisticated quantitative research, whereby correlation is assumed to equate to causation. In such studies, the 'black box' of explanation remains closed. In the case of research on environmental networks, such quantitative approaches might be able to tell us that there *exists* a relationship between formal organizational structure and proclivity to compete for resources, but they will fail to tell us *why* this is the case. This, of course, is less true of more sophisticated quantitative methodologies that aim to control for context and check for confounding variables.

Nonetheless, I would like to stress that I do not see my approach as entirely juxtaposed from the quantitative and interpretivist approaches against which mechanismic accounts have been contrasted. On the contrary, I would argue that it is important that an account of interaction in environmental networks incorporates some form of interpretivism, quantitative measurement or even both, for mixed methods can be useful tools to develop explanation. Neither am I universally opposed to the development of laws, even though I believe that broad or general laws cannot easily capture social and political dynamics at multiple levels required to explain interaction in environmental networks – hence the need for some form of systemism. I share with mechanisms-based researchers the desire to 'elaborate, sharpen, transpose and connect theories' (Weber 2006: 120).

The main advantage of my approach is that it is self-consciously aware of the need to *explain* observed phenomena by looking not only at structure or agency, but at both. Furthermore, I would argue that my approach is ideally suited to the exploratory empirical work I have carried out on environmental networks. Even though I cannot prove cause and effect, my exploratory empirical contribution can help move closer to developing explanatory hypotheses that can fully explain interaction in environmental networks and social movements. Thus, this is to take up an approach that straddles positivist hypothesis testing and constructivism. Lichbach (2008) is critical of such an approach, because it can only be put forward as a first step towards determining causation. I will be the first to admit the impossibility of confirming cause and effect with my relatively small survey sample of 149 environmental organizations. But I purport that exploratory research is at least a good way to *begin* to understand causation.

This book, then, uses mixed methods to explain my own empirical research findings from fieldwork in London in 2002–3. More specifically, the approach seeks to answer the question: 'Why do environmental organizations interact with one another in the way that they do?' To approach this question, I first had to ask myself, 'How do they interact?' To discover how they interact, I analyse results from a survey of 149 London-based environmental organizations. To answer the 'why' question, I deductively use previous theory and empirical research on social movements, and draw upon interviews and participant observation. In so doing, I tease out actions and interactions of actors at multiple levels that can help explain observed patterns.

For in-depth interviews and participant observation, I selected a sample of organizations across the spatial dimensions and the ideological spectrum of environmentalism. This allowed inclusion of radical groups that did not respond to the questionnaire. The interviews determined key campaigners' prior network links, extent of activism/involvement and perspective on interorganizational interactions. A full list of interviewees is given in Appendix 1.

I spent approximately one day per week for several months engaged in participant observation in three very different environmental organizations: Friends of the Earth (that is Friends of the Earth England, Wales and Northern Ireland, from here on simply 'Friends of the Earth'), the Environmental Direct Action Group,[9] and Chiswick Wildlife Group. Friends of the Earth is a national reformist organization, the Environmental Direct Action Group a regional (London-based) radical group and Chiswick Wildlife Group a local conservationist organization. As Friends of the Earth volunteer, I was responsible for implementing an action plan to involve local campaigners in the organization's (2003–8) strategic plan (Friends of the Earth 2002b). In the Environmental Direct Action Group, I attended meetings, and helped prepare and carry out actions. For Chiswick Wildlife Group, I helped with practical conservation tasks and butterfly transects at Gunnersbury Triangle Local Nature Reserve on volunteers' day (see Chapter 3 for more detail on these three organizations). Two key campaigning areas were studied in depth. Climate change and aviation were selected because of their central importance for London's activists and because an array of organizational types have been involved.

For the survey, a postal questionnaire (Appendix 2) was sent to 440 environmental organizations to discover their collaborative and information-passing networks, and organizational characteristics. Although only 34 per cent of those contacted responded to the survey, I ensured that prominent London based national environmental organizations and their local groups responded. The response rate compares favourably with other surveys of social movement organizations.[10] I also made sure to include a range of organizations across the environmental networks' spatial and ideological dimensions – even including a couple of radical organizations, traditionally considered least receptive to survey research. A list of the organizations that responded to the survey is given in Appendix 3.

Local environmental groups were sampled because there are so many environmental groups in London. Two locales were selected to explore the 'local' dimension of environmentalism: a pocket of southeast London, and an area in northwest London surrounding Heathrow Airport. The former has rich and lively local environmental networks, despite social deprivation and poor integration into Greater London's transport infrastructure (Rootes et al. 2001). The locale in northwest London was chosen because of its proximity to Heathrow airport and because its activist milieu is at least as, if not more, industrious than the southeast's. Having relatively recently lost a protracted campaigning battle against T5 (a fifth passenger Terminal at Heathrow Airport), action groups in the surrounding towns and villages were, at the time of field research, actively engaged in an on-going campaign against a third runway – an option that the then Labour government had, at that point, approved subject to operation of the airport remaining within emissions limits. Controversially, the Labour government argued that the new runway was important for economic prosperity, and that it would play a key role in meeting the predicted increase in aircraft demand as outlined in its aviation White Paper (Department for Transport 2003). After much campaigning, including a High Court Ruling in which the Labour government was found guilty of not properly consulting on a number of key issues, the plans were retracted. Anti-runway campaigners were delighted that the Conservative-Liberal Democrat coalition government, which came to power in 2010, dropped the plans.

The contents

Chapter 2 sets the scene by detailing the theoretical and empirical context. It defines environmental networks and gives a short history of their development. It includes some discussion of how environmental organizations might be categorized ideologically and spatially. Chapter 3 provides further contextual information on the campaigns and environmental organizations studied in depth. The following four chapters provide a critical evaluation of the major strands of social movement theory: resource mobilization, political opportunity structures, new social movement theory and the identity-oriented approach, respectively. Each of these chapters critiques and then contextualizes these theories in relation to environmental networks, illustrating them with examples of recent environmental campaigns in Britain. They then suggest how the different theories might anticipate environmental organizations to behave and to interact. Then, assessments are made of the theories' applicability to the interaction in environmental networks as uncovered by the London-based survey and fieldwork. More specifically, the empirical element of Chapter 4 explores the extent to which local groups find national and regional groups supportive and whether or not this is a result of national environmental organizations over-prioritizing organizational maintenance or being hampered by bureaucracy. Issues of resource constraints, funding, competition, conflict, reciprocity and the division of labour are investigated. Chapter 5 looks at the effects of political opportunities and structures at national and local levels upon network linkages between organizations that comprise environmental networks. Chapter 6 considers new social movement theory, evaluates its newness and discusses whether it can illuminate our understanding of environmental networks. In Chapter 7, individual activists' and organizational identities are considered. The development of organizational cultures and their impact upon networking is discussed.

As will be demonstrated, each theory has its strengths and weaknesses. To fully explain environmental networks requires considering aspects of all theories. Chapter 8 examines a significant attempt to unite the theories: the *Dynamics of Contention* research programme of McAdam et al. (2001). After evaluating McAdam et al.'s approach, it introduces an alternative analytical framework, which suggests that organizations' choices of allies might be determined on the basis of their relationships to society, the polity, their campaign targets, historic interactions with other environmental organizations and with individuals, both strategically and normatively. The synthetic approach is illustrated with reference to campaigns against climate change and aviation expansion.

The concluding chapter includes a comparison with observations of environmentalism in other countries to locate the findings and theoretical developments in the broader literature. To draw the book to a close, the key findings – both theoretical and empirical – are summarized and their implications for environmental networks and social movements more generally are discussed. I find that issues of resource maintenance influence environmental organizations' choices of allies. While well-financed moderate conservationist and reformist environmental groups will seek to maintain their office space, staff and reputations, radicals will want to maintain their strong sense of collective identity. This can set radicals and moderates apart from one another. However, this does not mean that large national environmental organizations are insensitive to grassroots campaigns. Particularly when environmental campaigns reach a democratic dead end, the ground for collaboration between radicals and reformists is fertile. Thus, to explain interaction between environmental organizations requires not only consideration of rational (resource mobilization and political process) and cultural theories (new social movements and identity). What is also required is consideration of the dynamic interplay between environmental organizations, the individuals that participate in them *and* those whom they challenge.

2 Environmental Movements or Networks?

This chapter, along with Chapter 3, sets the context of the book. It opens with a discussion of definitions of pressure and interest groups and social movements to make explicit what might be meant by the term 'environmental movement', and why I prefer instead to use the term 'environmental networks'. This is followed by an attempt to theoretically map out the possible ideological, strategic and spatial divisions within environmental networks. Finally, I look at survey results to see what sorts of organizations within environmental networks might be considered to be part of the environmental movement. In this book, I draw heavily on Diani's (1992a) consensual definition of a social movement (more on this, below), which is praiseworthy, even if one might suggest some slight modifications. Diani's definition is especially useful for those new to the study of social movements, to help them understand the parameters of the concept of a social movement. Nonetheless, one should always bear in mind that not all scholars use Diani's definition as a benchmark for what they refer to as social movements.

Defining movements

It is never easy to define or delineate social movements because theorists between and sometimes even within different theoretical branches of social movement theory use the term differently (Milton 1996: 79). To roughly illustrate how the concept is differentially used, I draw on different uses of the concept by the archetypal resource mobilization theorist and the typical new social movement theorist. Resource mobilization scholars frequently use the term to refer to organizational and at least internally institutionalized social movement organizations – in other words, organizations that have a formal structure. In this sense, a social movement can be considered to include organizations that others might call pressure groups. On the other hand, for some new social movement theorists this would be an anathema. New social movement theorists tend to prefer to use the term to denote informally organized horizontal networks of activists and consequently, give much less emphasis to the organizational dimension (see Chapter 6). Similarly, some political process theorists require that the components of a social movement are not externally institutionalized – that the organizations within a movement lack a close relationship to the government by virtue of being too immature or radical – whereas others will include organizations that have a close association with government. Because of these stark differences, I begin this discussion of what it means to be a social movement by comparing definitions of social movements according to the degree of internal *and* external institutionalization insisted upon.[1]

Early movement theorists (pre-1960s, for example, Turner and Killian 1957) saw social movements as non-institutionalized in both senses – that is, as fairly disorganized entities (internal) engaging in unconventional behaviour and having little access to policymaking circles (external). Thus, they contrasted them with pressure groups, which have been considered to be more organized and to have greater access to the polity. To some extent, this distinction between social movements and pressure groups stemmed from faith in the pluralist system in the United States, which hinged on a belief that rational[2] bodies could gain access to democratic decision-making processes. Less organized groups that lacked access and engaged instead in extra-institutional protest were regarded as separate from 'pluralist' politics, and misleadingly, but frequently, regarded as harbingers of irrational collective behaviour.

As social movement theory has developed (see Chapter 1) there has been a recognition that semi- or non-institutional protest activity can be rational *and* contribute to democracy. Gamson (1990: 138), for example, notes how the 'old duality' between institutional and non-institutional protest activity 'has been superseded by "simply politics"', recognizing that both social movement organizations and pressure groups seek to directly and indirectly influence policy (Goldstone 2003). Indeed, the idea that outsider groups can contribute to rational policymaking has recently been recognized by Labour Party leader Ed Miliband, who, in his address to the TUC rally in March 2011, alluded to the success of British suffragettes. The suffragettes appear to have been behaving rationally when viewed from the vantage point of the present day, but were deemed irrational by many at the time they were active. Indeed, modern day climate change activists justify their use of extra-institutional actions with reference to the alleged rationality of historically successful social movements that have used direct action, including the suffragettes and the civil rights movement. Inspired by the suffragettes, Climate Rush activists, for example, have adopted the slogan 'well-behaved women rarely make history'.

In practice, some environmental movement scholars, rather unhelpfully, use the terms 'social movement organization' and 'pressure group' interchangeably and seemingly indiscriminately. Rawcliffe (1998), for example, talks of 'environmental pressure groups' in reference to many of the same organizations that Rootes (2007) calls environmental movement organizations. As if to purposely confound, the term environmental non-governmental organizations (ENGOs) is also thrown in (Princen 1994; Biliouri 1999). I prefer to avoid the use of the term NGO because it is 'slippery' and 'over-used' – arguably, on both counts, even more so than the term 'social movement' (Saunders and Andretta 2009). To avoid confusion, I have adopted the more general term of 'environmental organizations' to refer to the individual groups that comprise environmental networks.

But what do others mean by the terms 'pressure groups' and 'social movement organizations'? Although the terms have frequently been used as synonyms, as shown in the previous paragraph, earlier scholarly work presented them as distinct entities. Turner and Killian (1957) and Smelser (1962), for example, view pressure groups as institutionalized and therefore as fodder for political scientists rather than for social movement scholars. But is it useful to make such a distinction between social movements and pressure groups?

According to Stewart, a pioneer in political sociology, pressure groups have two central characteristics – being formally organized and seeking to influence policy (Stewart 1958: 1). Confusingly, the terms 'pressure' and 'interest' groups are often treated as synonyms, while some regard interest groups as a specific subtype of pressure group, distinguished from cause groups.[3] Wilson (1990: 8) is among those who use the term 'interest group' as a synonym for pressure group. He distinguishes interest groups from social movements according to the degree of institutionalization:

> By requiring that for something to be an interest group, it must have an institutionalised existence, I distinguish interest groups from social movements (which need only have the most rudimentary linkages).

The purpose of this statement is to allow easy distinction between social movement organizations and interest groups. But where should one draw what seems to be a rather arbitrary line between rudimentary linkages with the polity, and constructive engagement? Is this really an important distinction to make between organizations fighting for the same cause? And in which pigeonhole do we put groups using a mixture of institutional and non-institutional tactics? The non-institutional view of social movements would imply that organizations like Friends of the Earth, Greenpeace and World Wide Fund for Nature (WWF)[4] are not part of an environmental movement because of their relatively involved level of engagement with the policymaking process, and formally organized structures.

Putting large influential groups outside of a study of environmental networks is inappropriate, not least because they set the environmental agenda and shape public perception of environmental issues by virtue of the press coverage they obtain. But such inclusion might upset a number of scholars who insist on a non-institutionalized approach. Yet in practice, what is often referred to as the environmental movement is certainly at least partially institutionalized (see Rootes 2007). Groups that were once considered radical, like Friends of the Earth, have become respected interlocutors in some decision-making circles. Now a semi-institutionalized entity, Friends of the Earth was, in 1970, merely a small group of activists excluded from formal political participation because of its radical viewpoint. Does that really mean that we should no longer view it as a social movement organization?

In the orthodox view, which insisted that social movements be non-institutional, an organization like Friends of the Earth would be promoted to the status of pressure group once it had taken on the characteristics of such, leaving behind the domain of social movements to find its place in the realm of 'proper' politics. I would argue that whether it is a pressure group or a social movement organization is somewhat immaterial – its role in environmental campaigning makes its inclusion in a study of environmental networks crucial.

Doherty's (2002) definition of what he calls the 'Green movement' emphasizes that organizations that are part of a movement must be at least externally non-institutionalized. Doherty adapts Diani's (1992a) definition of a social movement, which suggests that movements are semi- *or* non-institutionalized networks of organizations and individuals that share a collective identity, engage in collective action and have a common opponent. But Doherty's emphasis on the non-institutionalized element allows him to stress that to be part of the 'Green movement', organizations must engage in action outside of political institutions and challenge the basic principles upon which society is organized. On this basis, organizations like the Royal Society for the Protection of Birds (RSPB) and the Wildlife Trusts are excluded because (among other disqualifying factors) they do not engage mostly in non-institutionalized protest or challenge the social order. However, since Doherty wrote his book, the RSPB has been actively involved in protests, for example, against a proposed airport at Cliffe, Kent, and in the annual climate change marches that have taken place in London since 2006. Yet one might still question whether the RSPB has ever actually challenged the social order.

Nevertheless, these days, many social movement scholars consider social movement organizations to be entities that incorporate both non-institutionalized social movements and interest group politics (including see also McCarthy and Zald 1977; Diani 1992a; Dalton 1994; della Porta and Diani 1999; McAdam 2002: 282–3) (see Table 2.1). Burstein and Linton (2002), for example, regard social movement organizations and political organizations as part of a continuum without formal divisions. And for Diani and Donati (1999: 134), there are four main types of organization *within* a social movement including the 'public interest lobby' (i.e. a pressure group). Della Porta and Diani (1999: 16–19) similarly agree that pressure

Table 2.1 Pressure groups, non-institutionalized and modern concept of social movement compared

	What is a social movement?		
Characteristics	Pressure groups ⟶	Modern concept of social movement ⟵	Non-institutionalized social movements
Organization	Formal/ bureaucratic ⟶	**Both types of organization** ⟵	Informal, non-hierarchical and participatory. OR atomized individuals
Demands	Small scale change – usually related to specific interests of members ⟶	**Both types of demands** ⟵	Radical social change
Issues	Not system challenging ⟶	**Both types of issues** ⟵	System challenging
Strategy	Conventional/ insider ⟶	**Both types of challenges** ⟵	Unconventional/ outsider
Network links	None ⟶	**Must have network links** ⟵	Sometimes

groups and even political parties can be part of a social movement if they are linked through formal or informal networks to other movement organizations. However, they exclude them if specific organizations are the main source of participants' identities, assuming that this weakens loyalty to the movement as a whole (Diani 2003: 302–3). This may be problematic because it clashes with common usage of the term 'environmental movement'. For example, it assumes that a stalwart Friends of the Earth activist, who identifies only with Friends of the Earth, is not part of the movement and may well inappropriately exclude many activists who are active members in its local groups. Likewise, it might exclude a keen Climate Camp activist who identifies solely with the Camp.

In all, it appears that the terrains of political scientists and sociologists have merged and the divide between pressure groups and social movements has become increasingly viewed as an artificial construct. It could be argued that the qualifying factors in the distinction between a movement organization and an isolated pressure group are the existence of network links and a shared agenda. This modern conception of a social movement (cf. Snow et al. 2007) bridges the divide between pressure groups and social movements (Table 2.1). Yet we must remember that use of the term 'social movement' does not necessarily guarantee that scholars are always referring to the same class of phenomena. Occasionally, one sees scholars mistakenly referring to single organizations as if they are social movements. As Diani (1992b) states:

> In fact, social and political phenomena as heterogeneous as revolutions, religious sects, political organizations, single-issue campaigns are all, on occasion, defined as social movements.

Environmental networks

Given the quandary many movement theorists have got into over defining 'movements', it is perhaps not surprising that McCormick (1991: 29) used the term 'environmental lobby' instead, which he says is 'made up of individual environmental "interest groups"'. However, it is more constructive for the purposes of this book to view the object of study as 'networks'. The term 'lobby' is too restrictive because it excludes non-institutionalized environmental organizations and those that are not directly political. As identified above, the term 'movements' is equally, if not more, problematic because of the many different ways in which movements have been defined. Furthermore, this term is not necessarily suitable for the object of study in this book because some scholars insist that it evokes challenging the social order and/or insist on the use of protest as a key strategy, thus missing out conservation organizations and do-it-yourself groups.[5] Lofland (1996: 3), for example, suggests that social movement organizations 'are associations of persons making idealistic and moralistic claims about how human personal or group life ought to be organized that, at the time of their claims making, are marginal or excluded from mainstream society'.

Using the word networks also avoids use of awkward terms like environmental NGOs, environmental pressure groups and environmental movement organizations, eco-activist groups and so on, which among them have created a quagmire of confusion. To avoid confusion, I call all of these entities simply 'environmental organizations'.

Focusing on networks rather than movements also allows us to zoom in on the dynamics of temporary coalitions and what have been called, sometimes inappropriately, 'not in my back yard' (NIMBY) groups. Environmental organizations often form temporary coalitions against particular infrastructural developments, for environmental improvements or challenging a particular industrial sector (see Chapter 3). While these do not necessarily display social movement dynamics (see Diani and Bison 2004), they still reveal interesting patterns of interaction.

NIMBY groups are not universally considered part of the environmental movement. But Castells (1997: 173) includes them because of their focus on 'establishing control over the living environment on the behalf of the local community'. Strictly speaking, NIMBYs are local activists who claim a positive attitude to a development per se, but express aversion to it being located close to home (Wolsink 1994). Thus, they can work *against* the aims of a broader movement.

However, as Wolsink (2006) warns, it is dangerous to fall in to the trap of misrepresenting all local campaigns as NIMBY, or of viewing true NIMBY campaigns as inconsequential. Often, it is through NIMBY campaigns that activists begin to learn about the issues and controversies surrounding particular locally unwanted land uses (LULUs) (Carter 2001), and during this process they may begin to network with others and change from being egotistically NIMBY to genuinely NIABY (not in anybody's back yard). The result is a 'scale-shift' in local campaigners' discourse, whereby there is a significant 'change in the number and level of coordinated contentious actions leading to broader contention involving a wider range of actors and bridging their claims and identities' (McAdam et al. 2001: 331). In other words, NIMBYism can transform into broader campaigns. This is what has been found regarding contention over the siting of waste facilities (Rootes 1999, 2003a; and on roads protests (Robinson 1999)). Shemtov (2003) has found that friendship networks help NIMBY groups to expand their goals, whereas links with local political elite tend to keep NIMBY campaigns parochial. Therefore, while true NIMBY groups might not be part of an environmental movement *or* part of a broader environmental network, their interactions with other organizations can facilitate their transformation from NIMBYs to NIABYs. This makes them interesting to study from an environmental networks' perspective.

Environmental networks, then, consist of formal and informal organizations with a common concern to protect or preserve the environment, using a wide variety of tactics, from conservation work and conventional lobbying through to sabotage and forming, living in and maintaining eco-communes. They consist of organizations that are networked: the organizations within the networks share information, and collaborate with one another.

If Bosso (1995: 102) is correct to assert that it is wrong to view what is commonly called the environmental movement as a single movement, due to its various ideological and practical dimensions as separate movements, then the concept of environmental networks is useful to capture the plurality of movements he refers to. But Carter (2001: 134), on the other hand, concludes that there is enough unity to conceive of a single environmental movement due to shared concern about the environment, and the 'creative tension' that exists between organizations. The only way to see whether environmental networks really do constitute an environmental movement is to cast the net widely and then filter down on the basis of criteria for measuring the presence or absence of movement dynamics. A focus on environmental networks allows us to answer the empirical question of whether there are one or several networks/movements. I address this after delineating the boundaries of environmental networks.

Delineating the boundaries of environmental networks

Numerous attempts have been made to define the boundaries of the environmental movement. Lowe and Goyder (1983: 3) and Doyle and Kellow (1995) adopted an extensive definition including environmental organizations and the 'attentive public' (i.e. those sympathetic to the movement), while Rawcliffe (1998: 14) limits his definition to those committed or involved. Both definitions are empirically problematic because of the tendency to 'make the political personal' (Mooers and Sears 1992). Almanzar et al. (1998), for example, pose that engagement in pro environmental behaviours (such as recycling, energy conservation and green consumerism) are behavioural expressions of allegiance to and therefore participation in the movement. This is one reason why Haenfler et al. (2012) suggest a shift towards thinking about lifestyle movements so much as political ones. Furthermore, multitudes of people may be sympathetic to the movement, but not participate. The politics of the personal is one reason that, for Byrne (1997: 11), 'the environmental movement is perhaps the most extreme example of blurred boundaries'. That is not to say that defining movement boundaries is easy for any supposed social movement. The boundaries of the women's movement, in particular, have been heavily contested.[6] For practical, yet not entirely unproblematic purposes, this book focuses mostly on networks of active environmental organizations. Data collection would become unwieldy and unfocused if it considered all individuals with any form of movement allegiance.

To follow tradition in the study of environmental activism in Europe, organizations similar to those ruled out in the Transformation of Environmental Activism project have been excluded (see Rootes and Miller 2000; Rootes 2007). These include: natural science/technological groups; national or local governmental institutions; scientific associations; commercial organizations (and subgroups); and animal rights groups that do not explicitly mention the environment on their web pages. While in some European nations animal rights and anti-hunting organizations are considered to be environmental organizations, this is not the case in Britain. Rootes

(2000) shows that, on the basis of press reports in the *Guardian*, only 5 per cent of reported animal rights/welfare protests in Britain coincided with an environmental one. Rootes and Miller (2000) present network findings from a comprehensive survey of national environmental organizations, which similarly demonstrate the weakness of the connection between environmental and animal rights organizations.

For the Transformation of Environmental Activism project, building conservation organizations were also excluded. However, because the research on which this book is based focuses on an urban area with a proliferation of amenity societies and some well-established urban conservation associations, it was considered inappropriate to ignore them. It is also interesting to discover their position relative to other actors that constitute environmental networks. Building conservation organizations were surveyed, but their questionnaire responses were only analysed if the organizations considered themselves to be part of an environmental network and if they provided network data.

The fuzzy fringes of the environmental network (cf. Saunders 2003) overlap with what has been called the global justice movement, most especially its anarchistic elements and Do it Yourself (DIY) culture – often regarded as 'anarchism in all but name' (e.g. Purkiss 2000: 97). Pepper (1996: 45), for instance, claims that 'most radical greens are influenced by anarchism'. Epstein (2001) indicates that youth involved in the anti-globalization movement are mostly demanding human rights and environmental justice. To deal with these fuzzy fringes, radical anarchist groups and single-issue groups (e.g. transport groups, anti-incineration groups) have only been included in the study if they consider themselves to be part of a network of environmental organizations.

Spatial dimensions and ideological strands of the environmental networks

Environmental organizations that comprise environmental networks operate at a variety of levels – from very local guardians of single parks (e.g. Friends of Greenwich Park), to transnational organizations with worldwide influence (e.g. Friends of the Earth, Greenpeace and WWF). It is possible to make a useful distinction therefore, between the following types of environmental groups based on their sphere of operation:

1 Local – concerned with the environment at a particular site, within a street or, at the most, a borough. Examples include groups that steward a local park or nature reserve (the many Friends of . . .. Park groups in London), or campaign against a LULU. This category also includes local chapters of national environmental organizations, such as Greenwich Greenpeace.

2 Regional – representing the interests of at least two boroughs. An example is London Wildlife Trust.

3 National – concerned with national environmental politics throughout England/Britain. The main national environmental organizations are the National Trust, the RSPB, WWF, Friends of the Earth and Greenpeace. Most of them are also part of international networks, but it is beyond the scope of this study to consider the international dimension.

It is also useful to look at environmental ideological and tactical distinctions between environmental organizations. Following other literature on environmentalism, I suggest that, theoretically at least, it is possible to distinguish three *main* subtypes of environmentalism – conservationism, reformism and radical environmentalism. In contrast to other literature (e.g. O'Riordan 1981 [1976]; Dalton 1994), I argue that attempts to categorize environmental organizations into these camps should consider both ideology/beliefs *and* the loci of their challenges and strategies. While I look briefly at ideology in Chapter 6, strategies are emphasized in the analysis offered in Chapter 5. Later in this book, I show that the ideologies of environmental organizations are not easily distilled into three camps (Chapter 6), but strategies are much easier to distinguish (Chapter 5).

Let us begin by focusing on conservation organizations. Although there are precursors to nineteenth-century conservationism (Lowe 1983) and the 1970s manifestation of 'new' environmentalism (Grove 1990; Clapp 1994), these eras are generally considered significant milestones in the development of modern environmentalism (Dalton 1994: 27–39). The nature conservation movement began as a middle-class concern, initially fighting species loss and later concerned with urban sprawl and associated loss of countryside. As a result of its diverse history – stemming from, among other things, the clashing interests of hunting (Green 1981: 42) and humanitarianism – conservation organizations express 'a plurality of values' including preservationists and utilitarian/amenity groups (Green 1981: 42) and hence, 'not a little ambivalence' (Lowe 1983: 349).[7] Despite this, what conservationist groups do have in common is emphasis on 'the protection and preservation of flora, fauna and habitats perceived to be under threat' (Byrne 1997: 129). Often included in this category are groups like the Campaign to Protect Rural England (CPRE), the RSPB and the Wildlife Trusts. They share commitment to protection of natural countryside, but not necessarily the wider environment (Table 2.2). National conservation groups usually exhibit characteristics of archetypal insider-interest groups – showing respect for the established social and political order, having consultative status, and being conservative in both demands and political orientation (Atkinson 1991: 19). The words 'countryside', 'conservation' and 'nature' appear less frequently if at all in the

Table 2.2 Aims and objectives of conservation groups

GROUP	AIMS and OBJECTIVES
Campaign to Protect Rural England	'We . . . care passionately about our *countryside* and campaign for it to be protected and enhanced for the benefit of everyone. *The countryside* is one of England's most important resources but its *beauty, tranquillity and diversity* are threatened in many different ways' (Campaign to Protect Rural England, CPRE website 2004).
Royal Society for the Protection of Birds	'The RSPB is the UK charity working to secure a *healthy environment for birds and wildlife*, helping to create a better world for us all . . . (RSPB website 2004).
Wildlife Trusts	'The Wildlife Trusts partnership is the UK's leading conservation charity exclusively dedicated to *wildlife*. Our network of 47 local Wildlife Trusts and our junior branch, Wildlife Watch, work together to protect *wildlife in towns and the countryside* . . . The Wildlife Trusts lobby for better protection of the *UK's natural heritage* and are dedicated to protecting wildlife for the future' (Wildlife Trust website 2004).

Note: Italics are added to highlight conservation organizations' emphasis on nature and wildlife.

manifestos of political ecology organizations. As a result, conservationist groups might be considered too conventional to be considered part of a movement. Yet a network approach allows us to see the extent to which they interact with their more radical counterparts.

Conservation organizations are usually thought to be distinct from a new breed of environmental organization that emerged in the 1970s. During that decade, links were increasingly made between industrial expansion and environmental degradation. Political ecology (Atkinson 1991; Doyle and McEachern 1998) emerged as a critique of unsustainable consumption patterns, which were (and are still) regarded as having drastic global ramifications. Stimulated by visions of eco-crises put forward in publications from ecologically minded intellectuals such as Carson (1962), Ehrich (1968) and Meadows et al. (1972), the need for a New Ecological Paradigm (NEP) (Catton and Dunlap 1978, 1980) and a social movement to promote it were realized. For its realization the NEP requires fundamental change in the social and political order based on decentralized radical self-management of communities in line with a holistic environmental ethic. This formed the ideological backbone of the environmentalism that emerged in the 1970s, including, most prominently, Friends of the Earth and Greenpeace. The Friends of the Earth International website provides a good example of the range of social, political and global issues which political ecology addresses (Table 2.3), contrasting significantly with the nature-based focus of conservationism.

As a result of these two quite distinct waves in the development of environmentalism, commentators have distinguished between two main ideologies. Frequently cited is Dobson's (1990: 1) distinction between *environmentalism*, which seeks a 'managerial approach to environmental problems'; and *ecologism*, which holds that 'radical changes in our relationship with the natural world' are required to achieve sustainability. Like other similar distinctions (for instance Dalton's 1994 differentiation between *conservation* and *political ecology*), the categorization sometimes seems forced, resulting in artificial divisions because organizations do not always neatly correspond to ideal types. Most typologies imply a polarization of environmental attitudes, with conservationism as conservative (with a small 'c') and seeking to protect the environment as an aesthetic or amenity resource, and political ecology as a polar opposite – being radical and seeking fundamental change. In reality, many political ecology groups deal with nature conservation issues, while traditional conservation groups like WWF (Medley 1992) and the RSPB are becoming increasingly concerned with sustainable development (Rootes 2006).

These typologies also need modifying because they imply that political ecology groups are radical, which, in practice, is often only true in relation to their beliefs (see also Chapter 6). It is now recognized that groups with very similar ideology and goals may adopt drastically different strategies (Carmin and Balser 2002). Many groups with a radical ideology, including Friends of the Earth and Greenpeace believe that fundamental change is desirable. However, they consider that it can only be instituted through incremental, rather than radical, change. Therefore, they frequently, pragmatically target businesses and governments. In this respect, it is important to differentiate them from direct action networks (Doherty 1999; Doherty et al. 2007). Some have called the rise of direct action networks (Rootes and

Table 2.3 The remit of political ecology: The mission statement of Friends of the Earth International

---

We are the world's largest grassroots environmental network and we campaign on today's most urgent environmental and social issues. We challenge the current model of economic and corporate globalization, and promote solutions that will help to create environmentally sustainable and socially just societies. (//www.foei.org/en/what-we-do, last accessed 30 Nov 2010)

Saunders 2007) a third wave of environmentalism, which is also characterized by groups campaigning against LULUs and coalitions (Bosso 1997 in Carter 2001: 141). The radical element of the new wave makes political ecology appear moderate. While political ecologists call for fundamental societal change, they do not necessarily ideologically oppose the state as do some radicals. Neither do they 'engage in forms of action designed not principally to change government policy or to shift the climate of opinion, but to change environmental conditions around them *directly*' (Seel et al. 2000: 2). Earth First! literature, in contrast, makes it clear that there is 'no compromise in defence of Mother Earth' (Brower 1990, ix, xi) (Table 2.4). In practice though, many Earth First!ers in the United Kingdom steadfastly refuse to engage in violence against other human beings. These developments also suggest that Dalton's (1994) hypothesis that ideology is the key variable to distinguish between types of groups[8] requires modification. Despite ideological similarities, Friends of the Earth and other political-ecology-inspired organizations have vastly different action bases. Therefore, to avoid confusion, any typology needs to consider both ideology and strategy.

Before delving a little further into how the ideologies of the main types of environmentalism outlined above differ, it is necessary to clarify what might be meant by ideology in this context (Barker 2000: 64). Although often used to outline how society's hegemonic dominant ruling class' ideas are produced and become translated by the masses into 'constitutive values' (Heberle 1951: 12), what I am concerned with in this book is ideology at the organizational level. This refers to the way environmental organizations interpret reality and their cultural system of meanings. With reference to social movement studies, Snow (2004: 396) conceives of ideology as 'a cover term for a relatively stable and coherent set of values, beliefs and goals associated with a movement . . .'. Yet this definition only works if it is restricted to the group rather than applied at the movement or network level, because movements and networks can, and do, incorporate a multitude of

Table 2.4 Radical environmentalism: An example from Earth First! Literature

Earth First! formed in 1979, in response to an increasingly corporate, compromising and ineffective environmental community. It is not an organization, but a movement. There are no 'members' of EF!, only Earth First!ers. We believe in using all of the tools in the toolbox, from grassroots and legal organizing to civil disobedience and monkeywrenching. When the law won't fix the problem, we put our bodies on the line to stop the destruction. Earth First!'s direct-action approach draws attention to the crises facing the natural world, and it saves lives. (www.earthfirstjournal.org/section.php?id=1, accessed 30 Nov 2010.

ideologies, environmental networks especially so. According to Tucker (1989: 34), there are two main aspects of social movement ideology: debunking the claims of opposing groups, and defining how the state of affairs should preferably be run. For a more rounded outline of the ideology of types of environmentalists, I have added main issues of concern and perceived causes of environmental problems (Table 2.5).

Clearly these ideal types generalize about environmentalism and cannot fully reflect the diversity of organizations. Pepper (1983), for instance, is able to convincingly delineate at least four types of eco-anarchism, which is already a subtype. Nevertheless, such distinctions are useful as analytic tools. Dalton is, of course, right to suggest that 'pure, ideal-types [of environmentalists] exist only in the minds of social scientists' (Dalton 1994: 49). Just because it is possible to distinguish three waves of environmentalism does not guarantee that each of the three categories is a homogenous entity. For instance, the political ecology camp has internal conflict over the role that overpopulation has played in the environmental crisis, and the extent to which population control should be the solution (Kenward 2002). Similarly, among the radicals, deep ecologists have been satirized by social ecologists for their misanthropic tendencies (Devall 1991; Bookchin 1994; Gerber 2002).

A typology of strategies

The strategies used within environmental networks are diverse, ranging from radical (sometimes violent) confrontation to more moderate/conventional approaches – involving consultation, dialogue and compromise with authorities (Young 1993: 23), but also incorporating practical projects and cultural challenges. The latter are especially important fields of action for direct action and DIY networks (Melucci 1996; Doherty 2000). Most typologies of social movement strategies focus disproportionately on protest, ignoring the extreme forms of insider and outsider action such as acting as consultants/negotiating with government ministers, and the practical projects undertaken by DIY activists (Purdue et al. 1997; McKay 1998).

At the simplest level, environmental organizations can be classified according to the extent that they are 'insiders' or 'outsiders' (see Chapter 5); and according to the type of relationship that they have with the polity. The former distinguishes organizations by the actions that they use, the latter by the type and extent of contact that they have with official institutions. Insiders are viewed as legitimate, are widely consulted by the government and have access to the executive, whereas outsiders are those lacking access to the political system (Grant 1995). The types of actions associated with insiders, thresholders (those that use a mixture of insider and outsider strategies) and outsiders are shown in Table 2.6. Lhotka et al. (2008)

Table 2.5 A typology of environmentalist ideologies

Element of Ideology	Type of Environmental Ideology			
	Conservative		Radical	
	Conservationist	Reformist	Ecologist	Radical Environmentalist
Issues	• Nature protection • Emphasis on nature reserves and wilderness	• Tangible, often small-scale issues • Locally based, or issues that can be tackled piecemeal	• National and global issues • Mixture of urban and rural environmental issues	• National and global issues • Urban and rural environmental issues
Problem attribution	• Exploitation of nature • Interwar industrial development and loss due to urban sprawl	• Poor town/country planning decisions • Failure to cost environmental externalities	• Consumerist society • Over-consumption	• Domination of nature and society by an elite (artificial power structures) • Global capitalism
Perceived solution	• Practical conservation • Setting aside and managing reserves	• More careful planning decisions • Technocratic innovation/ ecological modernization	• Decentralized power • Participatory democracy • Restructuring of society piecemeal	• Autonomy • Anarchy • Revolution • Sense of urgency
Examples	RSPB, Wildlife Trusts	NIMBY or LULU groups	Friends of the Earth, Greenpeace	Earth First! Reclaim the Streets

Table 2.6 Campaigning activities and categorization of strategies

Category of Protest	Activities
Insider	Petitions, leafleting, press conferences, letter writing, researching and reporting, education and training, government consultee, LA21 involvement, procedural complaints, litigation, public meetings
Thresholder	Media stunts, marches, rallies, demonstrations, cultural performances and/or a mixture of insider and outsider activities
Outsider	Boycotts, disruption of events, blockades/occupations, ethical shoplifting, ecotage, adbusting, social events, practical conservation

use different labels but the same logic to categorize their sample of environmental organizations as neutral, intermediate and activist.

However, this ignores the differences between those that focus on the political system and those that seek self-directed change. Whereas reformists might be seeking to influence political institutions directly or indirectly, radicals often seek direct change through legal or illegal direct action and DIY or practical projects (Table 2.7). It is important to include all types of strategies to prevent accusations of state-centricity (see Chapter 8).

Groups from differing ideological persuasions share similar fields of action. In particular, radicals and conservationists both engage in practical grassroots localized projects, although radicals also engage in civil disobedience and direct action. Ecotage, for instance, involves sabotaging construction equipment used in the building of ecologically damaging developments, damaging computer files of environmental 'villains' during an office occupation, or ethical shoplifting to remove ecologically damaging products from supermarket shelves to prevent manufacturers profiting from environmental damage. What is distinct about political ecologists is that despite their radical ideology, their activity is typically geared towards influencing or reforming already existing institutions. While Friends of the Earth has a radical ideology, its strategy of seeking to force 'incremental change within an existing social order' (Weston 1989: 208) places it firmly in the reformist camp.

Radicals see the reformist approach as ineffective, comparing it to a hospital with only an emergency ward (Devall and Sessions 1985: 3) and are differentiated from other activists by focussing their efforts on self-directed autonomous change by means of direct action and practical projects. Thus, the key defining words are, for

Table 2.7 Typology of strategies

Directed at Institutions		Self-Directed Change	
Institutional	Indirect-Institutional	Direct Action	DIY/Practical Projects
Consultees	Marches	Ecotage	Practical conservation
Lobbying	Rallies	Occupations	Local exchange trading schemes
Negotiating	Vigils	Ethical shop lifting	Permaculture groups

conservationists – *conserve* (whether practically, or seeking changes in legislation), for political ecologists/reformists – *campaigning for change*, and for radicals – willingness to engage in *civil disobedience* or *alternative life-styles* (italicizations are from O'Riordan's [1981 (1976)] five-fold classification of environmentalists which also includes service groups). This demonstrates that while ideology might shape environmental organizations' strategies, it seems not to be, as Dalton (1994: 15) suggests with reservations, the main 'reason and logic'. Dalton's (1994) notion of ideologically structured action, which proposes that environmental organizations and activists select actions that fit their ideology, assumes more coherence than really exists, ignoring practical constraints that prevent ideology from dictating behaviour (Klandermans 2000; Snow 2004: 396, see also footnote 8). For reformists, pragmatism is the key; for radicals, direct action is the answer.

Thus, pragmatic reformists may seek positive relationships with government and/ or their local councils, whereas radicals will shun such associations. Thus, I have developed a set of idealized relationships that environmental organizations may have with various levels of governance, which I explore in more depth in Chapter 5.

1 **Positive** – the government/council frequently seeks the environmental organization's advice.

2 **Ambivalent** – the government/council is friendly, but the environmental organization itself initiates contact.

3 **Contingent** – government/council receptiveness depends on the issue(s) or department(s) involved.

4 **Negative** – the organization unsuccessfully attempts to influence the government/council, or has become blacklisted.

5 **No relationship** – the environmental organization has no relationship with government/council. It prefers alternative campaign targets or does not work at that level (e.g. local amenity societies are unlikely to have a relationship with national government because much of their work seeks to influence the local council instead).[9]

These five types expand upon the insider-outsider dichotomy used in the study of pressure groups, including institutional relationships that fall between the poles of the continuum. But which of these many different types of organizations that have been discussed above can be said to be 'in,' and which might be deemed 'out' of the environmental movement?

Who is part of the environmental movement?

Although an interesting academic exercise – even if just to ensure that the nature of the research object is clearly defined – not all activists regard it worthwhile to set movement boundaries. For many environmentalists, their primary concern is to improve the environment, and, for them, this often means collaborating with community groups, churches, elderly peoples' groups and, at times, anti-war and human rights organizations. Activists prioritizing other issues also work across movement boundaries. Inter-issue networking is especially evident in environmental direct action networks (Doherty et al. 2007). For Torrance (then Greenpeace Networker, now Sustrans Policy Manager):

> I don't think it's about building a wall around the environmental movement . . . it's more like a Venn diagram of interlaced circles . . . a kind of natural ecological system . . . There are relations with the peace movement, animal rights, environment, human rights, development movement etc. . . . it's unhealthy and not constructive to think who's in and who's out . . . Why not have just one social change movement? (interview June 2003)

The organizational types listed by Torrance are, in at least some strands of their work, fighting for related causes and therefore in real-world terms could be conceived of as part of a movement broader than environmental. Diani and Bison (2004) dealt with this in their study of civic organizations in the United Kingdom, by studying networking among organizations typically associated with a range of movements. And the broader literature on intra-movement interaction addresses the fact that networks extend beyond the remit of single movements. For example, Rose (2000) addresses the links between labour, peace and environmental movements; Ferree and Roth (1998) and Roth (2003) consider links between labour and women's movements; and Bystydzienski and Schacht (2001) have edited a collection that includes studies of interaction across many social movements. Consequently, Reinelt (1995), writing from the perspective of the women's movement, argues that it is problematic to exclude organizations that sit on the boundaries of movements. However, there are good reasons to focus on what has been purported to be a single movement: it prevents us selecting examples from across movements in support of a particular theory, allows us to question whether a movement exists or not and gives more focus to any discussion of political opportunities (see Chapter 5).

To see whether the environmental organizations I surveyed might be said to be social movement organizations, I look at their responses to four boundary demarcation questions. Do they consider themselves to be part of the movement? Do they have a main aim to protect or preserve the environment? Do they self-identify as part of a network of environmental organizations? And do they engage in at least some non-institutionalized activity?[10] (see Table 2.8). I find that, similar to Martin's (1990) research on feminist organizations, environmental organizations do not easily fit into ideal types, and that a variety of organizations exist within the milieu.

Overall, data shows high correspondence between the four boundary demarcation criteria and environmental organizations' own perceptions of whether they are a part of an environmental movement. Only nine organizations consider themselves part of the environmental movement, yet they also claim that their organization is *not* part of a network. These include one countryside protection organization, two working on food, farming or gardens and one working to protect a single species. A further two are transport organizations. There is not a single category of organizations that fails to meet the characteristics of social movement organizations. The most marginal are amenity societies, which are among the least likely to engage in non-institutionalized activity.

Of the 29 nature conservation organizations surveyed, many met all four criteria, perhaps suggesting that Doherty (2002) was a little too restrictive in his definition of the 'Green movement', which excluded conservation organizations on the grounds that they do not explicitly challenge the social order.

Despite high correspondence between boundary measures, there are important anomalies. While residents' associations have rarely been considered to be part of the environment movement, most of those that gave survey answers indicate the strong place of residents' associations in (local) environmental networks. Residents' associations in urban areas appear to have a strong input into local decision-making concerning the environment. Harmondsworth and Sipson Residents' Association and Longford Residents' Association, located close to Heathrow airport, both noted their primary concern for the environment, which was motivated by the threat of a new runway. Both had engaged in non-institutionalized activities including

Table 2.8 Boundary demarcation data by organizational aim type

Aim of Organization	Considers itself part of the environmental movement	Main aim to protect or preserve the environment	Part of a network of environmental organizations?	Some non-institutionalized activity?
	YES	YES	YES	YES
Air Pollution (2)	2	2	2	2
Amenities (34)	29	26	28	18
Anarchy (1)	1	1	1	1
Animal Rights (1)	1	1	1	1
Class (3)	1	1	1	1
Building Conservation/ Urban Landscapes (3)	3	3	3	2
Countryside Protection/ Conservation (29)	25	26	24	21
Energy (1)	1	1	0	1
Food/Farming/ Gardens (6)	6	6	4	6
Forests (1)	1	1	1	1
Land Rights (1)	1	0	0	1
Multi-issue (31)	26	26	25	24
Networking (2)	1	1	1	1
Single Species (12)	9	8	8	7
Transport (14)	13	10	11	10
Waste (3)	3	2	3	1
Non-environmental (5)	0	2	1	1
TOTALS YES	123	117	*114	99
NO	26	32	35	50

Note: * The analysis presented in the rest of the book is based on the 114 organizations that said they were part of a network and provided network data.

demonstrations, media work, public meetings and leafleting. While approximately three-quarters of amenity and residents associations considered themselves as having a main aim to protect or preserve the environment, 81 per cent perceived themselves to be part of the environmental movement and part of a network.

The case was less clear-cut for transport organizations. These include anti-airport expansion, anti-road groups, and those campaigning for better public transport, cycle lanes and walking conditions. Hillingdon Ramblers' Association responded, and answered all four questions in the affirmative, noting countryside protection and access to rights of way as key concerns. Sweeting, then coordinator of the Hillingdon Commuters' Association (and also of Hillingdon Friends of the Earth), claimed that although she is motivated by environmental concerns, the majority of the Association's members joined for the purpose of seeking improvement in their journeys to work, and not for environmental reasons. Rail Future's ambiguous connection to the environmental movement is similar. According to John Pitcher, organizer of the Kent Division of the London and South Eastern branch of Rail Future:

> Rail Future is on the edge of the environmental movement . . . I am in it for the right reasons but others are [in it] because their commuter train to London is always late, and others still have barely graduated from train spotting. Yet others welcome new airports because they usually promise new railway stations as crumbs! (personal correspondence January 2003)

Another interesting anomaly was the refusal of London Sustainability Exchange (LSx) to answer the questionnaire. Judging by its name, and information on its website (www.lsx.org.uk/), one would assume that it would consider itself to be part of an environmental network and that it would self-identify with the movement. Interestingly, Starr (2000) also regards the sustainability movement as distinct from the environmental movement. Chris Church of the Community Development Foundation argues along the same lines because of the tendency of the two types of environmentalism to work in relative isolation from each other (personal correspondence August 2003).

Environmental networks and environmental movements

Networking, then, is central to definitions of social movements and seems to cohere closely with environmental organizations self-perception as part of an environmental movement. But exactly how networked should organizations be to be considered part of an environmental movement?

Diani (1992a), in his 'emergent consensual' definition of social movements, argued that the network links between organizations (and individuals) can be informal or highly structured, frequent or infrequent, intense or cursory. These links, he suggested, mostly involve the sharing of information, expertise and materials, and are what lead movements to develop 'broader senses of meaning' (1992b, 8).

However, if the links are infrequent, brief and relaxed, they may amount to little more than a friendship between two people who may not share interests, and will not necessarily give the movement a sense of unity through shared meanings. The link could feasibly constitute just a brief consultation of a webpage, which, only at a stretch, would sufficiently network individuals. Moreover, the cursorily linked people could be engaging in completely non-compatible forms of action and have vastly different ideas regarding the need to protect or preserve the environment. Such cursory information sharing is a very weak network dimension, partly because it is informal and could be infrequent. I consider it too weak to measure meaningful networking – and especially to measure a social movement dynamic – because most people at best only skim read the information they receive. Rosy White, the Campaign to Protect Rural England Senior Development Officer, for example, said in an interview (in October 2003) that: 'Well, as a fairly typical member of these organizations, I don't read the stuff [received from other organizations] properly and possibly for not until about six months later'.

Within organizations, information from other organizations tends to get stockpiled, while the work demands of their own organizations and routines of everyday life are prioritized. Activists will not necessarily find information from other groups particularly informative or useful. According to Waugh (Volunteer Coordinator, London Wildlife Trust, interview, June 2003), much of the information she looks at from other organizations is 'fairly glib . . . and designed for a public audience and not of much use'. Similarly, Robertshaw (voluntary warden, Chiswick Wildlife Group), mostly finds the monthly glossy magazines she receives unhelpful to her conservation work:

> Mostly because we are at a stage where if we need information, we need specific information. And these magazines are for a public audience . . . they don't tell you how to do butterfly transects . . . because that would be deadly boring for the public. (Interview, February 2004)

I would, therefore, argue that Diani's (1992a) suggestion that the network dimension of a movement can be informal and irregular is too weak – especially for a study of environmental networks. Information often flows only one way and has no effect. If it is stockpiled, ignored or is too basic then it is clearly not leading to the development of the 'broader senses of meaning' deemed necessary to bind movements together

(Diani 1992a: 8). Although engagement in collective action is part of Diani's definition, he only recently came to insist on a collaborative network. In this book I shall look mostly at collaborative links between environmental organizations in London that are part of an environmental network, although I also consider the extent to which they share information. I suggest, in tune with Diani and Bison (2004) that collaborative networking is what really binds organizations together, not cursory or brief information passing links.

Concluding remarks

This chapter has defined environmental networks and stressed their relationship to definitions of social movements. Research which analyses the interaction between environmental organizations is better addressed through a study of environmental networks rather than environmental movements. It allows avoidance of conceptual confusion surrounding the term 'social movements'. This is a term sometimes used to talk only of organizations and activists that engage in non-institutional protest and which seek profound change to the social order via political conflict against an identifiable opponent. Viewing social movements as such precludes development of an understanding of the links that exist between different types of environmental organizations. Organizations using a wide variety of tactics that are, (a) networked; and (b) seek to preserve or protect the environment, are considered part of London's environmental networks. Tactics can vary from the pressure group-like approach taken by organizations like Friends of the Earth, to the practical conservation focus of groups like London Wildlife Trust, or the autonomous networking space found in radical social centres. I shall continue to include conservationists in the analysis that follows because I am interested to find out more about their extent of networking with other environmental organizations, even if they cannot be convincingly be considered part of an environmental movement.

Now that the scene has been set, I proceed in Chapter 3 to look in more detail at several key campaigns and environmental organizations in London.

3 Key Organizations and Campaigns in London's Environmental Networks

This chapter describes London's environmental networks in more detail. Although it focuses on the state of play in key environmental organizations in 2003 – the year the primary research for this book was conducted – it has been updated to include more recent developments. It provides background to the organizations that were selected for more in-depth study (see Table 3.1) and on two key campaigns – climate change and aviation – for which networking patterns are analysed in the chapters that follow. All of the organizations introduced in this chapter are part of London's environmental networks – they are based in London, are networked to others *and* seek to preserve or protect the environment. The campaigns that are introduced have involved a number of organizations working collaboratively, illustrating how environmental networks deploy their strengths. The chapter also demonstrates the diversity of approaches among environmental organizations, building on the previous chapters and setting the scene for the analysis that follows in the rest of the book.

Table 3.1 The ten study groups

	Conservationists	Reformists	Radicals
Southeast	Plumstead Common Environment Group	Greenwich Friends of the Earth	*
Northeast	Chiswick Wildlife Group	Hillingdon Friends of the Earth	*
Regional	London Wildlife Trust	London Friends of the Earth	Environmental Direct Action Group
National	Campaign to Protect Rural England	Friends of the Earth Greenpeace	*

Note: *Denotes that there were no environmental organizations of this type available to research

National environmental organizations
Campaign to Protect Rural England

The Campaign to Protect Rural England seeks to preserve and protect the countryside by preventing urban sprawl, supporting rural communities and their services and preventing developments that harm the 'beauty and tranquillity' of the countryside. It was established after the First World War, when England was being reconstructed with vigour, suburbanization was reshaping the landscape, ribbon developments were taking over the countryside and advertisement boards were creeping out of towns and cities onto rural roadsides. Under the leadership of well-known planners like Abercrombie and Williams-Ellis, it initially sought to redress suburbanization's adverse effects on the countryside (Campaign to Protect Rural England 2000: 3 cf. Williams-Ellis [1928] 1996). Building upon this, in 1940–60, it began actively opposing motorway and power station developments. By 1968, it had changed its name from the Council for the *Preservation* of Rural England, to Council for the *Protection* of Rural England, to reflect the more proactive role it was taking in countryside protection, having been instrumental in the establishment of the 1968 Countryside Act (Campaign to Protect Rural England 2000: 5).

By the 1990s, the Campaign was demonstrating broader commitment to sustainability (Campaign to Protect Rural England 1993), setting out how to make the most of the planning system its founders established. It also began with public engagement, improving its relations with the press. This change of focus is reflected in its more recent (2003) name change from *Council* for the Protection of Rural England, to *Campaign* to Protect Rural England.

The Campaign's strength lies in its strong relationship with government ministers and intricate knowledge of the planning system. In 2000, it took a lead role in campaigning alongside 10 other environment/planning organizations to reform the planning laws (Friends of the Earth 2002a).[1] This campaign was followed in 2002 with a successful attempt to prevent fast-tracking of the planning system for large infrastructural projects.[2] In the spring of 2012, it was once again actively campaigning against reforms to the planning system that would make it difficult for local authorities to oppose development. Despite its emphasis on the planning system, it has also worked on urban regeneration, rural policy, mineral extraction and energy use.

The organization consists of a national office, with a network of 43 county branches and 200 district groups that function as autonomous entities. County branches and local groups screen local planning applications, campaign against them if appropriate and promote positive solutions. Although tempting to classify the Campaign as 'reformist' because, among other things, it seeks policy gains via lobbying and joins reformist coalitions, the organization was selected as an organization for qualitative study because it is the best example of a London-based national conservation organization. As illustrated in Chapter 2, environmental organizations do not consistently match ideal types. But Campaign to Protect Rural England is the only London-based national organization with a conservationist ideology. It cannot be denied that the Campaign has overarching emphasis on the countryside. Its historical claim that it 'is the only independent organization concerned with the care and improvement of the whole of England's *countryside*' (Campaign to Protect Rural England 1993, emphasis added) is challenged today only by the Wildlife Trusts, whose headquarters is outside of London. The National Trust, based in Warrington, Cheshire, focuses much of its conservation efforts on heritage sites.

Friends of the Earth, England, Wales and Northern Ireland

Seeking to be '*the* environmental justice organisation', Friends of the Earth's mission statement (2003–8) stated that:

> Friends of the Earth will work with others to create a sustainable global community where protection of the environment and meeting people's needs go hand in hand. We strive for societies where people have decided to build the conditions for everyone to enjoy a dignified existence and good livelihood while not impinging on the rights of others to achieve a good life. (Friends of the Earth 2002b: 8)

Friends of the Earth England, Wales and Northern Ireland (ENWI, from here on simply 'Friends of the Earth') was established in 1971 by David Brower, founder of Friends of the Earth US. Its first high-profile media action involved dumping hundreds of non-returnable bottles on Schweppes' doorstep. Starting from a small office (less than a quarter of the size of the basement in their current six-floor building) with six desks, Friends of the Earth (EWNI) now has a staff of around 160. Its reputation, built upon long-standing emphasis on careful research, has been enhanced by on-going professionalization.

David Brower began the Friends of the Earth strategy of waging political battles to protect the environment back in 1970. Traditionally, Friends of the Earth worked at creating a climate of opinion to mobilize the public to pressurize institutions it considered most likely to have capacity to solve environmental issues. Its targets include political parties, government, international forums and businesses. The structure of the organization enables such activity at the national, international, regional and local levels under its motto of 'Thinking Globally, Acting Locally' (Lamb 1996: 50–1). However, there is an increasing tendency for Friends of the Earth to appeal directly to decision-makers: the parliamentary team tactically lobbies MPs, and drafts bills with the hope of instigating new environmental legislation. Examples include the Warm Homes (1990), Road Traffic Reduction (1997), Doorstep Recycling (2003) and Climate Change (2008) Acts. It works with businesses, but takes a cautious approach. In the main, it establishes relationships with ethical companies – working with the best to pressurize the rest (Juniper, 2000).

Friends of the Earth's main themes for 2003–8 were environmental justice, sustainable economies, environmental limits and accountability/participation. The environmental justice theme aimed to make issues of social, economic and racial equality central to the way the public and decision-makers viewed environmental issues. It incorporated a campaign for 'climate justice', seeking an equitable climate change treaty, and 'action for justice', working with community groups suffering from injustices. 'Environmental limits' incorporated campaigns against waste, recognizing the limits to what humans can extract from and dispose of in the environment. 'Sustainable economies' aimed to develop a sustainable economics agenda at technical and public levels, incorporating an attempt to 'curb the power of the supermarkets' and to 'derail the WTO'. Other aspects of sustainable economics included 'corporate accountability' and 'reducing resource use', which promoted zero waste policies. 'Accountability/participation' sought to improve grassroots capacity for environmental campaigning in and outside Friends of the Earth.

Ultimately, it is the board of directors, which is influenced by senior staff, that decides Friends of the Earth's formal policies. The board has a maximum of 17 members, 10 of whom are elected by local groups (Rootes 2002: 23). Between 2003 and 2008, campaigns were organized on the basis of the themes noted above, directed by team leaders. Paul De Zylva led (and in early 2012 continues to lead) the England team, coordinating 12 Regional Campaign Coordinators (RCCs) who seek a regional presence in strategic planning. Since 2002, there has been a concerted effort to involve local groups more effectively in strategic planning and a capacity building team exists to support local groups (Friends of the Earth 2002b). In 2003, Friends of the Earth had 193 local groups (but 229 were listed on the website in January 2011).

Friends of the Earth currently (in 2011) structures its work around the themes of futurity, equity and change. It is campaigning to 'fix the food chain', for warm homes, to persuade local councils to 'get serious' about CO_2, and for a secure international climate change agreement. Environmental justice remains central to its work.

Greenpeace UK

Greenpeace UK (from here on, simply Greenpeace) is probably Britain's most well-known environmental organization. Its principles are bearing witness, non-violence, direct action and internationality (Torrance, the Greenpeace Network Developer, interview 2003). Its current vision (2011) is to work towards 'a green and peaceful world – an earth that is ecologically healthy and able to nurture life in all its diversity' (Greenpeace website 2011[3]).

Greenpeace (International) began in 1971 when committed anti-nuclear activists hired a barely seaworthy boat attempting to bear witness and physically obstruct atomic tests off the coast of Amchitka, Alaska. Since then, Greenpeace has developed almost beyond recognition. The UK branch of Greenpeace International was established in 1977 and, unlike Friends of the Earth, initially prioritized bearing witness and direct action over research and lobbying. Over time, Greenpeace has become more committed to careful research, which now informs its policies and campaigns, establishing the Greenpeace Research Laboratories at London's Queen Mary's College in 1987, which relocated to the University of Exeter in 1992.

Unlike Friends of the Earth, which has a broad agenda for encouraging sustainability that encompasses environmental, economic and social themes, Greenpeace tends to focus on a few key global issues at a time, following a long established pattern of selecting just a handful of visible campaigns. In 2003, Greenpeace UK's campaigns were climate change/renewable energy, ancient forests, PVC, GM food, nuclear power and protection of the oceans. In 2011, it had moved on to climate change, 'beyond oil', protecting forests, defending oceans and working for peace.

Greenpeace's organizational structure has been likened to that of a corporate enterprise (Doyle and McEachern 1998). Campaign teams are centrally coordinated, with top-down management – from Greenpeace International, to the director, to the campaign team leaders, to local groups and 'active supporters'. In early 2012, there were 88 local groups listed on Greenpeace's website. Prior to 1995, Greenpeace local groups were confined to fund-raising and distributing Greenpeace literature. This has changed considerably as Greenpeace began to realize local groups' potential for raising awareness. By the early 2000s, Greenpeace local groups were actively campaigning. For example, in 2003, local groups participated in the Scary Dairy campaign targeting Sainsbury's stores. This involved dressing up as cows, drawing attention to GM animal feed, giving out free organic milk and asking customers to sign a postcard asking the store to stop selling GM-contaminated milk. In addition to local groups, Greenpeace has an active supporters' network, which contains activists not necessarily affiliated with a local group. Active supporters put themselves forward, usually via the Greenpeace website, to help with lobbying, or to offer their legal and media skills. At least until 2004, they received a monthly *Network* magazine including details of recent Greenpeace campaigning activities. Communication to and among Greenpeace activists increasingly takes place via the 'get active' section of the

Greenpeace website, which includes blogs and reports and posts opportunities for involvement.

Greenpeace's famous media stunts are carefully planned and coordinated by employed campaigners. If there is an outward appearance of fewer such stunts, it is because of the increasing emphasis placed on solutions-based campaigning (as evident in *Greenpeace Business* – the bi-monthly publication Greenpeace produces for a business audience – and declining media attention). According to Rootes (2002: 29) Greenpeace – although historically rarely invited to formal consultative meetings as a result of its critical stance towards them – has increasingly frequent meetings with government ministers and civil servants.

Although Doherty (2002) includes Greenpeace as part of his 'Green movement' because of its focus on direct action, for this study it is regarded as a reform organization, albeit a fairly radical one, not afraid to strategically break the law (Rucht 1995[4]). Although Greenpeace uses direct action, it tends not to do so in order to directly change things itself, but to levy pressure on governments and corporations via exposure in the media. In a reformist style, Greenpeace's direct actions are 'backed up by sophisticated political lobbying and scientific inquiry' (Brown and May 1991: 5).

Regional environmental organizations
London Wildlife Trust

Although the field of action for conservation organizations usually centres on practical projects and seeking changes in legislation (Chapter 2), London Wildlife Trust, one of the largest and strongest Trusts in the national network, has always been involved in fighting controversial planning applications (Dwyer and Hodge 1996). To an extent, this reflects the nature of the urban environment, which means that it acts in a very different manner to its counterparts in rural areas. In rural areas, there are considerably fewer controversial planning applications/decisions. The overarching aim of London Wildlife Trust is to sustain and enhance London's wildlife habitats. Although it engages in reformist strategies, it is clear that these are deployed in the interest of protecting sites that are important for wildlife. As its website[5] states:

> London Wildlife Trust is the only charity dedicated solely to protecting the capital's wildlife and wild spaces, engaging London's diverse communities through access to our nature reserves, campaigning, volunteering and education.

London Wildlife Trust was established in 1981. The first campaign it became involved in sought to prevent gravel extraction at the wildlife rich sites of Walthamstow

Marshes and Frays Farm Meadows. A practical project was embarked upon later that year and two acres of land were reclaimed from the rear of Kings Cross Station to create what is now the Trust's flagship reserve at Camley Street. In 2001, a Greater London Authority contract to resurvey London's wildlife sites was embarked upon, making London Wildlife Trust essentially an 'insider' – working *inside* the corridors of power – from a conservationist perspective at regional level. According to Gaines (Director of the Trust for five years before his secondment in 2002):

> What is undeniable is that the Trust has grown from a small committed group of people struggling to bring the capital's natural environment to the attention of all Londoners to a thriving and diverse organisation involved in all aspects of nature conservation. (Gaines 2003: 9)

In 2003, the Trust was concerned with the conservation implications of the UK Olympics bid, 'brownfield sites' (London Wildlife Trust 2002: 5), housing expansion in the Thames Gateway area and Stratford and a review of planning laws. Its campaigns in 2011 were for wildlife friendly gardens, against climate change and to 'save our seas'. The latter was part of a national Wildlife Trust campaign that sought to show public support for a robust network of Marine Protected Areas. Although the Trust garnered public support for Marine Protected Areas using a petition, it usually campaigns using insider strategies. In addition to campaigning, it also engages in practical conservation and supports local reserves. It opposes development on important wildlife sites, but has been working to make development more sustainable in certain areas, rather than opposing it point-blank.

The Trust is managed by a Council of Management, which sets policy and manages staff and budgets. Central Office facilitates information flows between Council, local groups, reserves and the national office. It also provides an overarching strategic perspective on London's nature conservation issues, raises funds, maintains membership databases, produces public information and delivers an education programme. Local groups consist of volunteers engaging in activities such as fund-raising, promotion, reserve management and local planning issues. In total, London Wildlife Trust manages 57 nature reserves, 6 of which are staffed, and the rest manned by dedicated volunteers (Hartley 1997: 1). The Hillingdon Group of the London Wildlife Trust, for example, is responsible for looking after wildlife sites in the Ickenham area – Gutteridge Wood and Yeading Brook Meadows.

London Friends of the Earth

London Friends of the Earth is one of nine regional Friends of the Earth offices based in the national Friends of the Earth office. The other regional Friends of the Earth groups have separate offices and are run by Regional Campaign

Coordinators who coordinate campaigns that affect their region, monitor policy developments within the English regions and play a support function for local groups. London Friends of the Earth has been constructive in developing London-wide networks of anti-GM campaigners in order to inject this issue into regional governance. In physical terms, London Friends of the Earth consists of only the Regional Campaign Coordinator, Jenny Bates, with support from national staff, the Capacity Building team[6] and local groups. Bates is responsible for 28 local Friends of the Earth groups.

Between 1997 and 2003, London Friends of the Earth was coordinated by Paul de Zylva, who in 1998–2000 worked extensively with a community in Enfield on the issue of contaminated land, culminating in the publication of the Friends of the Earth briefing *Safe as Houses*. During 2003, under Jennifer Bates, London Friends of the Earth was heavily involved in aviation campaigning and the Thames Gateway bridge proposals. It continues to work on both of these, and also seeks to make London a sustainable city: challenging the emphasis on economic growth in the London Development Masterplan, and helping to ensure that the 2012 Olympics become a 'beacon of sustainability'. It uses a very conventional form of campaigning activity, arguably more so than national Friends of the Earth. It has close links with the London Sustainability Exchange, and London 21 Sustainability Network.

Environmental Direct Action Group

The Environmental Direct Action Group is a small but active group of radical environmentalists who campaign 'against the root causes of climate change', which for them means government power structures and large corporations. It is hard to say much more about its origins without breaching the confidentiality promised to group members.[7]

The Environmental Direct Action Group works for climate justice and equality. Its protests are organized through weekly meetings, emails and some telephoning. Group decisions are made on a consensus basis and there is no leader. Naturally, as in most decentralized groups, certain individuals fall into roles suited to their skills and personalities (Saunders 2009b), including one activist who was particularly adept at leaflet design and another who most often compiled action reports for the Indymedia website. The group engages in a range of actions from Friends of the Earth-style street campaigning and Greenpeace-style banner hanging, through to office occupations and disruption of conferences (for more information, see 'climate change campaigning' section, below). During 2010, the group protested against consumerism and nuclear power and joined the Crude Awakening blockade of Coryton Oil Refinery.

Local environmental organizations
Plumstead Common Environment Group
Plumstead Common Environment Group was formed in the spring of 1991 by a small group of local people concerned about neglected local green spaces. A ravine that is now a beautiful nature reserve used to be a hotspot for fly tipping until group members cleared the area. The group have also restored a highly polluted pond in the heart of the Common that has since become a successful breeding site for ducks and moorhens.

More recently, Plumstead Common Environment Group turned its attention to trying to prevent dog defecation, litter and graffiti on the Common. To raise attention, offending faeces were marked with flags on a 'dog poo day' in 1999, alerting dog walkers and residents to the extent of spoilage. This was followed by a highly successful pooper-scooper display. Since then the amount of defecation has been significantly reduced, aided by Greenwich Borough Council's 'clear it up' logos painted on the main paths through the Common. Volunteers not only engage in the usual conservation tasks, but have on occasions been involved in mass litter clearance, sometimes removing an entire van load at a time. They also keep a watchful eye on planning applications affecting the Common, and successfully campaigned against a mobile phone mast in 2001. The group has a very close relationship with Greenwich Borough Council and frequently spurs it into taking positive action to assist with the management and conservation of the Common. Into the 2010s, it has continued to work on campaigns against environmental crime and to run conservation volunteer task days to maintain the ponds and nature reserve. As with other conservation-focused groups, there is something of tendency for it to engage in reformist-type actions, such as lobbying the council. But its overarching emphasis on the wildlife of the Common confirms that its field of action is very much conservationist.

Greenwich and Lewisham Friends of the Earth
Greenwich and Lewisham Friends of the Earth is bound by the Friends of the Earth Partnership Agreement that lays out expectations of local groups. This dictates that they should campaign on at least one national Friends of the Earth campaign, but can campaign on other issues depending on members' interests and opportunities. They are expected to have a public profile raised through the media, posters and leaflets or through staging stalls and events. All actions they carry out should be lawful, reflecting overall Friends of the Earth policy and be non-party political. Local group members should be encouraged to attend training events, conferences and consultation events and at minimum have a treasurer and coordinator. Group

members should be contactable by phone/email and local group meetings are to be welcoming and open to all. In return, Friends of the Earth provides public liability insurance, a range of support material, and invites groups to participate in strategy and policymaking. It also provides a Local Group's Support Fund, access to information and updates on campaigns via national campaigners, a local groups' community website, and publications (e.g. the bi-monthly *Change Your World* local groups' magazine). When local groups sign up to the agreement under these conditions, they are then granted the legal right to use the name 'Friends of the Earth' (Friends of the Earth 2002c).

In common with London Friends of the Earth, much of Greenwich and Lewisham Friends of the Earth's efforts in 2000–3 involved working to prevent construction of the Thames Gateway road bridge. The two groups share this concern partly because Jennifer Bates was, for a short while, coordinating both. It has also taken part in Stop Esso actions (see below). In 1999, Greenwich and Lewisham Friends of the Earth was heavily involved in opposing plans for the millennium dome site and the 'sustainable millennium village', which, according to campaigners, made a mockery of the principle of sustainability (cf. Gordon 1994, Bates interview, February 2001). As a result of her in-depth research and analysis into the issues surrounding the Greenwich Peninsular development, Bates became Friends of the Earth spokesperson on the issue. Since then, she has made an increasingly positive impact, culminating in her appointment as London Regional Campaigns Coordinator. Greenwich Friends of the Earth, typical of most local Friends of the Earth groups engages in lobbying, stalls, Friends of the Earth-designed days of action and fund-raising. Since 2003, it has been involved in the Big Ask campaign (see below) a 'Biofools' campaign – against biofuels – and in a live-local-shop-local campaign.

Chiswick Wildlife Group

Unlike most London Wildlife Trust 'branches', Chiswick Wildlife Group focuses on one nature reserve and only monitors local planning proposals likely to directly affect the reserve. It manages Gunnersbury Triangle Nature Reserve, Chiswick (northwest London), a triangular shaped green space wedged between a road, and two train tracks (the Piccadilly Line and a National Rail line). In total, the reserve covers six acres and is a patchwork of habitats – wild woodland, wetlands, pond and meadow. It is one of the London Wildlife Trust's Key Sites, and as such has a paid warden throughout the summer months of the year.

Chiswick Wildlife Group was established in 1984 when a group of local people vigorously campaigned to save from development what was then a piece of waste ground. London Wildlife Trust helped the campaigners, resulting in the site's designation as a nature reserve. It was a landmark case, being the first time a local council was forced to refuse planning permission due to newly founded nature reserve status.

Chiswick Wildlife Group has managerial control of the Gunnersbury reserve, but it is at the dictates of London Wildlife Trust, which had been working to keep a tighter rein on its local groups. The committee meets bi-monthly in a local public house and has an annual general meeting at which committee members are elected. The committee includes a chair, borough representative, events manager and voluntary warden.

Chiswick Wildlife Group and its summer warden follow the centrally coordinated management plan to create and maintain a bio-diverse haven. Volunteers engage in practical conservation work every Tuesday and on occasional Sundays. Pond clearance, bramble pruning, removal of invasive or non-native species, path maintenance, tree pruning/felling and wildlife monitoring are among the necessary tasks. Besides general maintenance of the Triangle, the group organizes a number of events to raise the profile of the reserve and generate community interest, hoping to recruit more volunteers. In summer 2003, the group ran a bird song evening, a butterfly and insect trail, a summer picnic and a guided walk focusing on mushrooms and other fungi. Numerous supervised visits from local schoolchildren were conducted. Chiswick Wildlife Group also write press releases to get local news coverage and leaflet the local community to raise awareness. Conservation volunteer days and education activities are scheduled to continue.

Hillingdon Friends of the Earth

At the start of its life, Hillingdon Friends of the Earth engaged in campaigns against whaling and used Greenpeace campaign materials to help spread its message. It used to show Greenpeace footage at its meetings to enthuse newcomers. In the early 1980s, the group was very active and relatively youthful, but over time, membership has dropped and the stalwarts have aged (Sweeting interview, February 2004).

The group was involved, in a supportive capacity, in the campaign against the third runway at Heathrow airport. Although members were encouraged to respond to the consultation and send a pre-printed Friends of the Earth postcard to their MPs, the main role Hillingdon Friends of the Earth played was the provision of a £200 donation to West London Friends of the Earth to pay for a new combined phone, fax and answering machine (Hillingdon Friends of the Earth 2003).

Monthly public meetings used to consist of talks from key speakers until the numbers attending meetings dwindled to seven or fewer. The group is a regular participant in Hillingdon Wildlife Week, an annual event to promote wildlife in the borough. It has also been working on producing a recycling directory which is to be posted on Hillingdon Borough Council's website. The group continues to promote itself at local fairs and fetes and was actively involved in the campaigns to introduce and then strengthen the Climate Change Act (2008).

Key environmental campaigns in London

Climate Change Campaigning

Climate change is emphasized in this book because of its significance as a major global environmental issue and the coinciding surge in the frequency of protests and campaigns on the issue. Climate change can be said to have to have replaced sustainable development as the defining environmental issue of this century (Connelly et al. 2012). The Intergovernmental Panel for Climate Change (IPCC), suggests that temperatures may rise between 1.1 and 6.4°C throughout the course of the twenty-first century, and that most of this rise is 'very likely' due to human activities. It reports that 'eleven of the twelve years (1995–2006) rank among the twelve warmest years in the instrumental record of global surface temperature (since 1850)' (IPCC 2007: 33). There is 'high confidence' that this will have a range of dramatic effects on weather patterns and ecosystems.

Given the severity of the issue, it is perhaps not surprising that a broad range of environmental organizations have played a role in campaigns against climate change. Before I detail campaigns, I present a brief précis of international policymaking on climate change as this provides useful contextual information for understanding the campaign responses. After discussing general climate change campaigning, the campaign against the Baku Ceyhan pipeline is outlined.

International policymaking

Annual international ministerial meetings entitled Conference(s) of the Parties to the Climate Convention Meeting (COP) have been held since 1995 to make progress on implementing the UN Framework Convention on Climate Change (UNFCCC), signed by over 150 nations at the Rio Earth Summit (1992). Until the Kyoto Protocol was ratified in 2004, the Convention amounted merely to a suggestion that parties to it make voluntary reductions of greenhouse gas emissions to 1990 levels by 2000.

At the first conference in Berlin (COP1), spring 1995, 116 nations agreed that climate change was the most pressing environmental policy field requiring partnership to achieve the Convention's objectives. The second conference (COP2), a year and a quarter later began to work on a protocol to ensure that nations fulfilled commitments. The Kyoto Protocol was christened at COP3, 1997, setting legally binding targets for emissions reductions.[8] Global reduction targets were set at approximately 5 per cent below 1990 levels by 2012, with Britain committed to a 12.5 per cent reduction (although Britain had an independent target of 20%).

By 2000, it was apparent to environmental organizations like Friends of the Earth and radical grassroots protesters that the negotiations were failing to bring about concrete agreements and that targets were either too weak, or, in the view of some, significantly diluted by flexible clauses. This perception was strengthened when the COP6 (2000) negotiations at The Hague collapsed due to vociferous demands made by the industrial lobby and the US government that emission reductions be lessened. According to a Rising Tide (2000a) briefing, 'COP6 looked more like a trade fair than an intergovernmental conference looking at ways to solve one of the world's most pressing environmental problems', as industrialists sought ways of profiteering from the 'carbon economy'. Indeed, it cannot be denied that economic concerns hampered the progress of the protocol, especially in the United States. Shortly before the then President Bush Jnr rejected the protocol, the Chairman and Chief Executive Officer of the US company Imperial Oil told a journalist:

Kyoto is an economic entity. It has nothing to do with the environment. It has to do with world trade. This is a wealth transfer scheme between developed and developing nations. And it's been couched and clothed in some kind of environmental movement. That's the dumbest-assed thing I've heard in a long time. (quoted in Greenpeace 2002a)

Many were not surprised when, in March 2001, Bush announced – under pressure from industry and oil companies (especially Exxon Mobil, more on this later) – that he would not ratify the Kyoto Protocol. This has rendered it virtually toothless to deal with climate change given that the United States produces around a quarter of global greenhouse gas emissions.

COP9, which coincided with the fieldwork reported upon in this book, was held in Milan in December 2003, by which time most of the rules on the operation of the protocol had been agreed. Media attention during COP9, however, was focused upon whether or not Russia would ratify the protocol. Until June 2004, Russia had still not ratified,[9] leading to consternation among campaigners that the agreement would not come into force, because to do so it needed to be ratified by enough industrialized countries to account for a total of 55 per cent of their collective emissions. Without Russia on board, the figure would have been only 44 per cent (Osborn and Castle 2004). Friends of the Earth campaigners from Russia claimed that Russia was playing a political game, using delaying tactics to seek further concessions from the European Union. Although Russia has now ratified, it continued to appear to campaigners that each round of COP negotiations resulted in a weakening of the Protocol.

Unfortunately, COP13 in Bali in 2007 did not reassure commentators, with Christoff (2008) branding the resultant Bali road map a 'rough goat track'. It did, however, set out that a future climate change strategy would be based on the four pillars of mitigation, adaptation, technology and finance. COP15 in Copenhagen in 2009 was hailed by many commentators as a last-ditch attempt to save the world from dangerous climate change. Unfortunately, it was a notable failure. The outcome of the conference was the Copenhagen Accord, a non-committal document, drafted by a small group of countries behind closed doors, and which parties to the conference agreed only to 'take note' of. Although developing countries agreed to reduce their emissions for the first time, the document lacked reference to specific emission reduction targets. It also opened up debates about the lack of democracy in the proceedings of the UNFCCC, with countries like Tuvalu, Venezuela, Bolivia, Cuba and Nicaragua dismissing the Accord on the grounds of collusion of a narrow group of states (Dimitrov 2010). Friends of the Earth was dismayed, but other more radical environmental organizations merely had their gloomy prognosis confirmed.

Campaign responses

One should not be surprised to note there is a general feeling among environmental campaigners that UNFCCC negotiations are resulting in little, if any, progress in preventing or halting climate change. For some organizations (such as the Environmental Direct Action Group), the UNFCCC framework was never anything more than a sinking ship. Others, including Friends of the Earth, Greenpeace and Campaign Against Climate Change, have, historically at least, regarded securing an international agreement on climate-changing emissions, no matter how weak, as an essential stepping stone towards achieving more stringent targets. A wide range of environmental organizations – whether or not they believe in incremental reformist change – argues the case for a rapid and significant reduction in emissions of greenhouse gases.

Since 1997, COP discussions have been visited by demonstrations, rallies, marches and media stunts highlighting the need for urgent action.[10] COP6 at The Hague saw the first International Environmental Direct Action Group festival as eco-anarchists engaged in direct action, from blockading to 'pieing'.[11] The Environmental Direct Action Group network originated in the Netherlands, and was at first a response to what its activists considered a flailing COP6. Shortly afterwards, it spread to Britain via ties between radical activists.

Also at COP6, Friends of the Earth campaigners created a mock dyke to draw media attention to the flooding issues associated with climate change (Rising Tide 2000b). London activists drawn from Reclaim the Streets joined in with solidarity actions in London attempting to alert the City of London to the causes of climate change. These included a festival style protest with a sound system and the

Rhythms of Resistance Samba Band. In addition, the Department of Environment, Transport and the Regions offices in London were occupied in opposition to the government's road building programme and, especially, to publicize links between increased traffic and climate change (Rising Tide 2000c).

The Campaign Against Climate Change was established in all but name in the aftermath of COP6 in The Hague. Inspired by his participation in the Hague protests, appalled by US attempts to weaken the Kyoto Protocol and dismayed with Friends of the Earth's lack of follow-up activity, Phil Thornhill, founder of the Campaign, on his return to London, began a one-man fortnight-long vigil outside the US Embassy. This was followed by a series of once-a-week vigils supported by the Green Party and some local Friends of the Earth activists. Describing himself as a 'sixties child', Thornhill had in mind to create a Campaign for Nuclear Disarmament-style protest organization. At the time of Bush's inauguration, the Campaign Against Climate Change staged a demonstration as a plea to him to take Kyoto more seriously, including a symbolic media action with 'Uncle Sam' setting fire to a globe. When Bush announced that he intended to reverse a US decision on the capping of power station emissions, the Campaign Against Climate Change mobilized 20 activists who sported Bush heads and carried placards proclaiming Bush a 'Global Village Idiot' (Thornhill interview, June 2003).

On the day that Bush announced his country's exit from the Kyoto protocol, 60 activists turned up outside the US Embassy for the Campaign Against Climate Change's Bush is a 'Dirty Rat' day of action. Annual Kyoto Marches were held between 2001 and 2005, involving a long march from Exxon Mobil's Headquarters to the US Embassy, with a rally en route. Since 2006, the Campaign Against Climate Change has (co)organized large-scale rallies and demonstrations to coincide with the annual COP meetings.

Stop Esso, like the Campaign Against Climate Change, was a response to Bush pulling out of the Kyoto Protocol. In particular, it drew attention to the relationship between Bush and Exxon Mobil (called Esso in Britain). Its key briefing (2001) stated that Esso had provided over $1,086,080 to the Republican Party in the 2000 US presidential election, that it funded and partook in expensive anti-environmental 'fronts' to discredit climate change science (including the infamous Global Climate Coalition[12]), dismissed the potential of renewable energy, and actively lobbied Bush to withdraw from Kyoto.

Stop Esso consisted of Greenpeace, Friends of the Earth and student environmentalist network People and Planet. For the first two years, local activists in the branches of these organizations engaged in national days of action, picketing Esso petrol stations around the country. In 2004, Stop Esso turned its attention towards the lingering environmental effects of the Exxon Valdez oil spill, by lobbying

Chief Executive Officer Lee Raymond and encouraging supporters to write to him demanding that the company pay fair mitigation costs. By 2006, the network had ceased to be active.

At the 2003 COP in Milan, which coincided with fieldwork reported in this book, the protests were much less significant than they had been in Bonn three years earlier. Friends of the Earth Italy organized a march and rally with the theme 'Stop CO2, Stop the Fossil Fuel Economy' and a student environmentalist network hung a banner proclaiming 'Stop Global War(m)'. A critical mass[13] was held attracting an impressive 2,000 cyclists, and Friends of the Earth International staged one of its annual 'Treetanic' award ceremonies, which attempt to expose industrial-scale timber plantations seeking to unjustly profit from the Kyoto Protocol. The winner was PLANTAR, a Brazilian company specializing in charcoal production for the steel industry and barbecues with apparently little concern for the environment (Friends of the Earth International 2003). Although Friends of the Earth (ENWI) was not present, some of its campaigners and activists were. London and Oxford Environmental Direct Action Group activists joined the festivities.

In solidarity with Milan-based protesters, Environmental Direct Action Group activists staged street theatre outside the London United Nation offices entitled 'What's the Big Deal [about Kyoto]'. The aim of the play was to show how carbon-traders, business interests and what they considered to be compromising NGOs hide under the UN's cloak of respectability, giving the public the false impression that prevention of climate change is in hand. The play highlighted the group's concern that the Kyoto agreement worked against the interests of poor people from southern countries who suffer the worst consequences of climate change. Leaflets detailing radical activists' concerns about the inefficacy of Kyoto entitled 'Why Kyoto is Pants' were distributed to UN staff and passers-by.

In its tradition of bearing witness, Greenpeace began climate campaigning activity on the eve of the Kyoto agreement by reporting the retreat of ice witnessed during its voyages to the Arctic and Antarctic and seeking the views of native peoples. Since 1997, Greenpeace has vociferously campaigned against the opening up of new frontiers for oil exploration, especially near the poles and in the North Sea. In the late 1990s, Greenpeace campaigned heavily against oil company British Petroleum's (BP, now Beyond Petroleum) plans to turn the remote arctic Northstar Island into a 'fossil fuel factory'. In addition to conventional campaigning activity, this involved establishing an ice camp to monitor the progress of the development (Greenpeace 2000). Greenpeace's *Carbon Logic* (Hare 1997), showed how burning existing fossil fuel reserves could lead to dangerous climate change without even beginning to open up new frontiers. This research is the impetus behind many Greenpeace climate campaigns, and was endorsed by the Beyond Oil coalition consisting of Friends of the Earth, Rising Tide, and Platform – an organization that works for social and ecological justice.

Using a multifaceted campaign approach that marks Greenpeace out as more reformist than radical, Greenpeace campaigners have purchased shares in companies like BP so that they can attend annual general and stakeholder meetings to raise the profile of environmental issues in corporate venues. Greenpeace has also been involved in COPs since the late 1990s and in solutions-based campaigning promoting renewable energy. Greenpeace helped launch a tidal power scheme, engaged in a partnership with Npower to help deliver 100 per cent wind-generated power, called Juice (Dorey interview, October 2003) and with the Peabody Trust, installed solar panels on Londoners' homes. In 2003 it became part of a Yes2Wind coalition, established to counteract what it considered to be misleading comments made by local anti-wind farm groups (one group, for example, was quoted making the claim that wind turbines cause grass-fires). Via the site, local people can meet up with others positively or negatively affected by wind farms, hear their views, arrange a visit to wind farms and make up their own minds about the effects.[14]

In addition to promoting renewables alongside Greenpeace, Friends of the Earth has been proactive in solutions campaigning by creating a Green Energy league table and encouraging people to choose greener suppliers (Friends of the Earth 2004). Friends of the Earth has also campaigned for the closure or conversion of the UK's remaining 16 coal-fired power stations, which it calls Carbon Dinosaurs. It has claimed that these old power stations produce over one-third more carbon dioxide than gas-fired alternatives and fail to meet EU efficiency standards (Friends of the Earth 2003a).

Since 2003, Friends of the Earth's most significant campaign on climate change has been the Big Ask. Friends of the Earth's parliamentary team drafted the legislation that is now the Climate Act (2008), and persuaded many of its local groups, including Greenwich and Lewisham Friends of the Earth and Hillingdon Friends of the Earth, to lobby MPs asking them to support the associated Early Day Motion. On 15 November 2006, the Queen announced to the opening of Parliament that 'my government will publish a bill on climate change as part of its policy to protect the environment' (Her Majesty, The Queen 2006). Friends of the Earth campaigners were subsequently successful in their lobbying efforts for more robust emission targets (from 60% on 1990 levels by 2050 to 80%) and the inclusion of aviation and shipping, but unable to secure desired year-on-year emission reduction targets.

The Campaign to Protect Rural England was slow to introduce climate change as a campaign issue but has been paying the issue increasing attention since 2004. Up until 2003, there was no mention of climate change in its transport policy statements (Campaign to Protect Rural England 2003a,b), although its energy statement noted that climate change poses threats to the countryside and wider environment (Campaign to Protect Rural England 2003c). According to the Campaign to Protect Rural England, solutions to climate change should be through appropriately sited renewable energy developments, management of energy demand, an increase in energy efficiency and reducing the need to travel. It is currently (2011) working for 'an urgent and independent review of aviation policy as we believe it to be as scientifically illiterate as it is democratically challenged' (Campaign to Protect Rural England website 2011).[15]

The Baku Ceyhan Campaign

Despite international agreement at COP7 that Export Credit Agencies should facilitate transfer of climate friendly energy, the Export Credit Guarantees Department (ECGD) had, according to Greenpeace, by early 2003, provided 193 guarantees of support to 140 fossil fuel projects in 38 countries including Zimbabwe, China and Turkey, effectively offsetting gains made by Kyoto. As of June 2002, the ECGD had apparently not provided even a penny of assistance to renewable energy projects (Greenpeace 2002b). The case of the Baku Ceyhan pipeline is a textbook example of an unpopular ECGD-funded fossil fuel project. It is also useful to focus on this campaign because it reveals interesting patterns of interaction that exist between conservationist, reformist and radical organizations in London's environmental networks. While the radicals remained critical of reformists, they were able to work collaboratively under certain conditions. Radicals and reformists were both critical of conservationists (such as the Worldwide Fund for Nature (WWF)), which appeared to have been co-opted by corporate sponsors (see also Chapter 8).

The Baku Ceyhan Campaign was a coalition of organizations working to prevent construction of a BP-managed oil pipeline project. Although human rights and conservation issues were at stake, the campaign was largely motivated by concern about climate change. As Rau, then Climate Change Campaigner at Friends of the Earth, stated 'this project will supply new oil to Western economies which should be cutting their fuel consumption, and fuelling the oil addiction of countries which refuse to sign the Kyoto climate treaty' (Friends of the Earth 2002d). Unfortunately, the Campaign was unsuccessful in preventing the pipeline from being constructed, although it continued, until 2006, to work on raising 'public awareness of the social problems, human rights abuses and environmental damage' caused by the development.

The Baku Ceyhan pipeline, totalling 1,087 miles in length, now exports crude oil from Azerbaijani oil fields in the Caspian Sea region, through Georgia to a new export terminal at Ceyhan on the Turkish Mediterranean coast. Approximately one million barrels of oil travel through it daily (Muttitt and Marriot 2002). Loans from international lending institutions have raised 66 per cent of the investment for the project. The Baku Ceyhan Campaign (2002) has estimated that the oil from the pipeline annually produces more carbon dioxide than all the road transport in California, or two and half times the gains the United Kingdom would make in meeting its 12.5 per cent Kyoto emissions reduction target.

The official Baku Ceyhan Campaign coalition consisted of Friends of the Earth (International), The Kurdish Human Rights Project (working to protect the human rights of people in Kurdish regions), Platform and The Corner House (a radical offshoot of *The Ecologist* magazine). Its international partners included CEE Bankwatch (an Eastern European organization working to minimize the social and environmental impacts of international development finance), Campagna per la Riforma della Banca Mondiale (a Rome-based environmental NGO that focuses on the role of international financial institutions) and Friend of the Earth International. In practice, Baku Ceyhan Campaign acted as two separate bodies – sometimes as a distinct organization with its own office, campaigners and constitution; other times as an umbrella organization for its collective members. Although not a part of the formal coalition, the Environmental Direct Action Group played a key role in protesting against the pipeline.

Most of the Campaign was focused on lobbying to prevent UK and European banks (including the UK Department for International Development [DFID], the European Bank for Reconstruction and Development [EBRD] and the World Bank's International Finance Corporation [IFC]) from providing £2.3 million in public money that the pipeline's construction depended on. The direct action protest to which the Environmental Direct Action Group contributed, however, was more diverse and radical. It sought to cause havoc at as many of BP's events as possible.

In response to a Baku Ceyhan Campaign call to lobby the European Bank of Reconstruction and Development, 900 people commented on the adverse effects of the pipeline. Affiliated organizations also asked their supporters to lobby the then Secretary of State for International Development, Hilary Benn, asking him to prevent the funding of climate change inducing developments and to invest in green energy instead (Friends of the Earth 2002e). Friends of the Earth collected as many as 4,000 letters objecting to the use of public money for the pipeline, made a section of mock pipeline out of them and presented it to the Department for International Development (Friends of the Earth 2003b).

By mid-June 2003, a 120-day European Bank for Reconstruction and Development consultation period for informing the pipeline funding decision was underway. Campaigners viewed this as a last chance to stop the pipeline. Monthly Baku Ceyhan Campaign demonstrations were held outside the bank headquarters in Exchange Square, London, from July onwards. Friends of the Earth organized the July protest and invited local group members and campaigners to come with a ready-made section of pipeline to symbolically link the European Bank for Reconstruction and Development offices with the BP offices and thereby raise public awareness of the funding issues. National Environmental Direct Action Group activists staged theirs in August, and the Baku Ceyhan Campaign was responsible for the September protest. The latter demonstration involved handing in signed letters from Turkish and Georgian people who would be negatively affected by the pipeline. This coincided with a Friends of the Earth organized mass fax action to the European Bank for Reconstruction and Development president, to arrive at 12 noon on the same day as the protest. The demonstrations included chanting, music and dancing and were visited by a range of activists with various ideological leanings. The formal representation of conservationist organizations was conspicuously absent.

Environmental Direct Action Group activists attempted to maintain a frequent presence by appearing almost every Thursday at the European Bank for Reconstruction and Development offices. The stifling hot summer, the Earth First! summer gathering, and activist burnout meant that this did not always happen as intended. A gas-masked penguin was seen handing out leaflets at one of these demonstrations. An attempted occupation of the World Bank London offices, Milbank, by Environmental Direct Action Group activists was unsuccessful due to relatively heavy-handed security, but a successful demonstration was held outside. In October 2003, five activists from the Environmental Direct Action Group succeeded in occupying the Export Credit Guarantee Department director Vivian Brown's office for the best part of a morning, barricading themselves in, while forcefully informing the staff about the pipeline's problems. An accompanying banner was hung using the ECGD acronym: 'Exporting Corruption, Guaranteeing Destruction'.

October 2003 witnessed a 'Climate Trasher's Critical Mass' involving a dozen activists cycling around the streets of London causing transport mayhem and trying to raise awareness of links between the BTC pipeline and climate change. The journey incorporated visits to the European Bank for Reconstruction and Development, the International Finance Corporation, the Export Credit Guarantee Department, BP, private banks and construction companies involved in the pipeline project and the fossil fuel industry. Shortly afterwards, despite these actions and a letter writing campaign to Benn (then Secretary of State for International Development), asking him to influence the decision in the favour of the campaigners, the European Bank for Reconstruction and Development (in October 2003) and the International Finance Corporation (in November 2003) announced at board meetings that they would provide funding (Friends of the Earth 2003a).

By winter 2003, attention shifted to private banks as the European Bank for Reconstruction and Development and the International Finance Corporation funding only contributed 10 per cent of the required sum. The BP-led consortium was in discussions with private banks including Barclays, Natwest, HSBC, Royal Bank of Scotland and Standard Chartered. Action shifted towards intensive letter writing (although by this stage many campaigners believed that the construction of the pipeline was a foregone conclusion). Under pressure from campaigners, Barclays refused to approve the loan for the project, but NatWest allegedly remained committed.

In addition to challenging international and British financial institutions, the Environmental Direct Action Group engaged in multifarious direct action stunts targeting BP. Only a couple of actions are chronicled here to give a flavour. In June 2004, they staged a greeting for BP at the BP-sponsored National Portrait Gallery. A leaflet was passed to attendees attempting to give 'a more accurate portrait' of BP than the harmless philanthropic art supporter it was purporting to be. The action involved activists wearing helios (BP logo) sunglasses and holding empty picture frames in front of their faces. Artists entering the awards were politely asked to refrain from attending future BP sponsored events and for help and support with a 'fossil-free' portrait award planned for summer 2004. The group also unfurled its large 'BP Sponsors Climate Change' banner at many BP sponsored events, including in the dinosaur hall of the Natural History Museum and outside the Tate Britain.

Aviation campaigning in London

Campaigning against climate change has taken a new focus in campaigns against aviation expansion, increasingly recognized as a significant contributor to greenhouse gas emissions. Along with major research institutes, environmental organizations have alleged that air travel is the fastest growing source of greenhouse gas emissions. Research sponsored by Friends of the Earth showed that, if the government goes ahead with its plans for airport expansion, greenhouse gas emissions from aircraft will increase by 350 per cent from 1990 levels by 2030, counteracting any positive effect in reducing emissions gained from increasing fuel tax, the climate change levy and Government promotion of renewables (Friends of the Earth 2003c). In other words, if the plans for runway expansion were to go ahead, this could 'totally destroy the Government's commitment to a 60% cut in carbon dioxide emissions by 2050' (Friends of the Earth 2003d). Note that the government has since committed to even higher greenhouse gas emission reductions of 80 per cent.

Setting the context

In July 2002, the government published its Regional Airport Studies consultation that assumed air travel demand will continue to grow and is best met by increasing capacity. It expected that between 2000 and 2020 the number of passengers passing

British airports would increase from 180 million annually to 400 million (Department for Transport 2003). To achieve this, airport capacity equivalent to Stansted airport would need to be built during each of the next 30 years (Airport Watch 2002). A second edition of the consultation document was produced in the autumn of 2003 after campaigners (especially from Cliffe and Stansted) successfully argued that Gatwick should be considered as an option for development after 2019. Gatwick was not included in the first consultation because of a legal agreement prohibiting expansion until 2019, secured by a campaign in the 1950s.

The *Southeast and East of England Regional Air Service Studies* (SERAS[16], DETR 2000) predicted that air travel in the southeast (including London) will increase from 117 billion passengers a year in 2000 to 300 billion in 2030, and therefore that four new runways are required. The initial options for expansion included a third runway at Heathrow, a second at Gatwick, a second at Stansted and a new London airport (Cliffe in Kent, or an artificial island in the Thames estuary) with a supporting role to be played by Luton, Manston, Southampton and London City airports. British Airport Authority's preferred sites for new runways were Stansted (two), Gatwick (one) and Heathrow (one).

Responses to SERAS

Environmental organizations across spatial and ideological divides are united in concern over large-scale airport expansion. The Campaign to Protect Rural England is quoted as saying that 'the main pressure for new runways arises in the Southeast and East of England . . . but . . . we consider that no site can be found for a new runway, let alone a new airport, which would be acceptable on environmental grounds' (Airport Watch 2002: 3). The Royal Commission on Environmental Pollution, which was shut down in 2011 due to budget cuts, used to provide the Queen, government and parliament with policy advice on environmental issues. It warned the government of the contribution that such increases in air traffic would make to climate change. English Nature, which was rebranded Natural England in 2006 and was responsible for conservation in the United Kingdom, including the designation of Sites of Special Scientific Interest, recommended an approach which 'dampens demand and sets environmental limits on airports' (Airport Watch 2002: 4).

The first national anti-aviation event after the release of the consultation document was the 'Airport Expansion: Options, Alternatives and Opportunities for Change' conference, in September 2002, organized by the London Green Party and Airport Watch – a then newly formed coalition consisting of Campaign to Protect Rural England, Friends of the Earth, Aviation Environment Federation, the National Society for Clean Air and Transport 2000 (now the Campaign for

Better Transport), set up to coordinate anti-aviation expansion groups. Its aims were twofold:

> One . . . was to ensure local protest groups weren't NIMBY – that they were perfectly entitled to fight for their own backyard, but not to put it in somebody else's. And secondly, [to] link them in with the national organisations, and make arguments against airport expansion. (Stewart interview, February 2001)

The overall purpose of the conference was to 'examine the options put forward by the Government . . . to identify and agree [on] . . . alternatives . . . and to explore the potential for some joint or coordinated national campaigns' (Lucas 2002). Besides setting the scene for cooperation between groups campaigning against different runway/airport options, the conference laid out weaknesses of the consultation, concerns about planning laws, and raised climate change and air pollution issues.

West London Friends of the Earth produced an extensive 71-page response to the consultation, commenting on sustainable development implications, noise, the environment (air pollution, climate change, habitat loss) and economics, and concluding that the solution lies with managing demand for flights by removing tax breaks and placing VAT on fuel (Ferriday interview, 2003).[17]

During the consultation period, Friends of the Earth ran a campaign entitled Brace Yourself, encouraging armchair activists[18] to put pressure on the Transport Secretary (then Alistair Darling) via Members of Parliament and by signing a pre-written letter raising concerns about the predict and provide approach, drawing attention to the need for removal of subsidies and tax breaks and recommending the replacement of short haul flights with high-speed rail alternatives. Subsequently, the Freedom to Fly coalition – the campaign's adversary – counterclaimed that everyone has the right to cheap flights and laid out a case for the economic importance of aviation. In retort, Friends of the Earth asked its supporters to sign a pre-printed letter to Richard Branson, Chairman of the Virgin Group (which includes Virgin Atlantic Airways) to alert him to public awareness that subsidies to the aviation industry come at the expense of people and the environment. During the consultation period, with a view to influencing people who may have been swayed by Freedom to Fly, Airport Watch issued an informative leaflet entitled The Plane Truth . . . Myths Busted.

For the Campaign to Protect Rural England, the main concern was that airport expansion would 'shatter the tranquillity of the countryside' (Campaign to Protect Rural England 2003d). Similar to its famous illustrated map comparing 'areas of tranquillity' in the 1960s to the 1990s, the Campaign drew up maps showing the areas that would be affected by flight paths and aircraft stacks in 2000 compared to 2030. The Campaign's consultants (TRL) showed that by 2030, 606,300 people in Britain would be seriously affected by aircraft noise – double current numbers. It asked the government to draw up more effective sound contours, adopt the World Health Organisation's guidelines for acceptable noise levels, and extend restrictions on night flights. In addition, the Campaign to Protect Rural England in its consultation submission raised issues of air pollution, climate change, development resulting in loss of wildlife and countryside, widening of roads and ribbon development and set out the case for removal of tax exemptions.

The White Paper

The Future of Air Transport White Paper (2002) set out the government's recommendations for air transport for the next 30 years, but had no statutory authority to determine which runways should or should not be built. The choice of plans was placed firmly in the hands of developers and depended on the planning process (DfT 2002: 2–3). It fell very short of the optimistic expectations of environmental organizations. It regarded emissions trading to be the primary solution to aviation's contribution to greenhouse gases, suggested airport noise could be reduced by ad hoc measures and that legislation be implemented only when parliamentary time is available. In the southeast, the government recommended making 'the best use of the existing runways at the major southeast airports', including a second runway at Stansted to be built as soon as possible and operating by 2012, and further development at Heathrow 'provided that strict environmental conditions are met' between 2015 and 2020. In other UK regions, the government favoured extra runways at Birmingham and Edinburgh and encouraged regional airports to make full use of their current runways (DfT 2002: 6–7). This contrasts with environmental campaigners' view that the solution lies in managing demand for aircraft via removal of subsidies and tax breaks.

White Paper responses

Nationally, a second Airport Watch conference was held to discuss post-White Paper campaigning. Stewart's opening discussion concluded that the focus of campaigning needed shifting from targeting government, which had made up its mind, towards airlines and airport operators. Airport Watch and the Aviation Environment Federation have since worked on developing policy arguments on high-speed rail alternatives, climate change, noise and air pollution and economics (Stewart 2004).

After the release of the White Paper, the campaign to Stop Stansted Expansion (SSE) pulled out all the stops to influence British Airports Authority, organizing weekly public meetings and getting press coverage to alert local people. A conventional mix of lobbying, influencing the planning process and taking the campaign to the city to question the dubious financial status of the airport was undertaken (Barbone

2004). As an act of solidarity with communities threatened with airport expansion, London Earth First! occupied the offices of British Airports Authority for most of a morning in January 2004 and staged a demonstration, brandishing a 'No More Airport Expansion' banner and handing out leaflets to alert the public to aviation's environmental implications.

In March 2004, judicial review proceedings were instigated against the British government by local campaigners to challenge the green light it gave to airport expansion. Supported by local authorities, campaigners argued that key information was excluded from consultation documents, especially regarding the possibility of new airports on the Isle of Sheppey and at Thames Reach. Stansted campaigners also launched a judicial review, but theirs was focused on the way in which the specificity of the White Paper might unfairly influence the planning process, and on the government's inadequate assessment of environmental impacts (Clark 2004).

Although Stansted campaigners were not keen to cooperate with radical activists, they did compose a direct action pledge along the lines of the earlier Oxleas Woods Campaign's 'Beat the Bulldozer Pledge', aiming to persuade thousands to pledge to promise that they would engage in direct action if airport expansion goes ahead at Stansted. The story ended happily for Stansted campaigners: in the 2010 general election, all three major political parties pledged their opposition to the building of a new runway at Stansted. The coalition government has, at the time of writing, stood by its promise.

Heathrow airport campaigns

Despite strong opposition from a well-organized campaign that made articulate arguments, used a range of appropriate campaigning strategies, and incorporated strategic networking among a variety of community, noise, health and environmental organizations, construction of Heathrow airport's fifth terminal (T5) was completed in 2008. The T5 campaign is important in the context of this book because the campaign networks that developed were still largely intact when fieldwork was undertaken, and were strengthened by the Third Runway campaign that followed. Further, it illustrates well the process whereby campaigners become disillusioned with conventional channels of influencing the policy process and begin to see direct action as the only way to get their voices heard.

According to British Airways, the purpose of T5 was to modernize the airport to facilitate its future growth. It accommodates approximately thirty million passengers and covers 260 acres of land – expanding the size of the airport by almost 25 per cent. T5 alone is one of the three largest airports in Europe second only to Heathrow Terminals 1–4 and Zurich (Aitken 2002).

The campaign was run largely by local organizations alongside Friends of the Earth (national, London, West London and local groups) Heathrow and Communities Against Noise and the Green Party. It was focused on influencing the public inquiry, which commenced in May 1995, lasted a record-breaking 3 years and 10 months and finally ended, after sitting for 525 days, in March 1999. Shortly before the inquiry decision was announced, four Environmental Direct Action Group activists occupied British Airport Authority's boardroom to raise the profile of the issue and make links with climate change. After the release of the White Paper, some of the same activists repeated the action as London Earth First!.

T5 was given a green light by the then Transport Secretary, Stephen Byers, in November 2001. This was no surprise given that government regards aviation crucial for Britain's economic prosperity. Byers suggested that 'for London to compete as a world player and for it to remain a major financial centre, Terminal 5 will help it stay competitive' (quoted in Aitken 2001).

At the public inquiry, British Airports Authority promised that a third runway would not be required, despite T5 accommodating an extra 30 million passengers. Hence, when the third runway was put forward as a possible option for meeting aircraft demand in the Regional Aircraft Summaries Assessment, some campaigners were shocked, while for others it was just another tally in the long string of broken promises from British Airports Authority. The inspector at the planning inquiry for Terminal 4, for example, was 'strongly of the opinion that all possible steps should be taken to satisfy those living around Heathrow that this is the last major expansion' (Glidewell 2004). At the time, British Airports Authority agreed, stating that 'there are multiple risks associated with a 5th terminal . . . They add up to a total risk which is completely unacceptable' (BAA, February 1983, NoTRAG website, no longer available). Heathrow residents who have lived near the runway for at least two decades were waiting with bated breath in anticipation of an announcement for a third runway, and, although most were unsurprised, it was regarded as an audacious move, which served to fuel campaigner's anger. Given recommendations for a third runway at Heathrow, the White Paper was giving an amber light for a sixth terminal: 'We . . . suggest that the operator should carry out further work on proposals for terminal capacity' (DfT 2002). British Airports Authority, too, has admitted that if it has a third runway at Heathrow, a sixth terminal will be 'required' (Campaign to Protect Rural England 2003e).

According to Friends of the Earth, the decision to go ahead with T5 shows that 'the only aviation strategy the Government has is constant expansion and more public subsidy. It's no wonder that people have little faith in the decision-making process and the public inquiry system' (Friends of the Earth quoted in Aitken 2001). In October 2003, there was direct action at the construction site of T5, which responded to the democratic deficit of planning inquiries reminiscent of the anti-roads protests of the nineties (see Chapter 5). In the autumn of 2003, eight activists, calling themselves Hounslow Against New Terminals (HANT) managed to outsmart security and scale 1 of the 22 cranes to erect a banner spelling out a demand for 'No Airport Expansion'. They kept a presence on site for over 100 hours after which they were brought before Uxbridge magistrate's court on charges of obstructing persons engaged in lawful activity and fined costs of £55.

HANT activists' court hearing was sympathetically supported by local residents and environmental organizations. Ferriday (coordinator of West London Friends of the Earth) told the local press how he would

> like to place on record our admiration for the courageous young people who were prepared to take considerable personal risks on behalf of all those who feel that this government does not care about the environment and residents who live near Heathrow. (quoted in Sharp 2003)

After having been misled by British Airport Authority's broken promises, subjected to a drawn-out and intensely fought public inquiry and feeling as if their public rights had been battered, Heathrow campaigners, after a cursory pit stop, were subjected to a second battle in the war against the expansion of Heathrow airport. The time had come to fight the Third Runway.

The campaign was kick-started by the publication of the government's consultation and the South East Regional Assessment which followed. It was a joint campaign between local residents' associations, supported by local MPs, local authorities, West London Friends of the Earth and Heathrow and Communities Against Noise. The No Third Runway Action Group, financed by Hillingdon Borough Council, acted as an umbrella group.

Shortly after the South East Regional Assessment document was issued, Heathrow and Communities Against Noise alerted the community to the loss of homes and increased noise and air pollution a third runway would cause. Leaflets containing this information were handed out at railway and tube stations throughout September 2002. During the course of the consultation, which took place in a London hotel, protesters posed for the local press with an 8-foot high aeroplane-winged shark that was, they claimed, 'flying out of control' and held a counter-consultation in the same hotel. In October, a demonstration and lobby of parliament was held, organized jointly by Heathrow and Communities Against Noise and the No Third Runway Action Group. Also in October 2002, Heathrow and Communities Against Noise arranged for an open-topped bus to travel along a section of the flight path with a sound system playing recorded aircraft noise to give the community 'a taste of what was to come' between the songs of a jazz band (Raymond 2002: 7). This was followed by a rally addressed by local politicians at Turnham Green and an opportunity for local people to sign a petition.

July 2003 saw at least a thousand people march along the route of the proposed runway followed by a rally in a local park. Speakers from Friends of the Earth, Heathrow and Communities Against Noise, No Third Runway Action Group and local churches addressed the rally (Grant 2003). In the same month, Heathrow and Communities Against Noise protesters dressed up in gas masks and boiler suits to draw attention to the predicted high air pollution.

Post White Paper (December 2003), Heathrow campaigners worked with their local authorities to ensure that pollution levels were monitored independently and not by British Airports Authority or its consultants, given that the future for a third runway was, then, dependent upon reduced air pollution levels by 2015. Efforts were also made to link up with European airport protest groups to try to achieve an EU ban on night flights.

From 2008, notably not earlier, Greenpeace contributed to campaigns against the third runway at Heathrow, instigating an ingenious 'airplot' campaign. For this, Greenpeace purchased a strip of land 'bang in the middle of the proposed third runway site at Heathrow',[19] and allowed supporters of the campaign to nominally purchase small chunks of it at no cost. Thus, the deeds to the land were owned by thousands of supporters who would have had a say in future land use.

Also in 2008, there was a week-long direct action-oriented Camp for Climate Action close to the airport, which culminated in a protest march and mass blockade of British Airport Authorities offices (August 2007). Climate Camp picnics at the new Terminal (early 2009), and a 'flash mob' (2009) – a group of people seemingly spontaneously congregating – followed. These actions, and those that preceded it, suggest that local people and climate change campaigners were not going to let the new runway be built without a fight.

Since the mid-2000s, environmental direct action, having reached a lull in Britain in the earlier part of the decade (Rootes 2007), appeared to be on the rise again, focussed, in particular, on climate change. This can be explained in a similar fashion to the emergence of the roads protests, which were also met with an apparent democratic dead end (see Chapter 5). Climate change campaigners and activists are frustrated by the government's apparent lack of commitment to reducing greenhouse gas emissions, which, despite the Climate Change Act 2008, is exemplified by its apparent willingness to give the go-ahead to coal-fired power stations and new airport runways. The new direct action networks, including Camp for Climate Action, The Coal Hole, Plane Stupid and Climate Rush, have engaged in all manner of direct action stunts: from blockading British Airport Authority's offices, to shutting down coal-fired power stations, disrupting the development of open cast coal mines, blockading coal freight trains, occupying airport runways and 'rushing' parliament (see also the beginning of Chapter 1).

Concluding remarks

This chapter has sought to illustrate the diverse nature of environmental organizations and campaigns in London. One thing it has demonstrated is the difficulty of pigeonholing organizations into ideal types. We can see that even radical groups like the Environmental Direct Action Group sometimes engage in more reformist strategies. And even the Campaign to Protect Rural England commonly viewed as conservationist has reformist tendencies. Although the previous chapter suggested that conservationists are not particularly well networked into the movement, the case study of the Campaign to Protect Rural England and its involvement in campaigns against aviation expansion demonstrates the difficulty of making such sweeping generalizations and illustrates how networking can be contingent upon the issue (see Chapter 5).

This background material also forms foundations I build upon in order to illuminate the patterns of interaction in environmental networks and assess the applicability of social movement theory to their praxis. In particular, we have seen that Greenpeace was slow to network with groups campaigning against the third runway, and that moderate environmental organizations are pushed to network with more radical direct activists upon meeting a democratic dead end. This happened in campaigns against the Baku Ceyhan pipeline and against aviation. I return to discuss such tendencies with reference to social movement theory in the chapters that follow. I shall look at the extent to which social movement theories can help explain and/or understand the networking among environmental organizations.

4 The Role of Resources in Relationships

This chapter focuses on the organizational approach to social movement theory, coupling organizational ecology and resource mobilization because of considerable overlap between them. Indeed, early proponents of resource mobilization theory (John McCarthy and Meyer Zald) were themselves once organizational scholars. The resource mobilization approach developed in the 1970s in the United States in response to perceived weaknesses of earlier theoretical approaches, partly spearheaded by Gamson's (1975) seminal study that sought to account for factors making supposedly *rational* social movement organizations *successful*.[1] Thus, it was viewed as a shift away from collective behaviour approaches' emphasis on the irrational – even if that aspect of collective behaviour has been exaggerated (Chapter 1). Given the centrality of debates around rationality and irrationality in the social movements' literature, I begin this chapter by exploring the meaning of the concept of rationality. I look at the micro-roots of the literature, before moving on to the organizational level.

According to resource mobilization theorists' conceptualization of a social movement, social movements are comprised of organizations with some degree of formality. These organizations are considered to be dependent on resources – in one shape or another – for their survival. It is suggested that organizations are likely to become preoccupied by the need to maintain themselves as organizations. This makes the battle to achieve or maintain resources pivotal for organizational survival. Consequently, organizations may compete for resources. Alternatively, they might, instead, collaborate as part of a shared strategy to mount effective campaigns and so indirectly increase resources by capitalizing on success. Organizational ecology is also concerned with explaining how organizations interact. It asks important questions about how it is that so many organizations can survive within a single organizational field. It uses the concept of niches to address these questions. Along with resource mobilization theory, the concepts of competition and collaboration are central to organizational ecology. The obvious coherence between resource mobilization and organizational ecology makes it somewhat surprising that little effort has been made, to date, to marry the two approaches. In this chapter, I begin to address this peculiar oversight.

After linking resource mobilization and organizational ecology and evaluating them, I tease out the implications of the theories for interaction in environmental networks. I illustrate the text with examples from recent scholarly accounts of environmental activism. I then explore whether these implications fit what we can glean about the environmental networks on the basis of my survey and interview data. I end the chapter with some concluding thoughts on the value of the resource mobilization/organizational ecology approach.

Resource mobilization theory and rationality

Whereas collective behaviour was criticized for stressing the irrationality of protest, much of the criticism directed towards resource mobilization centres was around its deployment of the concept of rationality. Hence, I visit debates surrounding that term first. The emphasis given to rationality means that research mobilization theory sits at some remove from the collective behaviour approach. To some extent, this reflects scholars' (over)reaction to the weaknesses of collective behaviour theory.

Generally, resource mobilization theory's proponents imply that the model is set within an economic or instrumental understanding of rationality, whereby actors seek the most cost-effective means for realizing interests (Crossley 2002: 58). This perspective constitutes the building blocks for rational actor theory, as incorporated into micro-level resource mobilization theory. It assumes, not unproblematically, that potential activists weigh up costs and benefits of movement participation and that a favourable balance needs to be struck before they join (Klandermans 1994). Klandermans' argument is based on an assessment of Olson's (1965) classic and hotly debated *Logic of Collective Action*. Olson believed that, strictly speaking, collective action[2] in the pursuit of collective goods was irrational, arguing that if collective actors were successful in achieving a collective good, individuals would stand to gain regardless of whether they participated or their extent of participation. On the other hand, unsuccessful collective actors would be left with a deficit in their cost-benefit balance, having invested in a cause to no avail, while still having to foot the bill for the cost of action. A rational actor would, in Olson's terms, *free-ride*, reaping benefits without personal commitment or outlay to the cause.

But why, then, have people persistently supported groups seeking collective goods such as environmental organizations? Olson's answer was that organizations persuade members to join via distribution of selective incentives – defined as material benefits exclusively for members providing incentives to join by swinging the cost-benefit ratio in members' favour. In reality, though, motivational bases for collective action, including participation in environmental organizations, are much broader than simple economic gain. People may, for example, join groups for a sense of belonging – to foster solidarity and develop consciousness or shared interests (Fireman and Gamson 1979). Consequently, some scholars have stretched the concept of selective incentives to include social, symbolic and normative incentives (e.g. Opp 1989; Cress and Snow 1996). Such generic use of the term is best avoided if we are to prevent loss of theoretical clarity; it implies that it is 'rational' for an actor to join a group seeking collective good in return for non-material incentives and without recourse to material costs and benefits. While such a statement may be true if one considers rationality to mean seeking the most appropriate course of action in the given circumstance, it twists the original meaning of rational-choice theories. Caution should also be exercised because broad use of the term 'selective incentives' means it has become sufficiently slippery to arouse suspicion that it is merely a means of justifying post-facto generated explanations.

Organizational-level resource mobilization theory

Decision-making individuals within 'rational' organizations[3] are assumed to weigh up the costs and benefits of cooperating with others. This kind of rationality applies to procedures under bureaucratic control, involves impersonal quantitative calculation and is what Weber (1971 [1922]) called 'formal rationality'. It stands poles apart from another type of rationality introduced by Weber: 'substantive rationality'. Whereas formal rationality is driven by calculations about success, substantive rationality is driven by values and norms (Kalberg 1980). Many variants of rationality exist on the continuum between these poles, but resource mobilization theorists' original application falls closer to the formal than the substantive. Unless otherwise specified, the term 'rational' will henceforth, for consistency, refer to the instrumental and economically guided rationality to which Weber's formal rationality and Olson's conception of rationality initially referred, and upon which most resource mobilization theorists built their theories (even though many later diverged from it).

Resource mobilization theory originally argued that emergence of movements was not due to strain, neither generalized beliefs, as in collective behaviour approaches (Chapter 1), but to an injection of external resources from elites. In their embryonic conception of the theory, McCarthy and Zald (1977: 1215) drew on Turner and Killian (1957) in their belief 'that there is always enough discontent in any society to supply grassroots support for a movement if the movement is efficiently organized and has at its disposal the power and resources of some established elite group'. They ventured even further to stress that 'grievances and discontent may be defined, created, and manipulated by issue entrepreneurs and associations' (ibid.). Nonetheless, it appears that resource mobilization theorists, at least sometimes, selectively chose examples of insurgency that fit the theory, at the expense of due consideration of wider movements (Crossley 2002: 84), or other case studies. There are quite possibly as many examples of social movements that do *not* fit the theory as ones that do, including Jenkins' (1985) farm workers' movement and the rise of black insurgency (McAdam 1982).

More than aspects of the theory that seek to explain movement emergence, of particular interest for this book are variables that affect social movement organizations' behaviour and choices of allies. In resource mobilization theory, such variables relate in some way or another to the broadly defined concept of resources. As Oberschall (1973: 28) suggests, 'resources are anything from material resources – jobs, incomes, savings and the rights to material goods and services – to non-material resources – authority, moral commitment, trust, friendship, skills, habits of industry',[4] and premised upon the notions of instrumental rationality and self-gain. Despite being a 'loose cluster of ideas that exponents use selectively and interpret idiosyncratically' (Turner 1981: 8–9), the theory can be especially useful for interpreting the activity of organizations that have a neo-corporatist structure (Dalton 1994: 10). Such groups – like Friends of the Earth, Greenpeace, the Campaign to Protect Rural England and the Wildlife Trusts – have to maintain themselves by seeking new members, encouraging existing members to re-subscribe, paying staff, funding research and so on, and this makes cost-benefit-type appraisals an inevitable and important part of daily organizational life.

Centrally important to the resource mobilization approach are strategic actions to secure a favourable resource balance, whether in members, money, press coverage and/or public sympathy. This apparently reveals itself through inter-movement competition or cooperation mimicking the marketplace. When demand for environmental organizations is high (when the issues are salient), product differentiation occurs, and new specialist groups emerge (Barman 2002: 1195). Rawcliffe (1998: 77), for example, notes that the early 1990s saw a dramatic rise in environmental organizations as demand surged. Consequently, more established organizations such as the Worldwide Fund for Nature (WWF) undoubtedly lost some of their members to more specialist groups (Rawcliffe 1998: 145). The problem was that supply began to outstrip demand, for when demand is high but only a few organizations exist, it is easier to obtain resources and there is consequently thought to be less competition and little need to specialize.

Links with organizational ecology

These implications of resource mobilization theory are closely related to the theory of organizational ecology (Hannan and Freeman 1977, 1989), which suggests that organizations are affected by the configuration of other organizations in their social environment. Rooted in arguments from neoclassical biology, but focused on corporate organizations, Hannan and Freeman sought to answer the question 'Why are there so many kinds of organizations?' Their answer was that organizational diversity exists because organizations search for their own unique niches for optimal survival. Niches balance supply and demand within multiple organizational fields; by carving out a target market, set of issues, an ideology and specific organizational forms, functional specialization/division of labour, and cooperation and/or competition emerge. An organization has found its niche when it is able to grow, or as a minimal requirement, sustain itself. The resultant configuration of organizational types is considered a direct result of competition and resource availability. Particular

> organisational forms presumably fail to flourish in certain environmental circumstances because other forms successfully compete with them for essential resources. As long as the resources which sustain organisations are finite, and populations have a limited capacity to expand, competition must ensue. (Hannan and Freeman 1977: 940)

Overall patterns of organizational diversity are considered the result of competitive and cooperative interdependencies that determine organizational survival and chances of prosperity as organizations 'find niches to protect themselves against competition' (Aldrich 1999: 43). Competition apparently occurs when the presence of one organization has an adverse effect upon another. Competition is pure when both organizations suffer, and a 'predator-prey relationship' describes the situation that occurs when competition benefits one actor but causes suffering to another. Symbiosis is where two organizations coexist to mutual benefit when interdependence is based on mutual need.

However, organizational ecology does not robustly predict the extent of inter-organizational competition. Perrow (1973: 241–2) is critical of the approach because it is difficult to extrapolate from the natural to the social environment. Furthermore, its central focus is not on interactions between organizations, but on determining the likelihood of organizational survival and adaptations to competition – as in population ecology. Particularly, he suggests that the central question, 'Why are there so many types of organisation?' is misdirected because, at least with firms, the market is dominated by large successful organizations that rarely die. This is of course also true of environmental organizations because a number of long-standing national and international environmental organizations flourish, some dating back to the nineteenth century. But even if large, established, environmental organizations are fairly ubiquitous, local groups and radical networks have high turnover, and frequently 'die' due to activist burnout, or a campaign reaching its natural end, rather than due to competition.

Young (1988) comprehensively critiques organizational ecology and most of its concepts. Young's most relevant criticism is that the concept of niche is difficult to define for organizations (4–5). How many dimensions should we include and which are most crucial? Another specific weakness is that it does not allow us to predict the type of collaboration that will occur as a result of niche overlap. Why does niche overlap just as easily result in cooperative symbiosis as in noncooperative competition?

The existing social movement literature tells us that there is a degree of competition between social movement organizations. But in the lesbian, gay, bisexual and transgender (LGBT) movement, 'niche activism' is thought to lead to cooperative – rather than competitive – interorganizational relationships (Levitsky 2008). Levitsky (2008: 272) offers this argument because organizations in the LGBT movement that have found their niches focus 'on very specific issues, strategies, or tactics' and therefore they 'increasingly rely on the proficiencies of differently specialized organizations in the movement'. Arguably, though, there are fewer organizations in the LGBT movement than in the environmental one, making it easier for them to each truly find their niches. In environmental networks, it seems fair to posit that the greater number of organizations means that there is more likelihood that a higher proportion of them are working in similar ways, thus increasing the chances of competition.

It may be that we can hypothesize that organizations similar to one another have a greater propensity for some form of interaction – whether cooperative or competitive. There is also the flip-side proposition to consider – seemingly disproved by Levitsky's (2008) LGBT study – which suggests that groups operating in distinct and independent niches neither compete nor cooperate. I show later in this book that answering the question about the actions that lead organizations to compete or cooperate requires looking beyond supposedly rational organizations towards environmental networks at large and their interrelationships with individuals, the polity and/or other campaign targets, involving insights from different social movement theories (Chapter 8).

Evaluating resource mobilization theory

Proponents of resource mobilization generally find *some* evidence that supports the theory, although social movements cannot be wholly explained by it (Dalton 1994: 10). This is partly because resource mobilization is not a grand narrative for which supporting evidence must be found, but rather an analytical tool to assist understanding of particular aspects of movements. However, resource mobilization is lacking because of the disproportional emphasis given to instrumentally rational organizations (Kitschelt 1991: 334–7). Via resource mobilization, social movements 'were quickly conceptualised in an insular way that privileged reform movements and formal organisations' (Buechler 2004: 54). Not all social movement activity focuses on reform, neither is it restricted to the activities of formal organizations. Piven and Cloward (1977), for example, emphasize the role of loosely organized protest and mass defiance in poor people's movements. 'In this view, resource mobilisation's emphasis on formal organisation amounts to conceptual blinders that preclude analysts from considering other forms of protest' (Buechler 2004: 56). This means that resource mobilization theory 'completely neglects spontaneous actions, newly emerging relations, and grassroots arrangements that are often critical to the successful development of social movements' (Bystydzienski and Schacht 2001: 3). According to McAdam et al. (2001: 15):

> Read 20 or 30 years later, early resource mobilisation models exaggerate the centrality of deliberate strategic decision to social movements. They downplay contingency, emotionality, plasticity and the interactive character of movement politics.

Crossley (2002: 66–7) suggests that the idea of selfish rational movement activity upon which resource mobilization is based, is equally as derisory as collective behaviour theory has been (exaggeratedly) alleged to be. Variables like solidarity, collective identity, consciousness and ideology are either ignored, or, at the other extreme, are incorporated under the broad umbrella of 'resources', stretching the concept to its limits. Selective incentives – in the economic sense – are infrequently provided by radical environmental organizations, yet these are furnished (at least during active protests) with healthy supporter levels. Furthermore, in a situation where a quick decision needs to made, it can be irrational to be instrumentally rational – it takes time to seek out all possible options (Turner 1981: 12), and, at the end of the day, subjective decisions will always be made by activists, who are inescapably social beings. This notion ties in with Simon's (1991) concept of 'bounded rationality', in which he provides examples of individuals' choosing courses of action that are 'good enough' rather than optimal. This is what he calls a tendency to 'satisfice'. It is, he suggests, the result of competing demands for time and attention and limits to individuals' cognitive abilities. This is yet another reason why it is necessary to look beyond a rational actor framework.

Resource mobilization theory was initially applied to movements of the 1960s and 1970s. This was the period during which organizational activities were regarded by newly emerging radical factions as unfashionable and ineffective. At that time, fluid and amorphous dissident subcultures were proliferating. Foss and Larkin (1986: 18–20) suggest that this means that resource mobilization theorists were focussing only on the more legitimate aspects of agitation during this important subcultural period, and that the approach makes social movements appear more cohesive and orderly than they really are. As resource mobilization theorists focussed on at least internally institutionalized 'social movement' organizational behaviour (which is what others have referred to as interest group politics), they have described the emergence and trajectory of something quite different from other social movement theorists who regarded being non-institutional as an essential factor for being considered a social movement. Zald (1992: 336), one of the founders of the approach, admits that resource mobilization theory may 'warp the analysis of the more unbounded and fragile forms of organizations often found in social movements'.

Competition, resource mobilization and implications for environmental networks

Despite the many weaknesses of resource mobilization theory, there is sufficient strength in the approach for it to be applied to environmental organizations that have interest-group type structures – such as Friends of the Earth and Greenpeace. The approach should not be thrown out for overemphasizing the rational and formal aspect. However, it should be recognized that such formal organizations are only *part* of the picture, and that rationality only partially dictates the behaviour of even formal environmental organizations. Indeed, we could argue that the approach deserves credit for asserting that collective action is not irrational and spontaneous, as painted by a *few* collective behaviour scholars, and for recognizing that organization underpins many social movements. What is particularly useful for this book is the approach's emphasis on the role of resources in dictating patterns of interaction. The theory talks directly to notions of competition and collaboration at the organizational level.

Resource mobilization theory argues that competition exists because the main goal of any movement organization is survival. Without survival, further movement goals cannot be sought (McCarthy and Zald 1977: 1220–4). To survive, resources – whether in the form of money or active support – are crucial. New social movement organizations – informal, participatory and non-hierarchical groups – tend to extract resources from members in the form of active participation (Chapter 6), whereas protest-businesses – formal organizations that mobilize money rather than active participation – mobilize direct-debit subscriptions to raise finances (Jordan and Maloney 1997).

For protest businesses, the majority of movement supporters tend to be mobilized through postal appeals, remain at a distance from the organization and tend not to interact (Jordan and Maloney 1997), resulting in little solidarity. In contrast, groups which can muster few monetary, material and professional resources, for various reasons – such as being newly formed or radical in outlook – will apparently attempt to generate more extensive network links 'as an essential replacement for the scarcity of organisational resources' (della Porta and Diani 1999: 88). They are thought to rely more heavily on social capital, preexisting networks or community relations, what Jenkins (1985) terms 'indigenous organisation'. According to this perspective, local, small-scale or radical grass-roots environmental groups would be expected to be embedded in denser networks than national groups as they strive to use limited resources to best effect (Edwards and McCarthy 2004: 141).[5] Previous research suggests that this supposition does not always match what has been empirically tested. Lhotka et al.'s (2008) study of environmental organizations in Alamaba, for example, found that environmental groups that were best resourced were also the best networked and that the outreach capacities of groups run by volunteers were much less effective.

We can also learn from the resource mobilization approach that national environmental organizations like Friends of the Earth, which acquire most of their funds from 'supporters'[6], will likely seek to keep them loyal in the face of high levels of multiple memberships. In 1997, 65.8 per cent of Friends of the Earth's paper membership belonged to at least one other environmental organization (Jordan and Maloney 1997: 82). As we have learned from organizational ecology, high levels of supply of environmental supporterships lead to variation in target constituencies, tactics and issues and dictate movement networks. Thus, McAdam et al. (1988: 715–16) suggest that

> the SMO [social movement organisation] must negotiate a niche for itself within the larger organisational environment within which it is embedded. This usually entails a complex set of relationships with other organisational actors representing the movement.

According to Tony Juniper, ex-Director of Friends of the Earth (Habitats Campaigner at time of interview), the result is 'regular informal liaison or coordination meetings with other major environmental . . . groups . . . [to] make sure that there isn't a duplication of efforts and resources . . .' (interview in Szerszynski 1995: 89, cited in Rootes 2007).

This liaison, historically at least, included the once-monthly 'Kentish Town Dinner', at which the executive directors of the big environmental organizations met to formulate policy, and decide how best to divide labour (Seel 2000). It certainly resulted in differentiation; while Greenpeace has had a historical tendency to mobilize money from its emergent action supporters network, to allow it to perform professional media-oriented stunts on global issues, Friends of the Earth has tended to focus more on locally based campaigning, offering direct involvement for local people. Consequently, Rootes (1999) suggests, rather as Levitsky does for the LGBT movement, that environmental organizations are not competitive so much as they increasingly cooperate on the basis of an accepted division of labour.

Diani and Donati (1999: 20), however, would argue that despite the existence of a consensually agreed division of labour, environmental organizations that seek finances continue to compete to attract new supporters. To do this, many groups offer, in the Olsonian sense, selective incentives – such as a monthly update, car stickers and free publications. They are also said to exaggerate the benefits of being a member, downplay the constraints they face and seek to maintain a favourable public image. Hannigan (1995: 94) suggests this is why 'big' groups tend to turn their backs on local issues (as Schlosberg 1999: 122 found in the United States) in favour of drastic doomsday-like, 'sexy', or winnable issues. Although this is probably exaggerated, it is certainly true that large environmental groups tend to cooperate more with other organizations most like themselves (Saunders 2007b). And, according to Weston (1989: 205), the two main factors that Friends of the Earth (at least in the past) used to select its key campaigns were funding availability and win-ability. More recent observers have added organizational maintenance to the pot. Rawcliffe (1998: 78), for example, notes how large environmental organizations like Greenpeace and Friends of the Earth seem increasingly motivated by self-investment, and that, consequently, their activities are becoming curtailed by their cumbersome budgets (Jordan and Maloney 1997: 18–25).[7] Certainly by 1992, ex-employees and ex-allies of Greenpeace thought that 'Greenpeace had become mired in its own bureaucracy and had lost touch with the grassroots, that it had become a cumbersome sluggish organization that decreased in effectiveness as it increased in size' (Dale 1996: 5).[8]

Thus, although local groups might often be whistle-blowers on important local issues (Friends of the Earth 2002a: 3), their campaigns may not always be fully supported nationally. Consequently, some local groups may feel that national groups do not give them sufficient support, engendering a sense of suspicion (DeShallit 2001). Although, as we shall see below, this is probably too harsh a judgement of Friends of the Earth and Greenpeace in the United Kingdom, Diani and Donati (1999: 23) report that it is true for the Italian environmental movement in which national environmental organizations apparently only support local mobilizations against high-risk plants 'to gain visibility for themselves [rather] than promoting the struggles in the first place'. At the very least, the literature on environmental movement organizations notes that large organizations must act in their self-interest in order to sustain themselves. Drawing on this idea, Tilly's (1985) interpretation of resource mobilization theory notes that self-interested groups are likely to engage in impromptu game analysis, estimating the optimistic best, and pessimistic worst likely outcomes of competition and/or cooperation (Forder 1996), with the overriding objective of self-gain.

For 'not in my back yard' (NIMBY) groups, logic would suggest that the best tactic would be to compete with other local groups to ensure that the locally unwanted land use (LULU) they are campaigning against is built in their competitors' constituency and not their own. An underlying economic motive may be the likely deleterious effect on property prices. This is common in the early stages of local campaigning, as evident in the 1980s Kent-based anti-Channel Tunnel Rail Link campaigns (Rootes and Saunders 2001), in which groups protesting against Routes 3 and 4 were, to the dismay of campaigners against Route 1 and 2, promoting any alternatives to save their own backyards. Similarly, in the early 1990s, the Greenwich Society promoted a bypass that would have increased total traffic volume throughout the borough, but removed congestion from their local patch (Connelly, interview June 2001). The immediate response to the late 1980s South Circular Assessment studies in London, which proposed a series of possible road schemes to relieve congestion, was outright hostility between groups representing different constituencies. The first meeting of the umbrella group ALARM (All London Against the Road Menace) was the scene of much bickering and 'nigh-on gang warfare' (Shields, interview June 2001). There was also a small amount of NIMBY rivalry in anti-waste facility campaigns in Kent (Rootes 2003a).

Sooner or later, NIMBY organizations usually begin to realize that there are wider issues that need to be articulated in order to win their campaign, and that their concern is only part of the broader picture. Rucht (1990: 171) suggests that if NIMBY groups are initially unsuccessful, they begin, perhaps out of desperation, to question the need for LULUs per se. Issues like exclusion from consultation and decision-making (procedural rhetoric), the search for alternatives, and the wider relationship of the issue to other policies (global rhetoric) begin to be addressed (Gordon and Jasper 1996). At the extreme, activists may even commence campaigning for a new social order. For instance, some activists in local anti-road action groups began to address the wider anti-car agenda by promoting green transport plans, while more radical anti-roads protesters began to engage with anti-capitalist protests, just as local anti-incineration campaigners have addressed wider waste management issues by coordinating local composting projects (Rootes 1999: 298). In this kind of scenario, the rationale of protecting one's own constituency gives way to the more comprehensive rationale of addressing broader concerns, so reducing propensity for inter-group conflict and competition.

The transition from NIMBY to NIABY (not in anybody's back yard) prevents local groups from competing and enables them to support one another instead. Rucht (1990: 171) calls this transition the 'principle of generalization', and suggests that it is most likely to happen when the conflict is lengthy, the activists involved are young and well-educated, protest groups and organizations are tightly inter-linked, and when groups with which the NIMBY group is networked have a well-developed ideology and much experience. Based on nine case studies of anti-nuclear and airport construction campaigns in West Germany, France and Switzerland, Rucht (1990) found that the 'principle of generalization' accurately reflected campaign groups' trajectories.

There is certainly a tendency to find that a lack of NIMBYism brings groups together and that a local case of contention can result in the integration of NIMBY groups into the NIABY (not-on-anybody's-back-yard) field (Robinson 1999). Local contentious issues are useful for bringing together groups from different ideological and strategic planes as groups either realize the benefits of cooperation, and/or feel too weak to fight the cause alone.

According to Tilly (1985), once groups realize that they can benefit from interaction, decisions on whether to cooperate are dictated by patterns of gains or no-gains, resulting in a process of trust-benefit generation. This he terms 'rational interaction', the result being that 'egoistic parties . . . recognise that cooperation suits their interests' (Tilly 1985: 735). It becomes tactically and strategically preferential for organizations to interact with those others with which they have a symmetric relationship of trust and gain (Todeva and Knoke 2002: 4). As Lhotka et al. (2008: 241) report, 'Trust between groups is a quality to be earned'. Positive interaction is required before more positive interaction can take place. Unfortunately, building positive relations is not always easy across ideological divides or even between similar groups.

The historic relationship between Friends of the Earth and Earth First! is a classic example of a marred trust-benefit relationship. In the early 1990s, Andrew Lees, Friends of the Earth's campaigns coordinator, was actively contacting local groups asking them to disengage or refrain from contact with Earth First! groups, fearing that it would spoil Friends of the Earth's reputation and credibility (Doherty 1998).[9] Earth First! and other anti-roads groups were dismayed with Friends of the Earth when it abandoned the anti-roads protest at Twyford Down in 1992 after being threatened with an injunction, which would have crippled the organization, forcing the choice of either pulling out or dealing with organizational collapse (Lamb 1996: 177). Needless to say, it chose the former course of action. In contrast, for Earth First!ers the singular objective was to prevent the road being built at all costs. Lush (quoted in Wall 1999b: 68), a sympathetic protester, had the following view:

> [Earth First!ers proclaimed] 'we're the best, Friends of the Earth copped off and f**ked off'. . . yet when you look at it, they really tried to help the Twyford Down Association. They set up this extremely bizarre 'we are the middle class, we are representative of middle England' and extremely media-obsessed camp. They found it uncomfortable, but they were f**king there . . . After three days the police cut through this very-easy-to-cut chain and they got slapped with this injunction [meaning that] they could be fined as a company and have their assets taken . . . but as a company they have to make decisions . . . unless they wanted to cease to be Friends of the Earth.

Unfortunately for Friends of the Earth, the majority of EarthFirst!ers were unsympathetic to its need for organizational maintenance, resulting in a chasm between the two which deepened when Friends of the Earth claimed the limelight for the victory of the East London River Crossing road campaign – which was really won by the Oxleas Alliance, a coalition including Earth First! and the Wildlife Trusts and sustained by local campaigners (Stewart in interview, June 2001).[10] Torrance, founding member of Earth First! and Oxleas Alliance representative, reprimanded Friends of the Earth for deviating from the planned strategy of shared victory and urged that caution should be exercised in future transactions (in interview, 2001). This has increased scepticism and distrust among EarthFirst!ers – many of whom were in the first instance wary of becoming involved in an alliance with what they deemed to be a competitive organization like Friends of the Earth, referring to them as '. . . namby pamby environmental organizations that are more worried about their image than saving wilderness' (Earth First! website 2004). On the other hand, the conservative (prefaced with both a lower- and upper-case 'C') Twyford Down Association did not feel as if Friends of the Earth had let them down; it considered that all legal means had been exhausted and thanked it for continued support through a tactical voting campaign (Porritt 1996). By contrast, some members of the Twyford Down Association regarded EarthFirst!ers as 'anarchists parachuting into the campaign', lacking both local knowledge and emotions (Bryant 1996).[11]

There have since been attempts to reconcile links between Friends of the Earth and Earth First! Ex-Friends of the Earth director, Charles Secrett, attended the 1995 Earth First! Summer Gathering, and relations at the 1995–6 Newbury Bypass protest were much more amenable, with Friends of the Earth staff present as legal observers. Yet, as Porritt admits (in Bryant 1996: 303), 'no-one can ever pretend that so diverse a range of tactics and organizations can hold together without a certain amount of internal strife'.

Indeed, Friends of the Earth has much more in common with Greenpeace than Earth First! and hence a greater inclination to cooperate, as Juniper (a more recent ex-director), relayed:

> although it [Greenpeace] does direct action, it does it in ways which enable it to function. . . like a national membership organisation with an office and everything . . . to that extent we're able to work with them. . . in a more upfront and open way than some other . . . more grassroots and informal networks are able to relate to us. (quoted in Seel 2000)

Previous research suggests that organizations with the same, or very similar organizational structures and ideologies are the most likely to gain from joint activity, and therefore cooperate, especially when not competing. Diani (1995) found that this rang true for the environmental movement in Milan. Similarly, Schlosberg (1999: 129) reports that networks of environmental organizations in the United States are based on 'rhizomatic organizing' – uniting around similarities. This might include local people networking to solve a local problem, or groups in different areas responding to similar circumstances. Although similar organizations tend to be the most likely candidates for cooperation, they are also, as we learn from organizational ecology, more prone to competition as they share a niche space. The circumstances that lead similar organizations to compete rather than cooperate require exploration. I now turn to see whether my primary research illuminates our understanding of the role of resources in relationships. The focus of this exploration is on the conditions under which NIMBY groups generalize, the role of niches in shaping competition or collaboration, whether national groups sideline their local counterparts and the extent to which resource-poor groups are able to foster network links.

Resource mobilization and networks in practice: The London data

Do NIMBY campaigns generalize?

There are countless examples of generalization in campaigns against roads and waste facilities. The example of aviation campaigning in London, however, demonstrates that this may be a long and drawn-out process. In aviation campaigning, the interactions between local and national organizations has not resulted in a NIABY attitude, but instead required national environmental organizations' to compromise their own NIABY stance. Thus, instead of outright opposition to new runways, the Airport Watch coalition initially agreed to an awkward compromise to promote a Thames Estuary airport as an alternative. National environmental organizations continue to emphasize the climate change implications and development pressures that expanded aviation capacity will bring wherever new runways are placed, but local groups have, in some cases, been slow to grab the baton. The No Third Runway Action Group at Heathrow was willing to use almost any ammunition it could find to prevent the construction of a third runway at Heathrow airport, without stepping outside of the law because it was dependent on its local council for financial support (more on this in Chapter 5). The No Third Runway Action Group's instrumental rationality, typical of NIMBY groups, may have been what prevented it adopting a NIABY stance. The Group's enthusiasm for an estuarine airport goes hand in hand with a weaker concern for the broader development and climate change implications it would have. Heathrow and Communities Against Noise, the aircraft noise organization, had been gradually introducing its newsletter readers to the grand-scale environmental implications of aviation expansion so as not to offend its largely Conservative supporter-base, and this is slowly having a noticeable effect. This suggests that, at least in some cases, relations between national and local environmental organizations need to endure over the long term for a NIABY scale-shift to occur. History seems to support this; it is probably no exaggeration to state that it was a matter of decades before local anti-roads campaigners coalesced into a network with common goals.

Do environmental organizations carve out a niche, and does this help them overcome competition?

The survey results provide very little evidence of competition between environmental organizations. But this does not prove that competition does not exist, but rather that competition is not best measured by a survey instrument. By contrast, qualitative interviews with key campaigners did reveal instances of competition. The questionnaire asked each respondent to list their organization's five most important competitors. Only 5 national, 1 regional and 2 local organizations claimed to have competitive relations with others, giving a total of 22 competitive relationships, as shown in Table 4.1.

Of these 22 competitive relationships, 15 did not have collaborative or information sharing links. This indicates that, in the survey sample at least, environmental organizations are most likely to admit to competitive relations with groups with which they entirely lack network relations. It could be that a lack of contact results in wariness and becomes self-reinforcing. Certainly trust-benefit relations will be absent in such situations because of the lack of opportunity to develop reciprocally supportive ties. Seven of these competitive relations exist between

Table 4.1 Competitive relationships in London's environmental network

1.	London Federation of City Farms/Groundwork
2.	League Against Cruel Sports[12]/International Fund for Animal Welfare
3.	League Against Cruel Sports/RSPCA
4.	League Against Cruel Sports/Hunt Saboteurs
5.	Ramblers Association/National Trust
6.	Ramblers Association/Youth Hostels Association
7.	Ramblers Association/Living Streets
8.	Ramblers Association/Transport 2000
9.	Women's Environmental Network/Friends of the Earth
10.	Women's Environmental Network/Greenpeace
11.	Street Tree/Groundwork
12.	Street Tree/Tree Council
13.	Street Tree/NUFU
14.	London Friends of the Earth/Greenpeace
15.	London Friends of the Earth/Campaign to Protect Rural England
16.	London Friends of the Earth/Transport 2000
17.	London Friends of the Earth/Royal Society for Nature Conservation
18.	Groundwork Southwark/SEA (acronym unknown)
19.	Groundwork Southwark/Planet Earth
20.	RSPB Bromley/British Trust for Ornithology
21.	RSPB Bromley/London Wildlife Trust
22.	RSPB Bromley/National Trust.

The organization listed first, in each case, is the one which listed the other as a competitor.

organizations in which both parties are specialist organizations, or which fill a similar organizational niche. League Against Cruel Sports (which considered itself part of an environmental network), for example, has a similar organizational remit to all three organizations it competes with, as do the Ramblers Association and Living Streets, and Bromley Royal Society for the Protection of Birds and the British Trust for Ornithology (see Table 4.1). However, this pattern is only seen in a minority of competitive organizational situations, which indicates that organizational ecology dynamics (Hannan and Freeman 1977, 1989), while they might be at play, appear not to be crucial in determining which organizations compete, or at least not in instances of competition that organizational representatives disclose.[13]

The few instances of competition disclosed in survey responses means that it is not possible, with the data I have, to accurately determine the conditions under which competition and cooperation occurs. Yet interviewees frequently discussed competition in in-depth interviews, whether this be for members, money, finance or to claim an issue as their 'property'. Schofield (Campaign to Protect Rural England Head of Regions) summed up the nature of competition between environmental organizations with the phrase: 'I think there is always competition by default between organizations for supporters and money and stuff' (in interview October 2003). Phil Thornhill (director of Campaign Against Climate Change) went so far as to suggest that Friends of the Earth may have been actively trying to stifle competition from Campaign Against Climate Change. Friends of the Earth had at one point in time allegedly made it awkward for Thornhill to draw on Friends of the Earth resources – such as use of the photocopier – for Campaign Against Climate Change promotional material, even though Thornhill was also a committed local Friends of the Earth campaigner. Indeed, Campaign Against Climate Change has continued to feel subject to a predator-prey relationship. While the relationship between Friends of the Earth and Campaign Against Climate Change appeared – at least at face value – to have improved by the time of the December 2010 National Climate March, at which Friends of the Earth director Andy Atkins gave a rousing and welcomed speech, other environmental organizations were not in its good books. At the post-march rally, a spokesperson for Campaign Against Climate Change took to the podium to thank Atkins for his speech, but also stated: 'Don't we know who our friends are. Thank you Andy. Campaign Against Climate Change is skint. Thank you Greenpeace for bringing your banner. Give us your f**king money'. The remark about Greenpeace was very sarcastic.

The Campaign to Protect Rural England has also sensed competition from Friends of the Earth and RSPB. In 2003, some of its campaigners were unhappy to see that those two organizations were taking up campaigns against reforms to the planning system, an area they deemed to be their speciality:

> I have heard through some of their [RSPB's] staff that they want to do more in London. And I thought 'Oh my God, no' they might start treading on our toes a bit in terms of supporter bases. But if they come to London . . . on the basis of their profile, members will go to them. I think they've already got something ridiculous like 27,000 members in London and we've got 6,000. They might take some of our members but it almost certainly would not be reciprocal. (Waugh interview June 2003)

While I do not have conclusive evidence that formation of niches prevents competition, it certainly seems to be the case that campaigners working within environmental organizations feel threatened when others begin to work in their niche area, even if this does at times strengthen the overall profile of their campaigns.

Are local groups sidelined?

Although national environmental organizations have considerably more links with other national organizations over local ones, it is unfair to suggest that they sideline local campaigners (Saunders 2007b). A scan of the DL list compiled for national environmental organizations[14] – a list of all connections that survey respondents of national organizations have with others – shows that they have more links with other national organizations than regional and local organizations. As each organization was given the opportunity to list five organizations at each spatial level (local, national and regional), it would be expected that there be the same number of links directed towards organizations at each of these spatial dimensions. However, national environmental organizations frequently named just one, two or even no local and regional organizations, but several national ones, showing that they have a clear bias towards exchanging information and collaborating with one another over local and regional groups.[15] In the information received and provided and in the collaboration networks, there are more than 50 linked pairs of national organizations (these networks are derived from questions 11–13 in the questionnaire, see Appendix 1). National group ties with regional and local groups are much fewer, with 17 pairs or less. This clearly shows a tendency for national groups to work together and share information with one another to a much greater extent than they do with their local and regional counterparts (Table 4.2).

But this does not straightforwardly translate to a conclusion that local organizations are ignored or feel sidelined. Greenpeace, Friends of the Earth and the Campaign to Protect Rural England all have strategies in place to involve local activists in their campaigns. Moreover, most of the local-level campaigners I interviewed were

Table 4.2 Pairs of ties in DL list by the sphere of operation

NETWORK	NO. PAIRS IN NATIONAL DLS			
	Southeast London	Northwest London	Regional (London-wide)	National (London-based)
Collaboration	12	8	11	62
Received-Information	12	8	12	67
Provided-Information	17	9	13	55

content with the support they received from national groups, generally having a nuanced understanding of the nature of resource constraints facing national organizations (Saunders 2007b). Indeed, during my participant observation for one day per week for a 6-month period at the national Friends of the Earth headquarters at Underwood Street, London, I was surprised to note how infrequent calls from local groups were. Sitting opposite the Local Groups Co-ordinator, I was able to see firsthand that she only received two or three calls from local groups per day.

Do resource-poor organizations have the most links?

To test della Porta's and Diani's (1999: 88) assertion that local grass-roots organizations have more ties to compensate for their lack of other resources, the average number of ties for national, regional, and local groups has been calculated on the basis of the DL lists. In the survey, local organizations could list a maximum of 60 organizations, and national organizations could list 75 organizations with which they have network links (that is with multiplex links counted more than once – so a link in each of the information providing, information receiving and collaboration matrices would lead to a score of 3).[16] By weighting the ties of London-based national organizations to make them equivalent to the maximum number of ties that local organizations could list,[17] southeast London environmental organizations listed on average 5.39 ties, northwest London organizations listed 5.5, regional (London-based) ones 5.75, and national organizations 11.73. Assuming that national organizations are the most resource-rich, it appears that resource-poor organizations have fewer ties than resource-rich ones, suggesting perhaps that the presence of resources, while it might stifle flexibility, actually facilitates networking, whereas a lack of resources hampers it, in tune with Lhotka et al.'s (2008) findings.

Despite this evidence, it is certainly not the case that a wealth of resources always leads to wide and inclusive networks. Although Greenpeace has an enormous stockpile of wealth compared to most other environmental organizations, it is a relatively marginal actor in all networks. This is because Greenpeace is very protective of its brand and appears to prefer to work collaboratively only when it can hold the reins. On the other hand, London Wildlife Trust was in a financial lull at the time of surveying,[18] but was the most popular organization for networking (whether in the receiving of information, or in collaboration), falling close behind Friends of the Earth only in information provision. The Campaign to Protect Rural England is also in the top ten most popular organizations in each network and yet its networking abilities, especially at the regional level, are allegedly constrained by a lack of funding (Schofield [Campaign to Protect Rural England] interview, October 2003).

Concluding remarks

This chapter has discussed resource mobilization theory in the frame of rational-actor theory. It has looked at individual and organizational level movement factors in this light, and drawn parallels with organizational ecology. It has considered networking implications of the theory and evaluated the approach. In conclusion to this chapter, we could argue that resource mobilization dynamics appear to go some way towards explaining how and why environmental organizations network in the manner in which they do. As I have shown, it can shed some light on the process by which NIMBY organizations can become embedded in broader environmental networks. Strategic thinking can lead to a scale-shift as they realize, through the process of generalization, that their campaign is just the thin edge of a much broader wedge. It also suggests to us that niches are important for environmental organizations seeking survival in the face of competition from others. The London data provides tentative support for the idea that similar organizations sometimes compete, especially when niches overlap. Similar organizations, though, also work better together than entirely dissimilar ones, especially when they are working under a mutually agreed division of labour. I also found that outright competition between very different types of organizations seems more common when organizations have had little historical contact. This could be because such organizations have lacked opportunities to build up mutually reciprocal trust-benefit relations. Networking also seems more likely when organizations have monetary or staffing resources to make it happen, and/or when the parties involved in collaborative efforts are willing to compromise stances. This latter qualifier is important because it can help explain why Greenpeace – ever protective of its own public reputation – has few network links despite it being one of the most resource-rich organizations in the sample.

Greenpeace appears to hold fast in its views, only entertaining entering coalitions when it can assert some control over them.

However, as has been routinely argued, resource mobilization focuses too much on individual organizations and assumes they take a coldly rational approach. Even Friends of the Earth and Greenpeace – among the most established and corporate-like environmental organizations in Britain – are much more altruistic towards fellow environmentalists than they would be if they were truly economically rational and absorbed by organizational maintenance. And if it *were* true that interaction in environmental networks was completely dictated by instrumental rationality, there would still need to be consideration of political processes and opportunities (Chapter 5). Given that environmental organizations are not entirely at the dictates of instrumental rationality, we also must consider culture, collective identity and solidarity (Chapter 6 and Chapter 7). Zald and McCarthy (1987: 180), key proponents of resource mobilization, would agree. They close their resource mobilization-based account of competition and conflict among social movement organizations stating that 'at some point, social movement analysis must join with cultural and linguistic analysis if it is to understand fully cooperation and conflict in its socially specific forms'. Therefore, although resource mobilization can provide us with some useful insights into understanding the rational side of environmental networking, we really need to look beyond it to get a fuller picture. The political environment is also important, and, in an environmental networks perspective, more fluid environmental groups also need to be considered. In the next chapter I turn attention to political opportunities.

5 Political Structures, Political Contingencies and Environmental Networks

This chapter introduces political opportunity structures and political process theories, and considers their implications for patterns of interaction in environmental networks. These theories essentially argue that political environments impact the emergence and development of social movements. In its simplest form, the key proposition is that relatively open states – those that are decentralized and which encourage participation – are likely to produce moderate movements that mobilize large numbers of protesters. At the extreme, the ideal open state would attract zero protest, as there would be no need for extra-institutional complaint. This is rather like Smelser's (1962) differentiated societies, which he considered create weaker movements than non-differentiated societies (see Chapter 1). In contrast, closed states – which are highly centralized and discourage or even repress political participation – are expected to be hostile terrains for movements, resulting in small, radical, or even violent movements. However, this simplistic explanation glosses over variation in the approach. To get around this, I distinguish between weak and strong versions of political opportunity structure theory. The strong version (e.g. Kitschelt 1986; Kriesi 1995) argues that characteristics of political structures principally determine the incidence and forms of social movements. Weaker versions of the approach – political process theory, especially in its later iterations (McAdam [1982] is an example) – merely assert that political structures and the relationships associated with them are *part* of the social and political environment that social movements must negotiate, and are important among the *many factors* that shape the incidence and forms of social movements (e.g. Tarrow 1998). The former approach is most problematic and is critiqued in this chapter.

Whichever approach is taken, we shall see that scholars have had a tendency to conflate structural and non-structural variables. This makes the name of the theory of political opportunity *structures* seem somewhat inappropriate. Some theorizing also displays a tendency to downplay the effect of organizations' strategy, status and choice of issues upon their actual opportunities for campaigning. To circumvent the latter problem, I draw on literature from pressure group theory to make the concept of political opportunities more useful for understanding environmental networks. Note that I am purposely omitting the word 'structures' in this part of the account.

After evaluating the theory and discussing its pertinence to extant literature on environmental movements, I tease out the implications of the theory for interaction in environmental networks. The empirical section focuses on the extent to which organizations' strategies (whether insiders, thresholders or outsiders) and self-perceived relationships to the polity (on a continuum from constructively engaged to actively opposed) affect the way in which environmental organizations network with one another. To avoid the charge of being overly statist – a well-versed critique of political opportunities literature – *and* to make the account relevant to local environmental organizations, I look at organizations' relationships with their local authorities in addition to central policymaking institutions.

The 'strong' approach

Political opportunity structure scholars argue that the emergence and behaviour of new social movements can be attributed to the 'structure' of national policymaking institutions (see Lentin 1999; Xie and Van der Heijden 2010). Kitschelt (1986) and Kriesi (1995) wrote the key defining works for the approach. They argued that social movement strategies are determined by the characteristics of the national polity within which they operate. Such theorists tend to imply that movements within a particular state are homogenous entities – that is that organizations and activists working within a given set of structural conditions behave similarly. This assumption is a major weakness of the theory. As Tarrow (1998: 91) suggests, 'If variations in movement structure and strategy could be predicted from differences in state structure, then all of a country's movements would resemble one another'. Yet it is a given fact that movements *within the same country* differ from one another. Furthermore, and more to the point for this chapter, movement organizations even *within the same movement* often have a variety of aims, structures and strategies. For example, animal rights activists include 'hard core vegans' *and* those who argue that 'you don't have to give up meat to care' (see Walls (2002) on the Campaign Against Live Exports in the United Kingdom). This has two important implications for social movement theory: first, that broad-brush approaches to theory gloss over the important differences between organizations and activists within movements in the same country, and second, that it is not feasible to rely on macro structural features of a polity as predictors of social movement behaviour. Decision-making procedures will probably always be more open to moderate groups than to their more radical counterparts. It scarcely needs pointing out that movements and/or organizations seeking fundamental changes to social structures are least likely to be granted access and are the most likely to be repressed (Tarrow 1998: 92). Thus, I postulate that a consideration of strategies of organizations and their relationship with the polity can tell us much more about environmental networking than any broad-brush theoretical approach. In other words, a more fine-tuned approach than the 'strong' one is needed to investigate how political opportunities shape movements.

The chapter also flags up another weakness of broad-brush approaches to political opportunity structures: they tend to assume that all campaigns are directed towards policy change at the national level. The targets of social movements may be considerably more multifaceted than this. Other targets, for example, include international financial institutions, corporations, and local governance (see Chapter 3). While this chapter does not, for reasons of space, address all possible targets, it does at least consider both the national *and* the local polity.[1] I first explore the 'strong' approach to political opportunities in more depth.

A critique of the 'strong' approach to political opportunity structures

Although it has precedents in the collective behaviour approach, and Lipsky (1970) suggested that fluctuations in political systems should be considered when explaining protest, it was a concept by most accounts coined and christened by Eisinger (1973 – in McAdam 1982, Tarrow 1998; Burnstein et al. 1995; Meyer 2004), who defined it as 'the openings, weak spots, barriers and resources of the political system itself' (Eisinger 1973: 11). Note that virtually all accounts entirely overlook Smelser's (1962) contribution to this branch of the literature. Much ground was made exploring the concept cross-nationally in the 1980s. However, different scholars seem to have adopted idiosyncratic approaches to the application of the theory, sometimes adding new variables more suitable to the particular movement or polity researched. As Staggenborg (2010: 17) states, 'specific definitions of political opportunity differ considerably'.

According to Tarrow's (1998) synthesis, political opportunity structure refers to variables that measure the presence or absence of political alliances, divisions within the elite, tolerance of the polity to protest, and repression or facilitation by the state. But this makes the approach seem more coherent than it really is and, in common with many who use the approach, might be considered to evoke improper use of the word *structure* (cf. Goodwin and Jasper 1999, 2004). To illustrate these issues, I explore two key contributions to political opportunity structure theory. Kitschelt (1986) looked not only at what he called 'input structures', but also at 'output structures'. Input structures, for him, were determined by a number of factors including the number of political parties – itself shaped by the nature of the electoral system – the degree of dependence of the legislature on the executive, and practices in place to deal with interest groups and to aggregate demands. Output structures involved the capacity of the state to implement policies demanded by social movements. Thus, strong centralized states that can govern markets and which have an independent judiciary were seen in a positive light. However, a strong state is not always beneficial for social movements because it has the capability to take strong action *against* the interests of social movements just as it is capable of bringing favourable policies to fruition.

Kriesi (1995), on the other hand, looked at the formal institutional structure (which included some of Kitschelt's input and output structures), and what he called informal elite strategies, which are either inclusive – facilitating, cooperating, assimilating – or exclusive – repressive, polarizing, confrontational. Along with Tarrow, both scholars make the mistake of lumping all these variables under the label of 'structure'. As Rootes (1998) argues, few of these variables are truly structural in nature – many are temporary and volatile. Thus, 'contingent political opportunities' might be a better label for many things miscategorized as structural.

Based upon structural and contingent types of political opportunities, it is possible, although not unproblematic, to conceptualize idealized 'open' and 'closed' polities (Table 5.1). Even though they are usually treated by scholars as if they can be neatly slotted into one category or the other, real life polities always fall some way between these two extreme types. To further complicate, they also change over time. The United Kingdom, for example, is seen to have practiced 'active exclusion' of environmental organizations under Margaret Thatcher (Dryzek et al. 2003), but has been viewed as accommodative under the latter years of her premiership (Rawcliffe 1998).

To generalize from the approaches described above, it might be suggested that idealized 'open' states have a decentralized structure, egalitarian ideology and proportional representation – allowing informal and formal access; thereby absorbing pressure before it builds up, resulting in moderate social movements. In this kind of polity, it is assumed that social movement activists regard negotiations and demonstrations as worthwhile as they will be likely to result in policy gains. As Kitschelt (1986: 302) sums up, those movements in a liberal egalitarian political culture are expected to be much less antagonistic, largely because they have less need to antagonize. By contrast, closed states – which at the extreme are centralized, corrupt and totalitarian – deny access, and activists regard conventional forms of political participation as time-wasting activities. Where protest is repressed, many find it too dangerous to take to the streets. According to this approach, when protest does occur in a closed polity, it tends to sway towards 'more direct forms of struggle such as land occupation, factory seizures, store-house raids and insurrections' (Boudreau 1996: 181) or go underground and be violent and sect-like.

Table 5.1 Idealized open and closed polities

Type of Political Opportunity	Indicator of Openness	Idealized Open Polity	Idealized Closed Polity
STRUCTURAL/ PERMANENT	Degree of centralization	Decentralized	Centralized
	Configuration of power	Proportional Representation	Totalitarian
CONTINGENT/ TEMPORARY *(ranked in order of durability)*	Political culture	Egalitarian	Corrupt/inegalitarian
	Policymaking capacity	Strong	Weak
	Elite divisions	Divided	Undivided
	Electoral stability	Unstable	Stable
	Policing/tolerance of protest	Tolerant	Repressive
	Alliances and counter-movements	Elite Alliances	No Alliances

A closed polity is most likely to engage in repression of social movement efforts. But heavy-handed policing and repression are thought to act as double-edged swords for social movements. For obvious reasons, they discourage social movement activity by increasing the costs for individual activists, yet could also serve as a stimulant to protest by reinforcing the identity, solidarity and sense of injustice felt by challengers (Kriesi 1995: 177–8; della Porta and Fillieule 2004: 233). Della Porta (1995: 80) sees protest policing as 'an important barometer of the political opportunities available for social movements'. Although perhaps overgeneralizing, she suggests that tolerant policing fosters diffuse movements, but harsh policing encourages smaller, more radical groups that are inclined to violence.

The contingent/temporary features of a polity are less stable and vary over time, but still impact upon the actual opportunities social movement organizations receive, albeit that these are not structural. Tarrow (1998) suggests that movements are more likely to be successful in gaining acceptance, or making material gains (Gamson 1975) when a political regime is unstable, or has elite divisions. When a government and a shadow government are in close competition, they will have greater proclivity to support the demands of popular social movements in an attempt to sway public demand in their favour (Maguire 1995). In the United Kingdom, for instance, the Labour Party in opposition has provided consistent support for social movements. Note, for example, Ed Miliband's overt support of the Trade Union Congress march in November 2010.

Unfortunately, Kitschelt (1986) and Kriesi (1995: 177–98) did not stick to the synthesized approach given in Table 5.1. Instead, it seems plausible that they may have cherry-picked variables that suited what they wanted to say about the movements they studied. Consequently, they reach different conclusions about which states are 'open' and which are 'closed'. Kitschelt (1986: 66), for example, described the German polity as closed because of its 'input structures' – having a centripetal party system and weak legislature – and 'output structures' – characterized by 'jurisdictional and territorial fragmentation of the state', an autonomous judiciary and little control over the private sector. Kriesi (1995), however, on the basis of more structural characteristics – such as Germany's decentralized federal system, which has multiple points of access – classified it, perhaps more accurately, as open. In addition, the work of Kitschelt and Kriesi can be viewed as outdated and overly focused on Western industrialized countries.

It is a shame that movement scholars remain unsure about which indicators can reliably be used to characterize a polity as open or closed. The fact is that no one has created a set of dimensions proved to reliably influence the opportunities open to social movements. As Opp (2009: 174) states:

> It is highly questionable to provide a priori lists of dimensions and claim that these are related to an increase or decrease in political opportunity structures. Dimensions involve empirical propositions, and it must therefore be tested empirically whether they affect the actual perceived goal attainment of groups.

The upshot is that this leads to the suspicion that Kitschelt's interpretation may have been coloured by his realization that German anti-nuclear organizations lacked access to the polity. However, a more convincing explanation for German anti-nuclear organizations' lack of access to the polity might have simply been the movement's system-challenging ideology and strategies – a contingent rather than structural factor.

Furthermore, as Welsh (2001) argues, not all organizations within a given movement in a particular country will share ideology and strategies. Welsh discusses this with reference to the British anti-nuclear movement, but the argument can be applied to movements more generally. Welsh bemoans that the British anti-nuclear movement is often misrepresented 'as if it corresponds with an actual, undifferentiated collective actor' (Welsh 2001: paragraph 2.1). In actual fact, the

British anti-nuclear movement, despite existing within a constant political structure, was historically split over both tactics and strategy. Whereas one faction focused on constitutional means of opposing nuclear energy, another turned towards education and direct action (ibid. paragraph 3.3). Thus, theories of macro-political opportunity structures neglect to take into account that different factions or even different organizations have varying behaviour that in turn influences strategies and status. As Rootes (1997a: 93) suggests, '[political opportunity] systems may be relatively open or closed to different kinds of issues and or groups, and this makes global categorization hazardous if not entirely arbitrary'.

Further, many variants of political opportunity structure theory assume that all movements depend on, or target, national political institutions to the same extent (Meyer and Staggenborg 1996: 134). In reality, sub- and counter-cultural movements are likely to have more autonomous targets and be considerably less affected than those instrumentally oriented organizations or movements with a 'highly focused problem structure' (Kriesi 1995: 193). What curtails one type of movement (e.g. a closed policy window) may be exactly the feature that spawns a different type (e.g. the rise of the UK's direct action movement) (see Saunders 2007c). This is why Tarrow (1998: 90) warns against what he calls 'the seduction of statism'.

The 'weak' approach

Despite my critique of the strong approach to political opportunity structures, I argue that the weak approach has merit. The weak approach suggests that *political processes* (not necessarily 'opportunities' or 'structures') impact organizations within movements to variable degrees. It is clear that there are many factors contributing to the making of *opportunities for campaigning* within environmental networks that are not structural. For example, Earth First! blossomed in the United Kingdom, when conventional campaigning appeared fruitless and direct action seemed the only viable course of action remaining. Although the political opportunity 'structure' of the state may have been relatively 'open', defeats at public inquiries and the apparent determination of the government to promote road building meant that, at least on the roads issue, channels for legal campaigning were 'closed'. This did not mean that legal avenues for campaigning were equally closed to all environmental groups across issues. At around the same time, the government was relatively open to the campaigning efforts of the Wildlife and Countryside Link and this resulted in a stronger Wildlife and Countryside Act (1990).

The concept of 'political process' is therefore useful for explaining some aspects of environmental activism in Britain. In this book, the concept of political opportunities is not used for cross-national comparison, so this means important politico-cultural differences between countries are not of concern. That does not mean that my approach is parochial, for I suggest that it can be applied more broadly across countries (see Conclusion). I purposly avoid giving the British polity a generic label as 'open' or 'closed', recognizing that it can be 'closed' in some respects and 'open' in others, and also 'open' to some environmental organizations or issues while being 'closed' to others. Furthermore, non-structural variables are not misrepresented as objectively structural, and I note that movement strategies can and do vary within a single supposedly relatively 'open' polity. Finally, inclusion of radical groups that seek to bypass the state in their campaigning demonstrates my awareness that achieving changes in policy is not the central aim of all environmental organizations. I also look at attempts to influence both state and local level policies. Thus, the caveats of the cross-national and 'strong' political opportunity structure approach are avoided.

In Britain, the electoral system is relatively closed, but this is allegedly balanced by a relatively open administrative system (Rootes 1992: 171–92). The electoral system – especially the first-past-the-post ballot – has stifled the progress of the Green Party of England and Wales, while the alleged relative openness of the governmental structure to representations by environmental organizations has arguably impacted the shape and form of the wider movement (although this may be less true of other issues). In his argument on British exceptionalism,[2] Rootes (1992) suggested that unconventional protest was largely absent from British environmentalism (as it was until just after the article was published, when direct action networks became prominent) because, among other things, the polity had broadly accepted environmentalism. That the political opportunity structure in Britain has been quite open to *moderate* green groups since the 1980s is indeed widely recognized, being 'sufficient for them [environmental organizations] to remain well-ordered and non-disruptive' (Rawcliffe 1998: 55).

Although the polity is allegedly relatively 'open' to moderate (but not radical) environmental organizations, this does not automatically guarantee success for moderate organizations. An open polity creates competition within the wider movement sector by increasing access for others. Olson (1965: 23) and Jordan (1999), for example, present evidence of 'demosclerosis'. This is the idea that the British policy arena has become so overcrowded and unresponsive to changing circumstances that it cannot effectively incorporate demands of pressure groups. For instance, the Organic Foods and Targets Bill proposed by Friends of the Earth (2000) was suppressed due to pressure from government whips. Harking back to Kitschelt's (1986) 'output structures', even if environmental organizations' Bills become law, they may lack adequate enforcement – as with the toothless Road Traffic Reduction Act of 1997. Contrary to the aims of the Bill, the government has refused to set targets for traffic reduction, and it can be considered as little more than lip service, in the light of the pro-car Ten Year Transport Plan (DETR 2000) that followed it, and the lack of emphasis on traffic reduction in the 2011 Carbon Plan (DECC 2011).[3] According to Porritt (1997: 64):

> With the exception of Mrs Thatcher's short-lived 'green period' in the late eighties . . . there has not been an ounce of heavyweight political leadership on environmental issues for the last 25 years.

After 1990, in light of the British government's apparent embrace of environmentalism, which failed to manifest itself in the implementation of new green policies or the more effective enforcement of current environmental legislation, environmentalists became more sceptical of the integrity of Thatcher's 1988 pledge to the environment. By the time of the Rio Earth Summit (1992), a large swathe of the British environmental movement, including environmental organizations that only a few years previously had been regarded as radical – such as Greenpeace and Friends of the Earth – was considered to have 'lost its critical voice, as states, corporations, and environmental organisations all appeared to share the same language, the same commitments and the same appeal to management as the way to solve environmental problems' (McNaughten and Urry 1988: 65).[4] Undoubtedly, the 1992 recession helped the environment slide down the political agenda. This combination of ineffective policy change and incorporation (some would say co-option) of the environmental movement, led to a perception among diehard activists and radical youth that the mainstream environmental organizations were impotent. Even activists within organizations like Friends of the Earth and Greenpeace were beginning to complain about a lack of action and commitment. Furthermore, a general disillusionment with politics had been steadily developing. Whereas in 1973, 49 per cent of the public believed the system of governing Britain 'could be improved' either 'quite a lot' or 'very much', the figure had risen to 75 per cent by 1995 (MORI 1998).[5]

This and other important events created a political environment ripe for the rise of radical environmentalism. The rights of young people had been infringed by several Thatcherite policies, including the removal of student grants, the implementation of the Criminal Justice and Public Order Act (CJA) (1994) and the elimination of unemployment benefits for 16–18-year-olds (Robinson 1999: 343). This created a pool of dissatisfied youth from which the personnel for direct action networks was drawn. It was also in the early 1990s that the government embarked upon its controversial UK-wide road expansion and 'improvement' programme. This resulted in high levels of public campaigning, but culminated in the defeat of objectors in 141 of 146 public inquiries (Must in McKay 1998: 128). Activists of all persuasions, witness to a democratic dead end, were realizing the inefficacy of official channels for halting roads, and sought alternative means. Relatively high rates of unemployment, and an emerging do it yourself youth counter-culture in the aftermath of the anti-poll tax campaigns that set a precedent for direct action, contributed to a new and much more radical protest culture. The development of do it yourself culture not only coincided with closed political opportunities that spurned extra-parliamentary campaign strategies, but also with an election year (1997) – two types of contingent political opportunities found to be significantly associated with greater networking among environmental groups in the United Kingdom (Poloni-Staudinger 2009: 387).[6]

The emergence of radical environmentalism in the United Kingdom seems to disprove Rootes' (1992) British exceptionalism thesis, which, according to Wall (1999a: 117), was a weak argument. Wall suggests that pre-1992 environmental activism in the United Kingdom was *not* exceptionally non-radical. He illustrates his argument with reference to the 1970s roads protests, the 1980s peace movements and previous spates of animal rights activism, each of which sometimes used militant direct action. What this case does show, however, is the danger of predicting movement trajectories on the basis of permanent political opportunity structure indicators alone, and that more volatile factors can have unexpected and sometimes drastic effects upon movements. As Rootes (2003b: 137) suggests, in his second and more convincing attempt to account for British exceptionalism, that changes in the nature of British environmental protest are better explained by

consideration of the legacies of other protest campaigns, more general changes in political culture, and by the contingent openness or closedness of governments to *particular issues* than by reference to political opportunity structures, *since the formal structures of the political system have remained relatively unchanged*. (my emphasis)

The reduction of direct action 1997–2007 can be explained by the government's withdrawal from the roads program, anticipation of the arrival in power of a potentially more environmentally conscious Labour Party, and the Labour Government's ability, at least at the start of its term of office, to defuse issues before eruption (Rootes 2003b). Tentative support for this is found in evidence that, by 1998, 54 per cent of the public believed the system of governing Britain 'could be improved' 'a lot' or 'very much', down from 76 per cent in 1995 (Ipsos MORI 1998). Similarly, shortly after the 2010–11 'winter of discontent' marked by a range of protests against government plans to reduce public sector spending, 55 per cent of the public were found to be dissatisfied with the government's performance (Ipsos MORI 2011[7]).

Since 2007, there has been a spell of direct action on climate change. Contingent political opportunities can also help to explain this. Activists, drawing on the failure of the anti-capitalist summit-hopping protests of the early 2000s to build an enduring movement (Mueller 2009, see also, Chapter 3), sought a new focus. Climate change provided them with just that. Activists were motivated to create the direct action focused Camp for Climate Action by virtue of what they perceived to be a disjuncture between the UK government's policy proposals and policy action (see Saunders 2012). While the input 'structures' allowed a Bill initially drafted by Friends of the Earth to become instituted in law (the Climate Change Act 2008), the output 'structures' are yet unable to deliver promised cuts to greenhouse gas emissions.

The case for looking at organizational strategy and status

The global/broad brush approach, as it stands, is barely useful for explaining interaction among environmental organizations, though the weak approach, which focuses on context and contingency is very useful. Dalton's (1994: 171) study of environmental organizations in Western Europe, for instance, concluded that local level factors which shape political opportunities – based on environmental organizations' external identity, ideologies and strategies – were more influential in determining the variety of movement activity within counties than macro-political opportunity factors were at explaining variation between countries. For instance, the lack of political acceptance of the radical environmental group, Earth First!, is more or less consistent across Western industrialized countries despite different political opportunity structures. Hence, political opportunities might be more accurately applied at the organizational level, rather than at the movement level.

Fortunately, we are not left in a theoretical abyss. The distinction between 'insiders' and 'outsiders', derived by scholars of pressure groups, provides a model which can be used to help fine-tune political opportunities theory. Environmental organizations can, like pressure groups have been, be categorized according to the extent to which their strategies reflect archetypal 'insider' or 'outsider' behaviour. Insiders are considered legitimate, are widely consulted by government and have access to the executive, whereas outsiders lack access (Grant 1989). Grant, however, has been criticized by Whiteley and Winyard (1987) for ignoring the differences between status and strategy – status can vary according to the strategy a group is pursuing, and may also depend on the political salience of issues being addressed.

For instance, in some of my early work (Saunders 2000: 74–5), I showed how the status of Greenpeace and Friends of the Earth varies according to strategies deployed and receptivity of the governmental department targeted. The contrasting views of the late Department of Trade and Industry and the Exports Credit Guarantee Department towards Friends of the Earth are shown as an example in Table 5.2. In

Table 5.2 The variable status of Friends of the Earth

	Example 1 : Friends of the Earth as legitimate	Example 2 : Friends of the Earth as incriminate
Department	Department of Trade and Industry	Export Credit Guarantee Department
Quote from Minister	'Friends of the Earth have an extremely important role to play in helping to shape policy on environmental issues. I value the contribution they are making to the debate on future waste and recycling measure legislation . . . I am determined to build on the good communication links that exist between Friends of the Earth and the DTI' **Consumer Affairs Minister Nigel Griffiths, 27 April 1998**	'Far from being a secretive or clandestine process, as alleged by Friends of the Earth, our approach to the Ilusi Dam project has from the outset been open and balanced. All the misinformation involved has flowed from Friends of the Earth, who at no point have sought a meeting with me or my officials' **Minister for Trade, Brian Wilson, 2 July 1999**

Source: Saunders (2000)

Example 1, Friends of the Earth pursued an insider strategy, resulting in favourable treatment from the Department of Trade and Industry. In Example 2, it deployed an outsider strategy, challenging the decision to fund the Ilusi Dam. The Export Credit Guarantees Department was put on the defensive and outwardly attacked Friends of the Earth, brandishing it a liar and awarding it contingent outsider status. As well as illuminating the importance of strategy for determining political opportunities available for challenging groups, this example also illustrates the importance of a more nuanced conception of political opportunities. Those challenging policy can rely on the receptivity of particular government departments or county/local councils as much, if not more, as on aggrandized nation-wide political opportunity structures.

By distinguishing between status and strategy, and appending the additional category of 'thresholder' to describe organizations using a mixture of insider and outsider strategies, like Friends of the Earth and Greenpeace (as suggested by Baggott 1995), some of the problems associated with oversimplifying the 'insider/ outsider' dichotomy are reduced.

An ideal-type insider group has a favourable status with the government, has access to the executive and works bureaucratically – in a manner amenable to the polity itself. Its strategy would largely be comprised of negotiations and consultations with ministers and it would deal with small-scale issues already on the policy agenda. It is to this type of organization that the polity, whether local or national, or a particular department, will be most open. At the opposite extreme, ideological outsiders would be met with a closed polity. They would be ideologically opposed to the state and therefore would have an unfavourable status. Their strategy bypasses the state – they may be a small violent group, or seeking self-directed change. Issues concerning them would be broad ranging and incompatible with bureaucratic polities (Table 5.3). This approach is useful for showing that groups facing an open political structure as 'insiders' (Grant 1995: 18–23) are likely to moderate their tactics. For such groups it becomes important to 'not jeopardize their relationship with government by attacking public policy openly' (Baggott 1995: 10). For this reason, ideological outsiders that regard the state as their adversary, and insiders who deem the state an ally and partner can be expected to dissociate.

This theory is reflected in what we already know about the environmental movement. Rawcliffe (1998: 17), for example, notes that the Royal Society for the Protection of Birds (RSPB) is an 'insider' environmental organization. As a result of its status, the RSPB is considered unlikely to network with radicals like Earth First!. Similarly, in their study of networking among environmental organizations in Alabama, Lhotka et al. (2008: 237) found that politically neutral groups chose to avoid working with activist groups to prevent themselves from being labelled as 'anti-business'.

Thresholders meeting a relatively inert set of political opportunities can be expected to network most extensively due to their unconstrained status and use of strategies. Greenpeace, for example, which uses mostly thresholder strategies, has denied any links with Sea Shepherd, a radical splinter group, so as to not further impair its already controversial reputation (Pearce 1991: 30–1). Although allying with a more radical group may be beneficial to Greenpeace through the radical flank effect – by making its own demands appear more practical and compromising – groups will also be likely to be wary of the 'negative radical flank effect', in which counter-movements or the state tarnish entire movements as deviant (Haines 1988: 167). This is likely to have implications for the way in which more radical groups are received by the mainstream movement, as well as on how the polity reacts to demands from the movement as a whole. In practice, a range of tactics across the insider-outsider spectrum can give social movements strength, even if it does provide tensions over credibility and funding (Spalter-Roth and Schreiber 1995).

Table 5.3 Implications for interaction in environmental networks based on strategy and status

Contingent opportunity 'structure'	Type of challenger	Status	Strategy	Issues	Network implications
MOST OPEN	Insider	Legitimate Has access to executive Bureaucratic and professional	Negotiates with ministers Works as a consultee	Seeks piecemeal, small incremental gains on issues already on the policy agenda	Few network links Some ties to insiders and thresholders Distanced from (ideological) outsiders
	Thresholder	Sometimes has insider status Sometimes has outsider status Semi-professional	Uses a mix of insider and outsider strategies	Works on issues that are usually already on the policy agenda Seeks to put new uncontroversial issues on to the policy agenda	Has strategic ties with others at all levels Is most central in networks due to flexible status
	Outsider	Not legitimate OR, lacks skills/ knowledge Amateur	Media, non-violent direct action Works to change public opinion	Seeks support for issues new to the policy agenda Many of these issues will be controversial	Has links with thresholders and ideological outsiders
MOST CLOSED	Ideological outsider	Ideologically opposed to the state	Direct action, possibly violent OR, seeking self-directed change	Works on issues outside of the state's remit Seeks radical social and/or political change	Small alienated cliques

Note: This model is based on categories of pressure groups suggested by Grant (1989) and Baggott (1995) but I developed the content.

Political opportunities and interaction in environmental networks: The London data

This section of the chapter takes a look at the findings of the survey of environmental organizations in London, and illustrates them with interview quotes as appropriate. It begins by looking at the extent to which organizations that use different types of strategies – as insiders, thresholders and outsiders – cooperate with each other, before turning to consider the extent to which status, measured by organizations' perceived relationships to local and national government, seems to determine patterns of collaborative networking. The section on status is split into two further subsections, looking at local and national governance in turn. The discussion of status with each of local and national governments begins with some contextual information gleaned from qualitative interviews, which illustrate the variable extent to which environmental activists consider local and national governance to be 'open' to their demands. This background information is included because it helps to further demonstrate why broad-brush approaches to political opportunities can be inappropriate, and helps explain why environmental organizations have a variety of types of relationship with local authorities and national governments. It also allows us to circumvent another issue with political opportunities theory. Objective political opportunities matter little if organizations and activists within them are unaware of them (Snow and Soule 2010: 84). As McAdam et al. (2001: 43) state: 'No opportunity, however objectively open will invite mobilization unless it is (a) visible to potential challengers and (b) perceived as an opportunity'. Thus, the emphasis here is on perceived openness rather than on any objective measure.

Organizational strategies and inter-organizational networking

In practice, very few organizations (only three in my sample) are pure outsiders. Even the radical anarchist environmental organization surveyed claimed in its survey response to engage in occasional lobbying. Unfortunately, this means that we are unable to draw particularly concrete conclusions about the behaviour of ideological outsiders. Nonetheless, consonant with expectations, all of the three collaborative ties that outsider groups admitted having to other environmental organizations were directed towards thresholder organizations. More importantly, *none* were with insiders. Of thresholders' 140 ties, a high majority (86%) were directed towards other thresholders (Table 5.4). This is likely to be because thresholders have similar political viewpoints and strategies. As they are not insiders, they are more likely to require support from allies and, unlike some radicals, are pragmatic enough to cooperate. This finding is supported by Poloni-Staudinger's (2009) research: Of

Table 5.4 Collaboration network by balance of activities

INITIATORS OF TIES (i)	RECEIVERS OF TIES (j)							
	Insiders		Thresholders		Outsiders		Total	
	n	%	n	%	n	%	n	%
Insiders	6	26	17	65	0	0	23	100
Thresholders	17	12	120	86	3	2	140	100
Outsiders	0	0	3	100	0	0	3	100

Note: the initiator of a tie is always the questionnaire respondent and receivers are the organizations that the respondents nominate.

all environmental protest collaboration reported in the Reuters Business Briefings 1980–2004, lobbying – a thresholder strategy – makes up 50 per cent of all cooperative protest acts. In contrast, only 8 per cent of the collaborative acts identified by Poloni-Staudinger were protest-based (an outsider strategy).

Collaborative ties from insiders to outsiders are missing, but we would not expect questionnaire respondents to admit to dealings with outsiders, at least not the most radical of them. Indeed, previous research has shown collaborative links have existed between radical outsiders and their more moderate counterparts, although the moderate parties are often unwilling to admit so. Seel and Plows (2000: 119), for example, noted that 'Greenpeace . . . sometimes gives "under the counter" financial assistance to local Earth First! groups or particular issue campaigns'. Yet Greenpeace is virtually silent over this cooperation. It may also be that thresholders perceive their links with insiders to be more important than their links with outsiders, thus the results might be considered to be partially an artefact of the question asked, which focused only on the top five collaborative links.

Relations with local borough councils
Open or closed?

Organizations within the same borough have different perceptions of the openness of local government. For instance, while Greenwich Friends of the Earth has, at best, a contingent relationship with Greenwich Borough Council (GBC), Plumstead Common Environmental Group, a conservation organization has a constructive one. The coordinator of Greenwich Friends of the Earth (Bates, interview February 2001) claims that 'to be frank, they [GBC] are barking up the wrong tree', that

GBC deprioritizes the environment by placing the economic agenda at the heart of decision-making, and views Greenwich Friends of the Earth as a 'thorn in their side'. Commenting on Plumstead Common Environment Group's constructive relationship with the council, Julia Cowdell, the group coordinator suggested in interview that 'they [GBC] are quite receptive to us, and they know us very well now and they do trust us, which is good to have'. Consequently, the group has seriously considered adopting a more formal partnership (Cowdell, interview, September 2003).

Environmental organizations in northwest London equally have contrasting views of the 'openness' of their local authority. In the Borough of Ealing, the Local Agenda 21 (LA21) group claimed that LA21 in Ealing amounted to 'words and not action' as annual pollution reports had not been produced by the council since 1997. This group is clearly dismayed by their local authority's apparent lack of concern for the environment. Yet a local conservation group, Friends of Blondin Park, has a very productive relationship with the local council, having won an Ealing Council Green Award for two years running.

Relationships with local polity and impacts on inter-organizational networking

The 69 organizations that were respondents *and* a part of the collaboration network[8] answered a survey question on their relationship with their local authority. Of these, 15 claimed to have a constructive relationship, 20 were ambivalent, 13 contingent and 11 had no relationship with their local authorities. Interestingly, not a single organization claimed to have a negative relationship (see Chapter 2 for the operationalization of constructive, ambivalent, contingent and negative relations with the polity). Of the 23 ties initiated by environmental organizations with a constructive relationship to their borough, the majority (44%) were directed towards organizations that lack a relationship with their local governors and 35 per cent towards organizations with an ambivalent relationship to them (Table 5.5). This collaboration network includes the national, regional and local groups, which is why such a high proportion of groups are claiming no relationship with their local authority – most national environmental organizations focus on the national level.

Although the relationship between the No Third Runway Action Group and Hillingdon Borough Council is best classified as 'ambivalent' because of the Council's initial reluctance to support the campaign, it is indicative of how an environmental organization's positive relationship with local government can constrain its activities *and* its network links. Hillingdon Borough Council had reportedly provided at least £50,000 for the anti-third runway campaign (Longhurst and Nadel 2002), including the funding of the anti-airport expansion group's road show that took to the streets

Table 5.5 Collaboration network by relationship to local authorities

INITIATOR OF TIES (i)	RECEIVER OF TIES (j)									
	Constructive		Ambivalent		Contingent		Non-Existent		Total	
	n	%	n	%	n	%	n	%	n	%
Constructive	2	9	8	35	3	13	10	44	23	100
Ambivalent	8	28	12	41	2	7	7	24	29	100
Contingent	7	44	3	19	0	0	6	38	16	100
Non-Existent	2	9	2	9	12	55	6	27	22	100

after the 2003 aviation White Paper was released to raise awareness of the issues. Because the group was dependent upon funding from its local council, it

> can't actually do anything illegal because if we do anything illegal, the council will cut off the money. At the same time, we appreciate the frustration of the people who want to take direct action, but we wouldn't at this stage want them on our committee, purely and simply on the grounds that . . . [the group] is funded by the council. (Sobey, Coordinator, anti-airport expansion group, No Third Runway Action Group] interview February 2004)

Being constrained by council funding in this manner caused a rift between those who wanted to take direct action, and those sought to abide by council rules. According to a local anti-third runway campaigner with Longford Residents' Association (local campaigner, LC):

> **LC** There were some people who really wanted to get up and be a bl***y pain in the arse and do things that the airport won't like. But you see the group itself didn't want to, and it split up a bit in that way. I was prepared to be one of those that was militant, but I kept on the ground and I said to the others, 'if you've got anything you want done, like being really militant, I am there with you'. So I tried to keep on both sides a bit.
>
> **I** What do you mean by being militant then?
>
> **LC** I mean if they wanted somebody to go and block the airport up, or drive really slowly around, or put posters up or, or just driving around the roads at 5mph for hours and hours in the morning. (interview, January 2004)

Although the anti-airport expansion group is somewhat constrained in what it can do as a coalition, this has not stopped its members from being highly supportive of direct action. Members have, for example, supported the court cases of direct activists who occupied the construction site of Terminal Five. However, even if the local council did not fund the group, it would probably continue to use conventional insider techniques because this allows for the possibility of a contingency plan should the development go ahead:

> If, in the final analysis, we lose, we have got to work with those blighters across the road, we have got to get all sorts of different types of facilities and amenities for the people left . . . the association has always been careful to keep the lines of communication open with BAA and people like that. (Sobey, coordinator, No Third Runway Action Group, interview, February 2004)

The highest figure in Table 5.5 is 55 per cent. It provides some indication that organizations lacking a relationship with their local council tend to select allies with a contingent relationship to it. National and regional organizations often lack a relationship with their own local borough councils, but if they have local groups, they are able to impact upon local authorities via these rather than through a centrally coordinated effort. For example, a branch of national Friends of the Earth in northwest London claims that national Friends of the Earth is one of its top five collaborative partners, but national Friends of the Earth itself has no contact with Hillingdon Borough Council either because of its more national focus or because it leaves this kind of work for its local groups. For instance, in their anti-GM campaign, Friends of the Earth called upon local Friends of the Earth groups (that mostly have contingent relationships with their local councils) to engage with their local councils to persuade them to become GM-Free Zones. By 2003, over half a dozen local authorities had voted for the exclusion of GM crops in their area.[9]

Greenpeace undertook a similar strategy in its Incineration Busters campaign (summer 2001–spring 2002). It produced postcards for on-street signing, asking local councils for more emphasis to be placed on the reduction, recycling and composting of waste as an alternative to incineration. Groups of Incinerator Busters were formed throughout the country, consisting mostly of pre-established non-Greenpeace incinerator action groups. Resources and training were provided for local activists. After long and thoughtful research, Greenpeace drew up a pro forma *Zero Waste* Strategy.[10] All local activists had to do was to change the details – for example, the total amount of waste produced by the local authority, the population size, the nature of local industry – and the result was a Zero Waste Strategy applicable to each district or county where activists participated in the campaign (Greenpeace 2001). The Zero Waste Charter that emerged from the Strategy was the result of wider collaboration involving Friends of the Earth, Communities Against Toxics and the UK Zero Waste Alliance. In England, at least one local authority (Bath and North East Somerset) and one county council (Essex) have adopted a Zero Waste policy. These successes are clearly the result of collaborative ties between (national) organizations that lack a relationship with their local council and local organizations that have at least a contingent relationship with them.

Relations with national government
Open or closed?

Just as with local governance, environmental campaigners' perceptions of national government vary according to organizational type and issue focus. According to a marine campaigner for Greenpeace:

> The UK government is pretty good from a climate change point of view. [They are] really up for pushing wind power and . . . when we did our No Nukes, Yes2Wind campaign, their White Paper changed completely . . . they decided that they could go with wind and that it was a viable alternative and . . . we were quite surprised at how good it was. (Dory, in interview January 2004)

But, on other issues, including wood procurement – for which the organization had embarrassed the government by exposing its use of illegally harvested wood from Cameroon to rebuild the Cabinet Office – and GM foods, the government were considered 'really, really bad'.

In terms of aviation, the policy arena is viewed as relatively closed by campaigners because the 2003 White Paper has left decisions more or less in the hands of the aviation industry. In his opening address to the Post White Paper Airport Watch conference, John Stewart, told the audience that:

> I think something fairly significant has probably happened as to who we will be focussing on post White Paper. We were focussing on government and civil servants because they were drawing up the White Paper . . . But post White Paper I think is different because we know what the government has said, it feels it has done its bit. It is now saying it is up to the aviation industry and developers to come up with proposals . . . And it seems to me that the key focus now of our campaign needs to be on the developers and the banks and the construction companies. (in interview 2004)

Even prior to the release of the White Paper, anti-airport expansion campaigners were sceptical of the government's stance on aviation. Mike Fawcett (then advisor for the Department for Transport) comment to the Airport Watch Conference in 2001, that 'Blair is committed to sustainable development', was met with raucous laughter from the audience.

The airport lobby have seemingly convinced the government of aviation's importance for the economic growth of the country, despite some contrary evidence. Friends of the Earth, for example, draw on the research of Professor Whitelegg, which illustrates that greener alternatives could bring greater economic return and employment (Whitelegg 2000). According to a Paul de Zylva, head of Friends of the Earth England:

> The government is supposed to have green ministers, but they rarely meet, have no weight and aren't reflecting green policies within their departments as they have to deliver on other, often contradictory, policies. Nor are there enough green departments. It is ridiculous having a single department to focus on the environment, which in itself is not green enough. The Department for Trade and Industry, the Department for Transport and the Treasury have few if any environmental and sustainable development concerns and are probably the worst culprits in the government. They are completely ignoring the sustainable development agenda or at best they are seeing sustainable development as a negative anti-progress ideology, which it is not. Either that or they hijack sustainable development so that it ends up meaning all the unsustainable things we are doing now i.e. 'sustainable development means building more runways'. (interview, January 2004)[11]

In line with the critique of macro political opportunity structures proffered earlier, these interview quotes neatly demonstrate that the openness of the government varies according to the organization involved, the nature of the issue, and the department being targeted. Additionally, we should bear in mind that individual activists' perceptions of the openness of the polity also matter for the actual uptake of political opportunities. I now turn to look at how perceived relationships with the national polity impact upon networking among environmental organizations.

Relationships with the national polity and impacts on inter-organizational networking

Of the 59 organizations in the collaboration network that answered a survey question about their relationship with national government, 6 claimed constructive ties, 7 were ambivalent, 11 contingent, 6 had a negative relationship and 29 had no relationship. Six organizations with constructive relations with the government have only a total of five ties directed to other organizations (at least one of them had no ties at all and the others averaged only one tie each), four to contingent ones and one shared with another organization with a constructive relationship to the government. This indicates tendency for those with constructive relationships with the government to work alone. Perhaps they have less need to collaborate because they are not, like thresholders, seeking to influence public opinion or generate a groundswell. Additionally, their status in policy circles is already assured. However, the Campaign to Protect Rural England (CPRE), which has a constructive relationship to the government – as a well-known saying goes: 'Ministers never refuse to meet CPRE' – works extensively with organizations with a contingent relationship to the government including Friends of the Earth (especially on the Planning Campaign) and the Campaign for Better Transport (then called Transport 2000) (David Conder, Campaign to Protect Rural England, in interview with Debbie Adams, June 2000). However, the Campaign to Protect Rural England, like other 'insider' organizations is unlikely to be more outrageous than this in its campaign alliances because its constructive relationship with the government makes it feel awkward about criticizing government schemes. As a staff member told me in an interview:

> You have to tread a very thin line when you have this type of relationship with the Government . . . When we are overly critical of their schemes, such as the Deputy Prime Ministers' Sustainable Communities Plan, it doesn't go down too well. (Rosy White, Campaign to Protect Rural England, December 2003)

Of the collaborative ties that organizations with a constructive relationship with the government extend, none of the ties are to organizations with a negative relationship to the government. The Campaign to Protect Rural England, for example, would avoid all contact with those with a negative relationship to the government. It was even concerned about working with Friends of the Earth, which has an ambivalent relationship with government, on a campaign to prevent dilution of planning laws. Paul de Zylva, head of Friends of the Earth England considered this clash between the organizations to be due to the Campaign to Protect Rural England's desire to protect its respectable political reputation:

> in government circles . . . CPRE is clearly the 'respected voice' and it felt that . . . Friends of the Earth was rocking the boat a little by being straight-up and forward about the issues . . . CPRE felt that their cosy relationship with the government may be threatened by . . . Friends of the Earth's approach. (interview January 2004)

Along similar lines to the Campaign to Protect Rural England's wanting to preserve its carefully crafted political reputation, the Environmental Direct Action Group tactfully decided not to be a formal part of a campaign coalition against the Baku Ceyhan oil and gas pipeline project so as not to tar the credibility of the coalition:

> Well, we discussed it within the campaign whether they should be officially part of the campaign and the decision was, that for both the coalition and for . . . [the Environmental Direct Action Group] it would impose restrictions. . . . [the Environmental Direct Action Group] wouldn't be able to behave in the ways they wanted to in terms of any dodgy stuff like office invasions or stuff

that might . . . run foul of the law. They wanted the freedom of not having to tell us every time they were going to do an action . . . obviously because of the way . . . [the Environmental Direct Action Group] works, it is on the spur of the moment and you can't cope with an approvals process on decision-making that takes ages. Partly for purely pragmatic reasons and I guess there is a whole thing about who might be liable for illegal actions. (Nic Rau, Climate Campaigner Friends of the Earth, in interview, January 2004)

In the same vein, while Friends of the Earth allegedly had great sympathy and admiration for the anti-capitalist demonstration in Seattle in 1999 (reportedly, Charles Secrett, then director, was 'really impressed by Seattle because it was such a broad range of people out in the streets'), it will not 'touch May Day [anti-capitalist demonstrations in London] with a barge pole' despite the fact that the organization has become

very interested in [the] anti-capitalist/globalisation . . . issue. In fact that has been the basis of some of our big campaigns. I mean . . . [our organisation] are of course very wary of throwing rocks at windows and getting lots of police out and any of that sort of thing, and as a big organisation, I think they have to be. (Sheila Freeman, post and volunteers coordinator, Friends of the Earth, February 2004)

Data in Table 5.6 further confirms that organizations with a flexible approach in their dealings with government have extensive inter-organizational linkages. Although organizations with a contingent relationship to government have many

Table 5.6 Collaboration network by relationship to national government

INITIATOR OF TIES (i)	RECEIVER OF TIES (j)										
	Constructive		Ambivalent		Contingent		Negative		Non-Existent		Total
	No.	%	No.	%	No.	%	No.	%	No.	%	No.	%
Constructive	1	20	0	0	4	80	0	0	0	0	5	100
Ambivalent	1	13	2	25	3	38	0	0	2	25	8	100
Contingent	6	22	2	7	13	48	3	11	3	11	27	100
Negative	1	10	1	10	5	50	0	0	3	30	10	N/A
Non-Existent	0	0	1	3	9	29	0	0	21	68	31	100

collaborative links with other organizations, most of their ties are directed towards other organizations like themselves. This may be because the contingency of their relationship with the government is a result of their range of insider and outsider campaigning strategies. Organizations with a contingent relationship are likely to be multi-issue, and therefore have more scope for collaborating. For example, as a multi-issue organization, Friends of the Earth cooperated with Stop Esso, the Campaign Against Climate Change and the Environment Direct Action Group on climate change, and WWF and Greenpeace on genetically modified food (The Five Year Freeze). In addition, each campaign team has a multitude of additional linkages. If it were a single-issue organization, it would likely only cooperate with one of those sets of partners.

While few organizations claimed a negative relationship with the government, there are actually 11 ties between these 6 organizations and groups with different configurations of relationships. But most of the links that such organizations have are directed towards organizations that have a contingent relationship to government. Contingent organizations make good allies when they are campaigning with organizations that have a negative relationship with the government on issues that the government is failing to address, and this is likely to be the case when outsider strategies are most appropriate and most popular.

The only striking relationship that organizations with an ambivalent relationship to the government have is with those with a negative relationship to the government. A quarter of their collaborative ties are directed towards organizations lacking government recognition, or preferring to campaign in different ways (Table 5.6). To refresh from Chapter 2, those with an ambivalent relationship to the government have contact with it but always initiate the contact themselves. Thus, they are likely to be whistle-blowers, bringing new issues to the attention of government. This makes others focusing on new or controversial issues likely allies.

Among organizations lacking a relationship with the government, 68 per cent of their collaborative connections are to other organizations like themselves. This is a meaningful percentage because there are 31 ties in this category – a little over 1 per organization. This is largely because of their local focus – of the 66 organizations that claimed to have no relationship with the government, all but 16 were local. Others were internationally focused conservation organizations like Save the Rhino, Rainforest Concern and regional reformist or conservation organizations (London Friends of the Earth and London Wildlife Trust), and radical organizations (e.g. London Anarchist Federation and Platform). There is, however, a high degree of collaboration between organizations with a constructive and contingent relationship to government. This is likely to be at its highest when those with a contingent relationship to the government are on favourable terms with a certain department, or are campaigning on relatively non-controversial issues.

Concluding remarks

This chapter has demonstrated problems that arise in comparative cross-national studies that use the 'strong' approach to political opportunity structures due to conflation of structures and contingent political variables, and the difficulty of prioritizing and operationalizing these concepts. This is not, however, to be totally dismissive of the broad-brush approach to political opportunity structures. Clearly, a polity that represses all protest movements will create movements much more sect-like and underground than one which facilitates them.

However, as I have shown, structural variables alone would wrongly predict that Britain's environmental networks be entirely moderate, given the relative ease with which environmental groups are able to make their representations heard (Rootes 1992). Although this is true for some environmental organizations, others are much more radical than would be predicted using a broad-brush approach. Generally speaking, when comparing environmental organizations *within* as well as *across* countries, it seems to make more sense to consider political opportunities based on strategies and status rather than on structures, or other features of the polity.

The chapter has also, importantly, illustrated that despite enduring and permanent political opportunity *structures,* individual activists have different perceptions of the openness of a particular polity, whether local or national. While some organizations and activists might believe that the polity is performing to the best of its ability and may be easily appeased by its rhetoric, others will scrutinize the gap between rhetoric and action. Yet when policy contradictions or inadequacies become widely known across environmental networks, things change. Upon reaching a perceived democratic dead end as formal routes for political participation fail, activists can come to view policy windows as closed. Upon perceiving few other worthwhile courses of action, direct action can become a matter of course for activists from many different persuasions. This is exactly what happened in the anti-roads campaigns and what has begun to happen in campaigns against climate change and against aviation.

As predicted by the modified theory, which incorporates pressure group theory, this chapter has shown that, within environmental networks, thresholders have the widest variety of ties across the insider-outsider continuum. Insiders and outsiders widely collaborate with thresholders. This, however, is at least partly due to the skew in the data towards thresholders (most respondents were thresholders). Nonetheless, the No Third Runway Action Group provides a textbook example of a local insider being constrained in its relations with outsiders due to fear that it will lose its income and status should it break the law or be associated with criminal activity. Similarly, the Campaign to Protect Rural England was wary about taking an aggressive stance in its campaigning and so was concerned about Friends of the Earth's more direct approach in the campaign to revoke the Planning Bill. Consequently, most organizations that have a constructive relationship with the government tend to work in relative isolation. The finding that organizations with a constructive relationship to the government rarely chose those with a non-existent or negative relationship as collaborators is congruent with expectations. As do strategically minded organizations (Chapter 4), insiders are concerned to protect their reputations.

In contrast, organizations with a contingent relationship collaborate with one another to a much greater extent. This is most likely to be because they have less need to be concerned about their reputation, which is flexible and issue/strategy-dependent or because their multi-issue focus makes them more likely collaborative partners on a wider range of campaigns. Friends of the Earth, for instance, has consultative status on waste issues and collaborates mostly with insider agencies, but has a radical agenda on 'corporates' with ideological (if not actual) links with the more radical anti-capitalist agenda. When outsiders collaborate with organizations with a contingent relationship to government, this is likely to be on issues that the government is failing to address, or which have become critical (Saunders 2007c). Organizations with an ambivalent relationship to the government appear to sit on the fence, and are in a position to keep radicals relatively content while maintaining a semi-cosy relationship with the government.

Perhaps the most important lesson to learn from this chapter is that a dynamic approach is required. Environmental networks focus on a range of issues, some of which are more warmly welcomed by the government than others. Furthermore, instead of looking just at governance as a target, it would be an interesting exercise to focus on other targets. For example, what effect does the type of relationship that environmental organizations have with *corporations* have on their status, strategies and networking patterns?

We should take note that there is also an emerging global political opportunity structure, focused on international financial institutions like the World Bank and World Trade Organization (van der Heijden 2006) that should be considered. The United Nations Framework Convention on Climate Change (UNFCCC), for example, is especially relevant to climate change protest (Chapter 3). Furthermore, we could take a leaf out of Melucci's book and begin consider 'cultural opportunities' (Melucci 1985) so much as political ones; never forgetting, of course, that movements are rarely, if ever, homogenous entities. On this note, I now turn to look towards those more cultural aspects of social movements as they relate to new social movement theory.

6 Environmental Networks and New Social Movement Theory

This chapter is centred on new social movement theory. This body of theory developed in the late 1960s as contention across Europe peaked. Contemporary social movements of the time were thought to have 'stretched the explanatory capacity of older theoretical perspectives' (Johnston et al. 1994: 3), particularly of collective behaviour. The theory is sometimes juxtaposed as being located poles apart from resource mobilization theory, which I discussed in Chapter 4. This is because resource mobilization theory emphasized the rational and formally organized aspects of social movements, while new social movement theory has largely focused on fluid participatory networks. Others make the distinction between resource mobilization theory and new social movement theory on the basis of their geographical roots. Thus, resource mobilization theory is often referred to as the 'US-approach' and new social movement theory as the 'European approach'. However, there has been a great deal of exchange across the Atlantic since the approaches emerged, and scholars now increasingly use concepts from both schools of thought.

As with other social movement theories, the strands of literature that are lumped together under the banner of new social movement theory are divergent. Scholars associated with the approach offer different reasons for movement emergence, assign different characteristics to new movements, and have been largely unable to agree on an overarching theory. I introduce the key strands of the theory, and supplement this with discussion of newer approaches to identity and subcultures. The diversity of approaches need not be viewed as a problem. Instead it could be conceived as a rich ecumenical approach that helps understand *aspects* of movements, which in themselves are complex.

I begin this chapter by introducing new social movements as distinct from old movements. In practice, though, scholars have tended to find that new movements are not actually all that novel. Therefore, I move on to a more thorough discussion of claims about 'newness'. The chapter then evaluates new social movement theory. I argue that a key weakness of new social movement theory is that it assumes – as do broad-brush approaches to political opportunities (Chapter 5) – that new social movements are homogenous. More specifically, it presupposes that all organizations that comprise new social movements are engaged in the work of seeking cultural change. Masking variation in this way is not useful for a study of environmental networks because it glosses over the fact that many environmental organizations are formally organized and *not* oriented towards social or cultural change as such.

After teasing out implications of the theory for interaction in environmental networks, I return to the London survey data. First, I explore whether the ideologies of organizations in environmental networks fit the new social movement archetype. I find much more homogeneity than I had expected given the different levels of resources (Chapter 4), strategies and statuses (Chapter 5) of environmental organizations. This suggests that it is not ideologies alone that determine whether environmental organizations will cooperate or compete. I then present network diagrams which illustrate how movement networks in southeast London have varied over time, by comparing a period in which protest was peaking to a spell of relative latency.

What is new social movement theory?

New social movement theory seeks to explain why 'new' movements formed in the 1960s, what their characteristics were, and their significance (Johnston et al. 1994: 9). Essentially, the theory acts as a bridge between macro-structuralist theories and micro-theories of identity formation. Previous theoretical approaches, especially collective behaviour, were, perhaps inappropriately (see Chapter 3), deemed inadequate for explaining 'new' protest manifestations in the late 1960s and 1970s, initially observed in the student movement, and succeeded by the peace, civil rights, feminist, ecologist and self-help movements. It was noted, perhaps exaggeratedly so, that these movements had commonalities distinguishing them from traditionally studied labour movements (Table 6.1) (Offe 1985; Pakulski 1991; Laraña and Gusfield 1992: 6–9). As Habermas (1981: 33) suggested, 'in short, the new conflicts are not sparked by problems of [labour and product] distribution, but concern for the grammar of forms of life'.

What is new?

Much scholarly attention has been focussed on questioning the extent of newness of so-called new social movements. As Steinmetz (1994: 179 in Wall 1999b) suggests, 'a cottage industry has grown up around the project of proving that new social movements were not really so new after all'. It is important to explore these arguments to allow for an assessment of the newness of environmental networks.

There are three main claims about newness. The first considers new social movements, including the environmental movement, to be 'new' in a metaphorical

Table 6.1 New social movement characteristics

Ideology
- Anti-modernism/anti-'progress'[1]

Form
- Decentralized, non-hierarchical, participatory
- Not class-based
- Amorphous/fluid
- Direct participation

Purpose
- Resist colonization of the life-world or manipulation of identity and needs
- Freedom of expression, communication and cultural reproduction
- Symbolic resistance
- Solidarity and autonomy as objectives in themselves

sense. According to this approach, they are new to the extent that they have only relatively recently come under scholars' radars because of the adoption of a new analytical lens. The second claim, which I already briefly visited in the introduction to this chapter, considers 1960s–1970s movements to be new in terms of their characteristics – especially, how they differ from the nineteenth century labour movement and other class-based conflicts. Third, they are classified as being new for the simple reason that we live in a 'new' type of society which has demanded a unique response from civil society (Melucci 1984, 1995a, 1995b). The third argument has been given the most emphasis in the literature.

Explaining 'newness' of NSMs by the emergence of a new scholarly lens

The study of social movements has been subject to the 'postmodern turn'. This has witnessed scholars interested in social movements looking beyond a Marxist approach. The Marxist approach focused on the meta-narrative of the labour movement as the source of a social revolution. Once scholars moved away from a near obsession with this idea, they were able to consider instead a broader range of influences upon society and politics. Although new movements may not be distinctly new in historical terms, or in their shape or form, the extent of scholarly interest that was generated in response to them and the emphasis on cultural aspects of social movements clearly was new. As Scott (1990: 24) states, '. . . what we see here is not a retreat from the political sphere, but an extension of politics to cover a wider range of concerns and social relations'.

The focus on the labour movement meant that nineteenth century manifestations of the women's movement and religious movements were largely ignored or, considerably later, passed to historians. Only relatively recently have they been a topic of post hoc analytical political sociology. According to Nash (2002a: 112), following Calhoun (1994), the overemphasis on the labour movement stems not only from the pre-1960s structural bias in sociology, but is also 'due to the rationalist, instrumental bias of sociology itself'. If sociology can be charged with this, political science can be criticized for being even more obsessed with instrumental political action. Yet the labour movement failed to bring about the revolution that many theorists had hoped for, thus beginning what has thus far has proven a wild goose chase of searching the broader social movement milieu for a revolutionary agent with which to replace it.

Hence, at least for European scholars of social movements, the labour movement became the benchmark against which 'new' movements were compared. It was not so much that these movements were actually regarded as new in themselves – their precedents cannot have gone unnoticed – but rather that scholars were exploring new ground. Certainly, the study of environmental movements is newer than the study of the labour movement. This is positively confirmed by comparing results of a British Library catalogue search under the exact terms 'environmental movement' and 'labour movement'. Particularly noteworthy is that the number of recorded entries in the British Library catalogue with a publication date pre-1970 is zero for the environmental movement compared to 171 for the labour movement.

The theory of 'protest cycles' (Tarrow 1998) further explains the degree of scholarly interest that different movements have ignited. Such cycles of protest 'correspond with moments of intensified collective action', which is clearly what was witnessed across Europe in the late 1960s (della Porta and Diani 1999: 189). The entire cycle is described 'as a parabola; from institutional conflict to enthusiastic peak to ultimate collapse' (Tarrow 1998: 168). The argument that Tarrow puts forward can be clearly represented in diagrammatic form, building upon his own parabola metaphor (Figure 6.1).

From this perspective, we might deduce that what was new about new social movements was that scholars followed them from virtually the beginning of this life-course, starting with the student movement that appeared to act as a springboard for a whole host of other related movements (see the explanation of phase 2, Figure 6.1). At the same time, the labour movement was clearly within the 'demise'[2] half of the life-course pattern. The notion of waves is more than a theory. It also appears to have a close fit with actual patterns of protest. Jai Kwan Jung's (2010) analysis of Kriesi et al.'s (1995) protest event data in the Netherlands, Germany, France and Switzerland illustrates how a favourable political

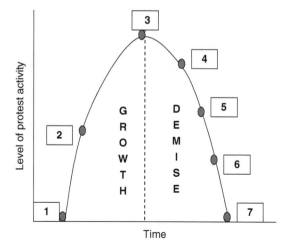

Key

1	Phase 1: a conflict of interests occurs and the affected begin to coalesce around the issues
2	Phase 2: coalitions of challengers organize themselves bringing together actors from different social movements
3	Phase 3: a coherent movement ideology is formed and the movement reaches its enthusiastic peak
4	Phase 4: the movement becomes increasingly channelled through organizations and has to defend itself against counter-movements
5	Phase 5: a violent minority group is instrumental in generating concerns over law and order, as a result it is suppressed and driven underground
6	Phase 6: the non-violent component of the movement becomes increasingly institutionalised
7	Phase 7: the movement winds down until it reaches its ultimate collapse

Figure 6.1 Tarrow's Protest Cycles

opportunity structure coupled with electoral competition appeared to stimulate the rise of protest, and that institutionalization and the emergence of radical protest accompany the dip after a peak. Patterns of environmental protest in Britain 1988–97 also seem to resemble small waves, although the end result has never been a dearth of contention on environmental issues. The steady march towards institutionalization in the early 1990s was broken by a wave of direct action before environmental protest began to tail away again in the late 1990s (see Rootes 2007: 25). Although no one has published in-depth environmental protest event analysis since 1997, it appears that environmental protest has risen again with the advent of annual marches and a host of direct actions networks forming to protest against climate change.[3]

Although such a theory can help explain why environmental movements did not receive a great deal of scholarly attention before the 1960s, this fact alone does not seem to justify the title 'new' in the light of historical evidence that environmental movements and networks have long histories and precedents (Nedelman 1984: 1033; Wall 2000). As Ray (1993: 60) suggests, 'movements like environmentalism, pacifism, feminism were significant around 1890–1900 or before'. As we saw in Chapter 3, first-wave environmentalism, which manifest as conservationism, was active in Britain in the early nineteenth century.

Explaining newness of NSMs by their distinction from old movements

Table 6.2 synthesizes a number of attempts to compare old and new movements (Cohen 1983: 98; Dalton et al. 1990: 13; Scott 1990) using the labour movement as the referent object for 'old' movements. Perhaps the largest problem with these types of comparisons is the way in which in which they convey old and new movements as polar opposites. In reality, movements that emerged in the 1960s and 1970s have features of the labour movement, and vice versa (Calhoun 1994). Thus, Touraine's (1981) distinction between (old) movements of organization and power, on the one hand, and (new) movements of cultural innovation and social movement, on the other, is an artificial bifurcation. Tucker (1991), for example, shows that the labour movement was not so far removed from the characteristics of new social movements as had been assumed. Syndicalists, for example, have coveted a new, decentralized democratic state and labour movements have used cultural symbols throughout history.

While old movements have some new movement characteristics, supposed new movements have some old movement characteristics, too. Rucht (1988) showed how ideologies and practices of the German women's and environmental movements failed to fit ascribed new social movements characteristics. He found differences in recruitment fields, organizational infrastructures and action and mobilization structures. While both movements had similar political and ideological orientations in that they sought widespread public participation, a democratic society and an improved quality of life within a holistic worldview, they differed drastically in other respects. The social base for the environmental movement was much more differentiated and diverse than the women's movement. He argued that this was due to mobilization potential of 'not in my back yard' (NIMBY) type campaigns. One could suggest that this was also the result of the low levels of demand placed upon supporters of environmental organizations, when often all that is required is a donation.[4] He also found that while the German women's movement had remained at the grass-roots level and been organized through informal networks at regional and local levels because of distrust for hierarchical structures, the German Green movement had developed many hierarchical and formal organizations, including large expert membership organizations that dominate the movement, and a political party: Die Grünen. To recapitulate from Chapter 5, this again illustrates why broad-brush approaches to political opportunity structures might be problematic. Finally, while the women's movement sought *quality* of membership, emphasizing values and demonstrating the locus of change through everyday behaviour, the environmental movement sought *quantity* of membership, using the weight of numbers of monetary supporters to help influence concrete policies. Rucht's use of these case studies serves well to remind us of the need to be wary of the differences between ideal-type new social movements and empirical reality.[5] Yet he also seems to gloss over differences *within* the two movements he examines.

Many of the environmental organizations I focus on in this book (see Chapter 3) have features of old movements, others have features of new movements and some have a mix and match of characteristics from both old and new. With reference to the 'old movements' column of Table 6.2, it would not take too much of a stretch of the imagination to claim that the Campaign to Protect Rural England is formal, Friends of the Earth works by way of instrumental reason and NIMBY groups are self-interested. In addition, climate campaigns might be thought of as oriented towards the universal, while Greenpeace strategically operates in the absence of

Table 6.2 Comparing the characteristics of 'old' and 'new' movements

Type of . . .	OLD MOVEMENTS	NEW MOVEMENTS
Rationality	Formal	Substantive
Reason	Instrumental	Value fundamentalism
Interest	Self-interest	Collective interests
Scope	Universalism	Particularism
Ethic	. . . of responsibility	. . . of ultimate needs
Action	Strategic	Exemplary
Organizational form	Hierarchical	Fluid
Democracy	Formal	Participatory
Milieu	Closed, class based	Open and supported by counter-cultural networks

democratic principles. On the other hand, looking now to the 'new movements' column of Table 6.2, the Environmental Direct Action Group practices value fundamentalism, climate campaigns press for collective interests, the Women's Environmental Network is 'particular' through its focus on women, the Climate Camp seeks to be exemplary, Earth First! and other radical networks are participatory (at least in theory, see Chapter 7), and the campaigns against the Criminal Justice Act (see Chapter 5) represented the sort of counter-cultural networks that new social movement scholars envisaged.

As environmental networks share characteristics of archetypal old *and* archetypal new movements, it is perhaps better to follow Scott's (1990: 133) line. Instead of trying to artificially force movements into one camp or the other, Scott sees the distinction as a useful way to divide the functions of different organizations within a single movement. This works especially well for the organizations included in the environmental networks I focus on in this book. However, even more dynamism needs to be built in because sometimes the *same* organization can behave both strategically and culturally (Chapter 8).

Explaining the newness of NSMs by their emergence in a new society

Partly in response to accounts that noted common features of both old and new movements, 'new' social movement theorists have sought other ways to account for the newness of the 1960s movements. Arguments focusing on the newness of society see new social movements as both symptoms and redressers of problems in post-industrial/programmed (Touraine), information (Melucci), late capitalistic (Habermas), or a range of other epithets ascribed to contemporary society.[6] Although scholars have idiosyncratic interpretations, Ray (1993: 59) usefully synthesizes the approaches, suggesting that they indicate a society with minimal class conflict, a growing tertiary sector or 'new middle class', expansion of cultural consumption and leisure, new types of social protest and an expanding welfare state. To complete the list, I would add the alleged importance of 'post-material' values and the processes that have led to increasing state surveillance and domination of politics and lifestyles by corporate interests, which (at the state level) Habermas (1981) has called the 'commodification' of culture and the 'juridification' of politics.

These aspects of 'modern' societies are neatly encapsulated in four key theoretical contributions, which I briefly visit: the new middle class thesis (Offe 1985), the post-material thesis (Inglehart 1971, 1987), the process of 'colonization of the lifeworld' (Habermas 1981) and the Meluccian notion of the 'information society' (Melucci 1985).

The new middle class

If we were to step back in time and ask a nineteenth- or early twentieth-century political scientist to describe the main features of the political landscape *at that point in time*, they would note that political parties were class-based – defined in terms of the division of labour between owners of the means of production, and the bearers of the work load. Such a politics was concerned with the sectional interests of classes, dominated by the elites, with the corporatist state at its heart. Hence, during that period, the labour movement was the key focus of much research (see above). By contrast, contemporary society has a 'new' kind of politics (Crook et al. 1992), sometimes called 'disorganized capitalism' (Lash and Urry 1987). Traditional class identity has been lost through fragmentation of regulated markets, the institutionalization of production, capital accumulation and markets, and the shrinking of the semi-skilled and working-class occupational base (Lash and Urry 1987). New politics is multifaceted. Disintegration of standard conceptions of social class has led to social differentiation and, consequently, diversity of lifestyles.

This new politics is thought to have allowed for the emergence of a 'new middle class' – a new class of people working in services and welfare professions (Offe 1985; Lash and Urry 1987). These people are considered responsible for propagating values espoused by social movements. Their employment in services and welfare positions is thought to be both consequence and cause of their resistance to the state. On the one hand, individuals in the new middle class are thought to take up their chosen employment positions because 'welfare and creative professions provide acceptable sanctuaries to those who wish to avoid direct involvement in capitalist enterprises' (Parkin quoted in Rohrschneider 1990: 4). On the other hand, their lack of a strong and binding traditional class identity is thought to allow them to develop universalistic concerns based on human rights (Cotgrove and Duff 1980). So while new social movements are not *on behalf of* a class, they remain a politics *of* class (Offe 1985).

The evidence in support of the new middle class thesis is in the balance. Rohrschneider (1990) in his exploration of the basis for environmental concern found that there is only a slight relationship between new middle class membership and support for environmental groups. And Bagguley (1992: 30) shows, using cross-national comparisons of social movements, that those countries with strong service classes do not have the strongest new social movements. Part of the problem might be, as Nash (2002a: 106–7) says, that the diverse group classified as 'the new middle class' do not share similar backgrounds, conditions of employment or opportunities in the way we would expect from the term 'class'. Despite findings that seem to contradict the new middle class thesis, a recent survey of five climate protests in four countries – London, Utrecht, Copenhagen and Brussels throughout

2009 and 2010 – finds that 75.3 per cent of participants self-identify with the upper- or lower-middle class.[7]

New Values and the post-materialism thesis

The debate on new values is essentially based on Ingelhart's (1971, 1990) post-materialism thesis, which argues that new values developed across Western democracies in the post–Second World War period as a result of unprecedented levels of economic security. Through his broad surveying of the values of the populace of European societies, he noted an increasing trend towards economic goals – measured through indicators like military security and availability of provisions essential for survival – to be supplanted by quality of life concerns, such as equality and concern for the environment. He made explicit the exponentially cumulative impact of generational change, arguing that over time larger proportions of the population of Western societies develop post-material concerns. Hence, they come to express these concerns through 'new' social movements.

At least by 2050, according to Inglehart's crude calculations, we should have a whole population of post-materialists, but that fact alone does not necessarily mean that everyone will be involved in every type of social movement that reflects post-materialist concerns. Thus, Inglehart's thesis fails to shed any light on differential rates of involvement in social movements among those with post-material concerns – why do some people choose to support the peace movement rather than organizations within environmental networks, whereas others choose not to be involved at all? And just because someone is concerned about the environment, for example, does not mean that they will become involved in environmental organizations or environmental protest. The relationship between values and protest action is actually rather weak. Klandermans and Oegema (1987), for example, found that while three-quarters of a random sample of residents of a community near Amsterdam were sympathetic to a protest against cruise missiles, only 1 in 20 actually participated in the protest. A final criticism is that Inglehart takes it as given that the correlation between the emergence of new values and the upsurge of new movements implies cause and effect. As we all know, correlation does not imply causation, and who is to say that new movements were not responsible for bringing about new values rather than vice versa?

Social change

Broader social changes are regarded by many to be responsible for the emergence of new social movements. The key theorists are Habermas (1981), Touraine (1981, 1984), Offe (1985) and Melucci (1989, 1996), who, despite disagreeing on details, present similar theoretical arguments. They document shifts in society that have implications for social control that new social movements react against. Even though they are not strictly new social movement theorists, sociologists from Marcuse to Foucault and Althusser to Bourdieu make claims consistent with Touraine, who argues that 'contemporary society is subjecting itself to even stricter control and surveillance in such a way that social life is nothing more than the system of signs of an unrelenting domination' (Touraine 1984: 71). This well-documented trend is the cornerstone of much new social movement theorizing.

Social control, it is argued, has changed from being class based, broadening and deepening to expend influence over organizational systems, symbol formation and even interpersonal relations (Melucci 1980: 218), invading – or as Habermas would put it 'colonizing' – the everyday lives of individuals and making society culturally impoverished (Habermas [1981, 1992], see also Edwards' 2004 reworking of Habermas' theory). In this complex society, which Melucci calls the 'information society', goods are mass produced, based on 'information systems and symbolic universes controlled by huge [branded] organisations' (Melucci 1994: 109; Klein 2000; Edwards 2007). In the relentless push for progress and profit, these systems and symbolic universes are thought to erode self-help systems while the state placates society through the welfare state, despite its inability to halt or reverse embedded problems including environmental destruction, poverty and military superfluity. The moral duties of the state go wanting because of the increasing plurality of sites of power. Melucci, in particular, identifies multinationals, health experts and the world media systems as sources of 'dominant' codes, while Offe, Habermas and Touraine hang onto neo-Marxist notions of class- and system-based domination. Whatever the source of domination, new movements are seen to result. They are thought to act as magnets for seeds of discontent that the system cannot integrate. The discontented respond by forming new identities and alternative ways of organizing for positive change, purposely bypassing the state (Melucci 1984: 829). The theory seems to chime with some radical activists' concerns. A radical environmentalist, writing about his/her observations on society, for example, wrote the following for the Earth First! journal.

Around us has grown a web of domination, a web of mediation that limits our experience, defining the boundaries of acceptable production and consumption. Domesticating authority takes many forms, some of which are difficult to recognise. Government and religion are some of the more obvious faces of authority. But technology, work, language with its conceptual limits, the ingrained habits of etiquette and propriety – these too are domesticating authorities which transform us from wild, playful unruly animals into bored unhappy producers and consumers. (Anon. 2000: 171)

Let us turn to examine Melucci's (1984, 1995a, 1995b) theory of new social movements in a little more depth. He sought to defend the concept of a new social movement – a concept he claimed to have been responsible for introducing. According to Melucci, the 'real' way to tell whether a movement is 'new' was to consider if the meanings behind the movement and the movement's place in the system of social relations are new. Since we live in the information society, movements that have arisen in this new historical time period are by implication 'new' in relative terms (even if they do have characteristics of old movements). 'Old movements' – by which he means labour movement *and* pre-1960s manifestations of the women's movement – were, he suggests 'about the quest for citizenship and their identity was already given' (Melucci 1994: 116). He suggests this because they sought enfranchisement of already defined social groups. In comparison, in contemporary society, a degree of emancipation is already manifest in that we all are enfranchized to vote. This has weakened social divisions that pervaded life in the old politics. Hence, 'in new movements, citizens form themselves into social networks where a collective identity is negotiated and given shape' (1994: 117). What is different is that this identity is not ascribed. I return to discuss identity within environmental networks in Chapter 7.

In his 1995 essay, 'The New Social Movements Revisited: Reflections on a Sociological Misunderstanding', Melucci (1995a) explicitly lays out seven ways of conceptualizing the newness of new social movements:

1 Information resources are at the centre of new conflicts. Activists now have much more self-reflexivity as a consequence of the wide availability of information and conflicts are no longer solely about production and distribution of material goods.

2 Action becomes self-reflexive with positive action played out through lifestyles and the wider cultural habitus.

3 Movements now have a planetary dimension. Partly due to the availability of information, there is awareness of global issues. As information can be condensed and can travel at high speeds, movements are able also to sustain informal global networks.

4 For new movements, there is an important relationship between latency and visibility. They act as 'laboratories in which other views of reality are created [during latency]. They emerge [i.e. become visible] only on specific grounds to confront a public authority of a given issue' (114).

5   The effects of movements cannot be measured on a political level; they have immeasurable effects too, such as the reversal of cultural codes – a slow but pervasive process.

6   They provide public space and express the double meaning of the terms representation and participation. Representation means both presenting your interests, but also means that your arguments become watered down as they travel through political channels. Participation means taking part, but also belonging to the system and community. New social movements emphasize the latter in favour of the former.

7   New social movements 'raise the challenge that recasts the language and cultural codes that organise information' (Melucci 1994: 102), creating new meaning that challenges master codes.

The first two arguments characterize newness in terms of the type of society that we live in. Unfortunately, defending newness in this manner amounts to what could be considered a circular argument. It could lead sceptics to the conclusion that, since new movements have wide-ranging precedents and many features common with old movements, the *new* society creates similar movement forms to those which the *old* or industrial society did and therefore explains little, if anything, about social movement shape or emergence. Information and resources may be central to our society, so why do new (in temporal terms) movements form that do not match the ideal-type characteristics of new social movements shown in Table 6.1?

Arguments 4–7 fall flat because old movements also have some, if not all of these characteristics – for instance, labour movements also exhibited an important relationship between latency and visibility (Scott 1990). Latency possibly acted as a laboratory for the formation of views of the world through workingmen's clubs, pubs and other work-based social events for the labour movement. The dissent only made itself visible through actions such as strikes, sit-ins and boycotts. As the work of Tucker (1991), Ray (1993) and Nedelmann (1984) showed the impacts of 'old' movements could be measured beyond the political level – some were indeed culturally and identity oriented. Due to the class-based nature of industrial society, the conflict between representation and participation was most probably also evident to working-class men and women in industrial society. Frequently excluded from formal representation, the limits of representation were at least to some extent countered by the strong sense of working-class solidarity and a stronger, not weaker, sense of community.

So what then is the big deal about new social movements? This leaves defenders of the 'newness' argument with only one string left for their bow; only Melucci's third point on the newness of social movements remains unscathed. The point he is making there is that movements now have a planetary dimension and an unprecedentedly large scale of action and scope of issues. Many agree (e.g. Brand 1990; Inglehart 1990; Rochon 1990) that this was what was new about new social movements. Student, environmental and peace movements were, indeed, working on global issues. Yet, had not the anti-slavery movement done that decades earlier? The archetypal old movement, the labour movement, also has a planetary dimension, having spawned campaigns against sweatshops and for human rights (Waterman 2001). And Rupp has shown how the women's (1994) and lesbian, gay and bi-sexual rights (2011) movements both have long transnational histories.

Are environmental networks new social movements?

Environmental networks writ large *cannot* be labelled as new social movements because of the many different types of organizations involved – from insider pressure group organizations through to radical protest networks (see Chapter 3). Scott (1990) looked at the German Greens and came to the conclusion that 'new' movements only manifest in real life at the early stages of the protest lifecycle, with a permanent state of 'newness' restricted to movements' fundamentalist wings.

Despite a general consensus that radical environmental organizations – the more fundamentalist wing of environmental networks – are new social movements, some fit a particular conception of a new social movement better than others. In this section, I show that attempts to find textbook examples of new social movements can be viewed as problematic because they can be too easily accused of cherry-picking evidence to fit. It is also worth stressing that equating a single group or organization with a movement is to blur the concept of a movement, which, in most accounts is considered to be a *network* of several organizations. In the examples I explore below, Clark (2000) and Storr (2002) suggest that particular organizations – the Exodus Collective and Reclaim the Streets, respectively – are social movements.

Storr (2002: 193–4) notes how Reclaim the Streets has the new social movement characteristics that Melucci emphasizes. She regards Reclaim the Streets to be a reaction against the information society. She illustrates its concern with ownership, control, the distribution of alternative information and redressing master codes to reveal underlying truths about cars, roads and capitalism. Reclaim the Streets uses the symbolism of the car as a means of attacking wider car culture and the 'insidious'[8] capitalism that it supports. Reclaim the Streets, she suggests, also exhibits signs of antagonism towards the corporate ownership of information resources (via hostility to professional journalism), it is self-reflexive, has a planetary dimension (e.g. international networks and concern for global issues) and displays the relationship between latency and visibility – being drawn from counter-cultural networks of squatters, travellers, hunt saboteurs and ravers.

For Clark (1990), the Luton-based Exodus Collective – which provided communal living space, workshops and parties and engaged in environmental projects for activists and youth – is an almost perfectly fitting example of resistance to Habermasian colonization of the lifeworld. This, he argues, is because it is active in producing 'cultural moments of resistance', has created a discursive space, resists formal political institutions and has an egalitarian structure.

Unfortunately, such analyses leave us with grounds for some suspicion that the authors are not robustly testing the theories' relevance for modern environmental protest. These could, instead, be seen as generalizations made from case studies that authors have purposely selected with prior knowledge that they will be fitting cases. A further problem is that they assume that all radical activists within these networks share the same principles. However, in-depth interviews I have conducted with Climate Camp activists have shown that even within a supposedly radical environmental organization, activists hold a variety of green positions, from reformist and instrumental through to deep green and cultural (Saunders 2012). Even though it is great to see these complex theories being related to real life examples of contention, studies like Storr's and Clark's unfortunately do little to further theoretical developments within the field of social movements. Part of the problem is that they look at individual organizations, not the broader networks required to talk of environmental networks, or, indeed environmental movements (Chapter 2). At best, these studies – and my own – therefore suggest that it is difficult to classify any movement or even a sub-movement as a fully fledged new social movement.

Alternative ways of understanding contemporary movements

Although new social movement theory is useful for studying environmental networks to the extent that it introduces useful concepts – such as solidarity and identity – the practice of trying to decide whether environmental networks constitute a new social movement is mired with difficulties. This is especially so when we consider two major caveats: first, theorists are unable to agree on the defining characteristics of a new social movement and second, so many different types of environmental organization are involved in the so-called environmental movement that it cannot be easily applied to the wide variety of organizations we find in environmental networks.

Consequently, scholars have reacted against the concept of new social movements and have tried to find a better alternative. Alternatives include identity politics, subcultures (Hebdige 1979), DIY culture (Purdue et al. 1997; McKay 1998), neo-tribalism (Maffesoli 1996) and expressive identities (Hetherington 1998).

Identity politics best represents those networks of individuals and/or organizations that are united by common ascribed identities such as age, gender, ethnic background or skin colour. To the extent that some environmentalists manufacture an identity (for instance, they refuse to buy a car, become vegetarian and may even grow dreadlocks), the term identity politics can be useful. However, some radical environmentalists promote localization that supports *difference* between localities as a counter trend to corporatist globalization. In some situations, ascribed identities do not bring radical activists together, but actually keep them apart.

For McKay (1998) who writes about the DIY culture, radical environmentalism of the 1990s is seen as part of a wider counter-culture incorporating 'party and protest'. The DIY culture includes such arenas as self-organized workers, unemployment centres, activist spaces, squats, protests, street parties and free festivals. As with the concept of 'subculture', the notion of a DIY culture is useful for uncovering those latent networks – that is, networking behind the scenes that sustains activity during periods when protest is less visible. For the purposes of this book though, it is too broad to be useful since it includes a wide variety of types of social groupings that are not embedded in environmental networks. While some radical environmentalists live in squats and attend free parties, not all of them do. Nonetheless, it is worth documenting that there are some important overlaps between DIY culture and the type of social movements Habermas and Melucci envisaged. Within DIY culture, activists really do live out experiments at the seam of society, spreading cultural innovations. The actions that DIY activists engage in have an end in themselves.

Although some of the earlier writers on subcultures had been misled into believing that subcultures were based on the 'profoundly superficial level of appearances' (Hebdige 1979: 17) which leads to the tendency to preconceive subcultures with a 'decorative sociology' mindset, at least some aspects of subcultural studies are useful in the study of radical environmentalism. Especially useful are the concepts of 'bricolage' and 'homology'. Bricolage is a term that originated in the visual arts to refer to the way in which artefacts can be gathered and given new meaning. It was adapted by scholars of cultural studies to understand youth subcultures. As Moore (2004: 312) writes with reference to the 1980s punk subculture:

> Punk style shocked, parodied, and conveyed ambiguity by appropriating banal commodities (safety pins, vegetable dye, Vaseline), essential badges of Britishness (the Union Jack, the Queen), and the tools of conventional gender roles and sexuality (cosmetics, pornography), thus disorienting the 'natural' uses and meanings of those by situating them with a new 'bricolage' of fashion and attitude.

Environmental activists have, similarly, sought to shock and parody using art forms. Art not Oil, for example, campaigns against the sponsorship of art galleries by oil companies using alternative art to spread its message. In April 2011, around 100 Art not Oil activists staged a 'sleep-in' at the Tate Modern dressed in 'BP-branded sleeping gear', changing the usual meaning of the BP logo.[9]

Whereas bricolage refers to unusual use of common artefacts, homology, refers to some coherence in the use of artefacts. As such, it refers to the link between values, 'lifestyles . . . subjective experiences and musical forms to express or reinforce . . . focal concerns' (Hebdige 1979: 135). Hebdige commented that homology existed in punk subculture only to the extent that chaos ruled. By contrast, radical environmental activists share, to an extent, an alternative value system and lifestyle which makes their subculture cohere as a way of life (this is followed up in Chapter 7). Activists' use of bicycles instead of cars (Horton 2011), for example, has a meaning beyond the chaotic bricolage of punk.

Despite suggestions that subcultures are not real entities but merely constructs of socio-analysts, as 'catch-all terms for any aspect of social life in which young people, style and music interact' (Bennett 1999: 599), subcultures are 'real' for some of the people involved in them. Neal, a 'hippy traveller' interviewed by Muggleton (2000), for example, remarked that one's clothes reflect one's lifestyle and values – similar to the idea of subcultural capital. This insight from subcultural studies reinforces the idea that lifestyles and appearances associated with subcultures are important to participants, not forgetting that they might be able to help us predict the degree of exclusivity of subcultural groupings.

A further critique of subcultural studies is their tendency to view subcultures as temporary but nonetheless static phenomenon. In reality, there is much less coherence between lifestyle, symbolism and values than subcultural theory allows for. Maffesoli's concept of 'neo-tribes' can be applied in order to bolster subcultural theory. Maffesoli embraces the idea that modern subcultural groupings are not stable entities, but are instead characterized by their instability and fluidity manifest in occasional gatherings followed by dispersal (Maffesoli 1996: 76) – pretty much like the annual Earth First! Summer Gatherings and Climate Camps, which are frequently attended by some stalwarts, but consist mostly of a dynamic and changing attendee base. According to Maffesoli (1996: xi) 'as the highest social good, the members of [neo-]tribes are marked by wearing particular types of dress, exhibiting group specific styles of adornment and espousing the shared values and ideals of the collectivity'. What distinguishes Maffesoli's argument from the concept of subcultures is recognition of the fluidity and dynamism of modern collectivities. Maffessoli's argument also avoids presenting a false clear-cut distinction between mainstream culture and subcultures, neither of which are easy entities to define (Clarke 1990: 180). The implication is that any research focused on fluid entities would do best to study them over time.

Hetherington (1998) takes a similar stance to Maffesoli with his concept of 'expressive identities'. This term covers a wide range of modern radical and expressive movement arenas that closely match a list of (aspects of) movements originally designated as new social movements – for example gay rights, environmentalists, youth culturalists, and new ageists. He suggests that they all have in common the search for 'authentic experiences and personal growth' based on identification with and empathy for the rights and freedom of marginalized groups. They meet and protest in self-liberated autonomous spaces. Activists are glued together by emotional and moral solidarity, have an emphasis on the body as an expressive source of communication and identification with others, and focus on aspects of social life that are regarded as irrational by modern societal institutions (Hetherington 1998: 5). The reference to the body might seem strange in reference to environmental activism. However, he defends its use in this context with reference to how activists use their bodies in direct actions. For example, in the anti-roads protests of the 1990s, many physically blockaded sites for new roads against the bulldozers. More recently, in 2010, Climate Camp activists super glued themselves to the front doors of several Royal Bank of Scotland branches to protest against its investment in tar sands.

Certain radical environmental groups are clearly within a DIY space, are associated with subcultures – such as the squatters subculture – resemble a neo-tribe and/or share expressive identities. These theoretical concepts are all useful for understanding elements of radical environmentalism. They are not necessarily useful as an alternative label to new social movements for, as with social movement theories, textbook examples can be cherry-picked at the expense of generalizable theory. What they are most useful for is sharpening awareness of the identity-based, fluid and amorphous nature of the radical elements in environmental networks.

Evaluating new social movement theory

There is much that can be said in praise of new social movement theory. It has brought the cultural aspects of social movements to the fore, and has offered many useful insights that resonate with the practices and experiences of some social movements and/or activists. However, its biggest weakness is overemphasis on culturally challenging participatory aspects of social movements at the expense of the formally organized and rational. Strictly following a new social movement theory approach would lead us to the mistaken position that all environmental campaigning groups are fluid participatory networks, which, of course, they are not (see Chapter 3).

Another weakness is the assumption that broad shifts in politics and society alone are adequate for the emergence of new social movements. The debates about new types of society refer solely to Western industrialized societies, thus making new social movement theory unable to account for protests spawned by conflicts in less developed countries, such as the Brazilian landless movement, which encouraged radical environmentalists from the West to join protests labelled 'anti-globalisation' (Crossley 2003[10]), or even the more recent uprisings in the Middle East. By doing this, it ignores the importance of resources, mobilization processes, opportunities and organization. These weaknesses are heightened by a general disregard of the relationship between cause and effect (Hannigan 1985: 446–7; Bagguley 1992: 28). Equally, new social movement theorists are especially vague about the features of a so-called post-industrial society. This leads them to misleadingly propose that all post-industrial societies create similar movements, overlooking domestic differences between countries and undermining important lessons from critiques of the political opportunity approach (Chapter 5). One thing new social movement theory is unable to do is to account for the presence of very different types of environmental organizations (Chapter 3) within the 'environmental movement', which has been labelled 'new'.

A final criticism relates to the concept of newness being outdated. Many of the new social movements that emerged in the 1960s have now become at least partly institutionalized (Scott 1990: 90). It can also be argued that the 1960s new social movements' critique of the welfare state gave governments a valid excuse to begin to dismantle it, which has created a newer cohort of social movements among the marginalized – with focuses such as AIDS and homelessness (Lentin 1999: 6.2). Although I have been able to quote a radical environmental activist talking about processes that seem akin to colonization of the lifeworld, Crossley (2003: 298) argues that the anti-corporate protests of the 1990s and early 2000s (which included radical environmental activists) have only a 'basic "fit"' with the theory. He argues this because Habermas, in the 1980s, was talking about the *state* as the agent responsible for colonization of the lifeworld under welfare capitalism. Times have moved on. Crossley argues that we no longer live under welfare capitalism, but instead under corporate capitalism. After a period of intense and intensifying privatization, modern activists see themselves as subject to colonization of the lifeworld due to pressures from markets, transnational corporations and the international financial institutions that support them, not so much from states.

Implications for environmental networks

If protest really does come in waves as Tarrow (1998) proposed, then we would expect organizations involved in environmental networks to collaborate most when a protest cycle is peaking (at Phase 3 of Figure 6.1). Indeed, this is the point at which movements are thought to be increasingly channelled through organizations. However, as the protest cycle enters the demise phase, cooperation tails off. Tarrow suggests that at Phase 5, many organizations within a movement become institutionalized, while the radical organizations become violent, generating concern over law and order. This would suggest that, as we explored in Chapter 5, radical outsiders and institutionalized insiders dissociate when protest tails off.

Tarrow's concept of protest cycles illustrates the dynamic nature of social movements, which Hetherington and Maffesoli also emphasize. Movements are not always visible: they also, during troughs in protests cycles, go through spells of latency. Latency does not signify a lack of activity, but rather involves 'the daily production of alternative frameworks of meaning, on which networks themselves are founded and live from day to day . . . [and] potential for resistance or opposition is sewn into the very fabric of life' (Melucci 1989: 70–1). Latency can be sustained by emotions. As Taylor (1995: 224) explains, with reference to feminist movements, women who remain committed during periods of latency 'have often been motivated not only by a deep sense of anger at gender injustice, but by the joy of participation, the love and friendship of other women, and the pride at having maintained their feminist convictions in the face of strong opposition'.

Committed activists from previous waves of protest are regarded as the fertile seeds from which new waves of protest grow (Hetherington 1998: 3). Even when a particular political challenge has ended and movements themselves become latent (through victory or failure), wider subcultural networking remains active, providing the context for new waves of protest on related themes. McAdam (1989) for example, in his study of activists' post-Mississippi Freedom Summer Project (1964) biographies in the United States, found that a sample of past activists were more likely to become involved in other related counter-cultural movements. Of the activists, 79 per cent had previously been involved in the civil rights movement. In 1984, 22 years later, 11 per cent claimed to be very involved in the environmental movement, compared to 3 per cent in the sample of those who were invited to, but *did not* participate in Freedom Summer. Of Freedom Summer Participants, 60 per cent, as compared to 41 per cent of non-participants, claimed to have leftist political orientations. McAdam (1989: 754) concludes that 'activism by its very nature broadens the base of the activists' links to movement organizations and other activists'. Similarly, McNaughten and Urry (1998) cite Bramwell's (1994) research that showed a huge crossover of supporters between the student and environmental movements as part of a wider counter-culture. In the early days of Earth First!, nearly all of the founding members (a group of 12 activists whom Wall (1999a) refers to as 'the first cohort') came from previously latent, or at least lower key green, peace and animal rights networks. This results in the extraction of resources and repertoires from the wider amorphous counter-culture. Similar can be said of the non-violent direct action protest repertoire of the anti-roads movement. Melucci (1994: 831) suggests that the passage from latency to visibility is carried out by umbrella organizations that provide the finance and organization, yet respect the autonomy of submerged groups – the exact same role ALARM-UK and Road Alert! played for the anti-roads movement in the 1990s.

Alex Plows (2006) predicted a 're-emergence of Eco-action' after the Blackwood roads protest of 2004. She predicted that the 'latent/emergent (Melucci 2006) networks and campaigns are starting to become more visible as they build up capacity' (Plows 2006: 463). Thus, she anticipated a '(re)cycle' of direct action campaigning over roads or airport expansion on the basis of the success of camp strategies and the discursive linkages made between issues like globalization, oil and climate change. Her assessment was not far off the mark. What actually manifested was a spate of direct action on climate change, supported by the Camps for Climate Action (Saunders and Price 2009; Saunders 2012). The Camps for Climate Action drew on submerged networks, and played a crucial role in bringing climate change protest into visibility.

If we were to believe that the organizations comprising environmental networks were a new social movement, we might expect them to be fairly homogenous. We would anticipate shared ideological standpoints, organizational strategies and democratic principles. We know from Chapters 3, 4 and 5 that organizations within environmental networks have very different democratic structures, and that strategies vary across the insider-outsider continuum. But do they share ideological positions? I answer this question in the empirical section of this chapter (below).

On the other hand, we might expect there to be distance between organizations that have a hierarchical 'old' movement structure and those that have a participatory and open structure. That the old and new are sometimes seen as polar opposites suggests that they might have little to do with one another. However, as we already know, many environmental organizations mix and match features of old and new movements. It is also true that, in practice if not in theory, participatory radical environmental organizations are considerably more closed than they aspire to be. Radical environmental networks are strange creatures in that, quite paradoxically, they are both closed and open to outsider participation. On the one hand, they practically involve small affinity groups working together on direct actions. These bring together a small hardcore of activists who often know one another well and who generate the type of expressive identities to which Hetherington refers. They often keep their actions secret to everyone outside of these small groups for fear of having their plans rumbled by the police. This has the effect of making it hard for newcomers to feel comfortable or learn the ropes. One likely effect is the development of – as both colloquialists and social network analysts would term it – cliques. On the other hand, they have a Melucian neo-tribe dynamic, which involves large numbers of less committed activists dipping in and out of participation in certain of their meetings or gatherings, which are open to anyone. The solidarity generated in the former may militate against the building of broad and open networks in the latter. It also has negative ramifications because cliques may develop at the expense of antagonistic relations with other movement organizations.

In contrast, passive membership, or even working as a staff member in groups like Friends of the Earth precludes the need for underground meetings. It also requires little behavioural conformity or identity transformation. This makes cliquey behaviour much less likely, especially so for Friends of the Earth, which aims to be the 'broad church' of the environmental movement. At the polar opposite are green communal living type groups, which, again, are likely to be much less inviting towards the inquisitive individual, especially if s/he lacks subcultural credibility. The implications of the effect of identity transformation, or the lack of it, in environmental networks are fully explored in the next chapter.

New social movement theory in practice: The London data

Ideological factions?

An exploration of measures of ideology from the survey of London's environmental network shows some surprising similarities between new social movement theory's idealized new social movement ideology and elements of the ideologies of environmental networks. To try to capture ideology, the survey asked a number of questions about possible causes and consequences of environmental problems (Table 6.3). This draws on my typology of environmental ideologies, developed in Chapter 2 (see Table 2.5). The two most commonly given causes of environmental problems were: 'poor planning decisions' (42.9%) and 'over-consumption in consumerist society' (32.1%). The most popular solutions were: 'improved planning decisions' (52.7%), participatory democracy (36.6%) and reduction of consumption (22.3%) (see Table 6.3). While predominance of reformist/instrumental causes

Table 6.3 Measuring the ideologies within environmental networks

Question	% of environmental organizations (*n*=114)
Which one or two* *categories best represents the underlying sources of environmental problem(s) that your organization works to resolve?*	
Erosion of nature/wilderness	13.3
Urban growth	20.5
Poor planning decisions	42.9
Failure to cost environmental goods	13.4
Over-consumption in consumerist society	32.1
Unequal distribution of resources	13.4
Domination of nature under capitalism	14.3
Globalization	11.6
Which one or two *categories best represent the overall solution to the environmental problem(s) that your organization works to resolve?*	
Practical conservation/management of reserves	18.8
Halting building on Greenfield sites	16.1
Improved planning decisions	52.7
Technological innovation	11.6
Participatory democracy	36.6
Reallocation of resources	6.3
Reduction of consumption	22.3
Self-sufficient communities (i.e. bioregions)	8.9
Anarchy	3.6
Revolution	3.6

Note: many organizations did not follow these instructions literally. Some identified just one cause and solution, others identified up to three of each.

and solutions as expressed by the prominence of planning negates new social movement theory, a different pattern emerges when we subject the results to a principal component analysis.

Principal component analysis allows us to simplify data from a multiple battery of questions (like those shown in Table 6.3) allowing us to point to a smaller number of categories. In particular, it is a useful exercise to conduct in order to check for the presence of the three distinct ideologies – the conservationist, reformist and radical ideologies I explored in Chapter 2. For a conservationist ideology, we would expect erosion of nature/wilderness and urban growth as causes of environmental problems to be paired up with practical conservation/management of reserves and halting building on Greenfield sites as solutions. For a reformist, we would expect the causes of poor planning decisions and failure to cost environmental goods to load – or be paired – with improved planning decisions and technological innovation. The radical ideology – which most closely matches what we would expect of a new social movement – would ascribe over consumption, unequal resource distribution, domination of nature under capitalism and/or globalization as responsible for causing environmental problems that are solvable by a mix of participatory democracy, resource reallocation, reduction of consumption, self-sufficiency, anarchy and/or revolution. Is this how the factors ended up being grouped in factor analysis?

The component matrix is shown in Table 6.4. The most significant component, which explains 18.9 per cent of the variance in the data, has positive coefficients for all four causes and three of the solutions to environmental problems that we would ascribe to radicals, and which would identify environmental networks as ideologically in tune with an ideal new social movement. This is the only component that loads neatly in tune with what we would expect were there three distinct ideologies in London's environmental network. In other words, only the presence of a radical – or new social movement type – ideology is confirmed. Component two loads positively on the causes and solutions of environmental problems that we would expect of conservationists, but these coincide with some more radical causes (domination of nature under capitalism and globalization). All of the other components mix and match items from different ideologies. Important in all but component 6 (the component that explains the least variance – just 5.9% – in the data) is globalization as a cause of environmental problems. Thus, Melucci's (1995a) emphasis of the planetary dimension in new social movements seems highly applicable for environmental networks, regardless of other aspects of their ideologies. Most strikingly, this would suggest that it is *not* ideological difference that determines the networking patterns to which I referred in Chapters 4 and 5. As suggested in Chapter 2, the concept of ideologically structured action (Dalton 1994)

Table 6.4 Component matrix for the ideologies of environmental networks

	1	2	3	4	5	6
Variance explained*	18.9	11.2	10.6	8.7	7.2	5.6
Environmental problems are caused by . . . erosion of nature	−.213	.061	−.697	.059	.150	−.095
. . . urban growth	−.346	.316	−.163	−.355	−.063	.518
. . . poor planning decisions	−.549	.106	.676	.029	−.010	−.058
. . . failure to cost environmental goods	−.173	−.107	.438	.505	.255	.235
. . . over-consumption	.343	−.433	−.010	−.434	.050	−.413
. . . unequal access to resources	.142	−.427	−.394	.266	−.402	.036
. . . domination of nature under capitalism	.708	.209	.000	−.045	−.025	.326
. . . globalization	.690	.415	.150	.017	.024	−.138
Environmental problems can be solved by . . . practical conservation	−.215	.140	−.380	.296	.203	.014
. . . halting building on greenfield sites	−.341	.230	−.430	−.174	.422	−.074
. . . improving planning decisions	−.644	.093	.386	−.201	−.042	−.146
. . . technological innovation	−.198	−.066	−.046	.095	−.831	.055
. . . participatory democracy	.525	−.419	.268	−.055	.207	−.143
. . . reallocation of resources	.123	−.360	.060	.428	.259	.372
. . . reducing consumption	.546	−.438	−.048	−.014	.033	.131
. . . self-sufficient communities	.332	.055	.114	−.592	.019	.416
. . . anarchy	.542	.562	.078	.115	−.079	−.062
. . . revolution	.427	.639	.016	.320	−.085	−.196

Note: Items that load positively are highlighted to ease interpretation.

*The six components together account for 62.0 per cent of variance.

seems to overlook practical constraints that prevent ideology dictating the behaviour of social movement organizations (Klandermans 2000; Snow 2004: 396).

Latency and visibility

It is quite clear that many of the ties between environmental groups that were generated during the anti-roads protests of the 1990s, and which spent a decade being latent, were reinvigorated in the course of anti-aviation and climate change campaigning. As predicted by Melucci, the two umbrella groups, Alarm-UK and Airport Watch, have been important in preventing NIMBYism and bringing these networks back into visibility. John Stewart, chair of Airport Watch (see concluding remarks to Chapter 1) has been able to draw on previous links that were established throughout the course of his campaigning against road building. Stewart had been responsible for circulating information on direct action techniques from Road Alert around the network of aviation campaigners. He has maintained links with the Royal Society for the Protection of Birds (RSPB) which was very active in the successful campaign against an airport at Cliffe. Many organizations became linked through their association with Airport Watch, which transformed certain parts of environmental networks from latency allowing for the emergence of a powerful and highly visible campaign force.

Network maps based on data collected at two different points in time (Figures 6.2 and 6.3) further illustrate the importance of key campaigns and umbrella organizations in bringing environmental networks into fully fledged visibility. In these network maps, each circle (or node) represents an environmental organization that answered the questionnaire and which claimed to be part of a network. If a node has an arrow pointing towards it, this indicates that another organization claimed it was one of its top five collaborative partners. The size of each node is scaled to give an indication of the popularity of each node (i.e. how many times the organization was listed by another).

Figure 6.2 shows the environmental network in southeast London in February 2001. At this point in time, a large-scale community campaign was just coming to a head. Numerous local groups, many of which were supporters of the Crystal Palace Campaign, were vigorously campaigning against Bromley Council's decision to build a 14-screen multiplex cinema on the site of the ancient Palace (for more detail on this campaign, see Saunders 2007c).

The same network questions were asked in a survey of the same organizations nearly two years later, once the campaign had been won. In January 2003, even the once popular Crystal Palace Campaign did not consider itself to be part of a network of environmental organizations, and the rest of the movement was considerably more fragmented (Figure 6.3).

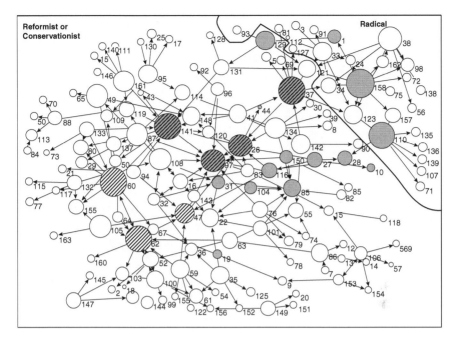

Key

⬤ Organizations campaigning against Crystal Palace Multiplex park

▨ Organizations with a key brokerage role[11]

See Appendix 4 for a key that gives labels for the nodes.

Figure 6.2 Southeast London's environmental network, February 2001

We could argue that Figure 6.2 illustrates cooperative interactions in the local environmental network of southeast London at a peak of a 'wave' of protest. Yet although the protest was in apparent decline two years later (Figure 6.3), it certainly had not followed the trajectory set out by Tarrow (1998. See Figure 6.1 of this book). There was, for example, no evidence of a counter movement, the non-violent parts of the movement did not become institutionalized, and complete collapse has *not* been the end result. However, what these networks do confirm, as new social movement theory would predict, is the fluid and amorphous nature of movement networks, which seem to change over time depending on the grievance base, political opportunities, the networking capabilities of key activists and social capital in the community. We should also note the presence of a number of key brokers – organizations that brought together a substantial number of others in the network, thus putting them into indirect contact. Of the top seven brokers, five of them were directly involved in the Crystal Palace Campaign. These brokerage organizations ceased to work in the same way once the Crystal Palace Campaign had been won.

Much of the impetus for their action had been removed. Brokerage organizations can be thought of as bridging organizations (Roth 2003), which strive to overcome factionalism. In this regard, note, in particular, how the Environment Office (node 37 in Figure 6.2) bridges the radical and reformist organizations.

The Crystal Palace Campaign was clearly a temporary coming together of a variety of organizations and individuals. Certainly, the capturing of networks in two different points in time shows the limits of adopting a synchronic approach to them – a warning I take from Hetherington (1998). Despite their temporary nature, local campaigns, like the Crystal Palace campaign, do not meet the characteristics of a neo-tribe. Most significantly, many participants did not share subcultural traits. Instead, the participants of the Crystal Palace campaign had a plethora of styles and beliefs. Importantly, I should stress that what brought the Crystal Palace campaigners and the protests against roads and aviation expansion into fruition was not only the umbrella organizations and the reinvigoration of latent networks. The lack of formal political opportunities also spurred these networks into action (Chapter 5). At Crystal Palace, three local authorities (the site bordered three southeast London boroughs) supported the plans for a multiplex cinema and rooftop car park. As with the roads protests, the absence of opportunities to bring about change through the democratic system led to a very active protest wave that brought direct activists and more conventional campaigners together in a pitched battle against the local authorities and developers (Saunders 2007c). This story warns us against reading new social movement theory in isolation from other social movement theories like political opportunity/process

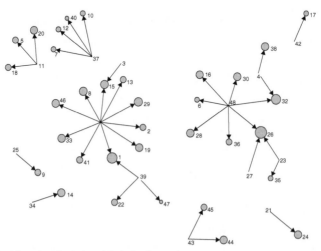

See Appendix 4 for a key that gives labels for the nodes.

Figure 6.3 Southeast London's environmental network, January 2003

theories (Chapter 5). Upon winning or conclusive failure of a campaign, the capacity for bridging seems to break down, resulting in network fragmentation.

Although the network looked sparse and segmented once the Crystal Palace campaign had ended (Figure 6.3), there were latent networks that my study – limited by its focus on entities at least informally organized – was unable to pick up on. By 2003, many of the radical activists that had been living at the Big Willow Protest Camp at Crystal Palace had moved on to squats in the surrounding area. A key informant advised me that this group of activists would feel uncomfortable with a researcher in their midst. Although I was unable to gain access to these undercover networks, it is clear that such 'invisible' or 'latent' networks are important in keeping radical activists together and helping them retain solidarity in the interim period between more visible waves of protest. Thus, we are also warned against focusing too heavily on the visible networks at the expense of the submerged. To study the latter, however, would require in-depth ethnographic research, which would depend heavily upon gaining the trust of activists in the network under study. Examples of ethnographic studies of activism include those by Graeber (2009) and Juris (2008), both of whom have successfully embedded themselves in the protests against economic globalization.

Concluding remarks

This chapter has introduced many strands of new social movement theory. This is a challenge because of the diversity of approaches. But what really ties the various strands together is a belief that something 'new' was afoot with the emergence of 'new' radical movements of the 1960s and 1970s. Although it is difficult to prove what was actually new, the most commonly used arguments refer to either a cultural turn in social sciences, changes in modern society, or both. However, even these sets of arguments have their weaknesses, for how do we explain earlier manifestations of these movements in an 'older' society?

Nonetheless, I have shown that some aspects of newness chime fairly well with elements of the praxis of more radical organizations in environmental networks. Somewhat surprisingly, the ideological element seems to have a more generic fit right the way across environmental networks than we might have initially expected. Ideologically structured action (Dalton 1994) cannot be said, therefore, to dictate the shape of environmental networks. Thus, new social movement theory cannot, alone, account for patterns of interaction in environmental networks – other factors besides ideology must be at play. Strategically oriented actions perhaps play a much more significant role than new social movement theory is able to account for. Moreover, collective identity is shaped by activists' perceptions of political opportunities and constraints just as the contingent political opportunities an environmental organization faces depend on its external image that is crafted as part of its mission to 'survive'.

Despite the need for new social movement theory to be supplemented by other theories, it should be stressed that it has been useful for emphasizing the role of informal networks in seeking cultural change – something that resource mobilization theory overlooks. The attention given to dynamism and fluidarity draws our attention to the fact that environmental networks are constantly evolving and warns us against taking a static approach. The theory also resurrects, from collective behaviour theory, the notion of strain. For example, new social movements, like the environmental movement, are thought to be a response to changes in society that have brought environmental issues into sharp relief.

We now look in more depth at a particular aspect of new social movement theory, the nature and role of which is also contested: identity. After that, I turn to consider how the different theories I have discussed might be integrated to provide a more thorough explanation for the shape and form of environmental networks.

7 Collective Identity and Solidarity: Unity or Factionalism?

This chapter picks up where Chapter 6 ended by considering, in more depth, collective identity and solidarity, and how they impact upon interactions between groups in environmental networks. Perhaps by virtue of its theoretical slipperiness, collective identity is often hailed an important feature of social movements for the role it plays in unifying activists and organizations, and so helping them develop solidarity, agree on shared concerns and engage in collective action. Environmental networks are broader than movements, consisting of a multiplicity of groups, some of which *do not* challenge the social order. Party because of the broad range of groups that exist within environmental networks, I diverge from the view that collective identity is a movement-level process. Instead, I argue that collective identity is a *group*-level process. I suggest that although it can unite activists within a *group*, it is not always beneficial for broader *environmental networks*. Although organizations within environmental networks have a broad shared concern, I show in this chapter how their differing collective identities can actually be quite divisive. Those activists who are highly committed to an organization with an encompassing collective identity will be likely to develop a strong sense of solidarity with other activists similarly committed to that organization. The resultant solidarity can lead to the construction of a 'we-them' dichotomy between organizations working to the same ends. This increases the chances of hostility between organizations, and can cause factions within environmental networks.

The empirical part of this chapter is based on case studies of the three environmental organizations in which I conducted participant observation. To reiterate, these are Chiswick Wildlife Group, Friends of the Earth and the Environmental Direct Action Group (see Chapters 1 and 3 for more information on these organizations). The organizations were selected because they broadly represent the three main fields of action of organizations within environmental networks; conservationism, which, to recapitulate from Chapter 2, involves a direct concern for hands-on protection of natural sites, reformism, which seeks to bring about change by incremental reform, and radicalism, which seeks fundamental systemic change and engages in direct action and lifestyle change to achieve it.

Note here that the reference is to fields of actions rather than to ideologies (see Chapters 2 and 6). The Environmental Direct Action Group did not respond to the survey as group members felt uncomfortable in doing so.[1] However, it was clearly one of the most radical environmental groups active in London at the time of fieldwork. London Reclaim the Streets (RTS) had recently folded, and London Earth First! had not yet been re-formed (it existed in the 1990s and re-formed during the period of study). According to survey responses, the other two groups have very different ideologies measured by the indicators I explored in Chapter 6 (Table 6.3). Chiswick Wildlife Group believed that the environmental problems it works to address are caused by erosion of countryside and overconsumption, and that these problems could be solved by practical conservation. For Friends of the Earth, overconsumption and globalization were considered to be the main causes of environmental problems, whereas participatory democracy and reducing consumption were considered solutions.

What is identity?

Identity is a knotty concept. Essentially, it is the basis for recognizing others and recognizing the self. It is permanent yet fluid, individual yet collective, and a precursor to social movement formation yet also a barrier. Three types of identity are important in the study of social movements: individual, collective and public identities (Jasper 1997: 87). This chapter is concerned with individual identity – to the extent that it contributes to and is affected by social movement participation (Klandermans and De Weerd 2000) – and also with collective identity. Despite conceptual confusion in the literature (Polletta and Jasper 2001: 285), many studies of collective identity have suggested that it is something that should be highly valued for its binding effects on social movements. Collective identity has been presented as both a process and an outcome, apparently as a precondition for collective action, to help overcome the free-rider problem (Polletta and Jasper 2001) and to give activists a shared senses of meaning and a sense of belonging (Diani 1995; Hetherington 1998). The concept of collective identity is so central to the literature on social movements, and new social movements in particular, that it has been suggested that the networks of organizations and individuals that constitute movements cannot be deemed to be part of a movement unless they also share a collective identity (Diani 1992a; Diani and Bison 2004).

Regardless of the importance of collective identities in definitions of movements, it is clear from the literature that there is some confusion over whether 'collective identity' is a term best applied to the movement organization (or group) level, or to whole movements. As we shall see in this chapter, the term is more frequently used to refer, and – particularly for the case of environmental networks – seems better applied, to the group level rather than the movement level. Far from uniting environmental networks, this actually gives collective identity the potential to create conflicts between organizations that define themselves differently and have different fields of action, even if they, as part of the same movement, share a more broadly conceived concern.

It will be argued that when an individual becomes thoroughly immersed in a movement organization and where collective identities are encompassing, strong solidarity is the net result. Strong solidarity exists when individuals within a collective have shared behaviour that differentiates them from other groups and from the norms of society. Strong solidarity evolves from the process of developing an encompassing collective identity in which there are high levels of commitment from activists who spend a considerable amount of time together, and who tend to identify solely with a particular movement organization and so develop a cliquey and exclusive movement culture. Solidarity is weak or absent when activists exhibit few behavioural differences from societal norms and where movement organizational culture is easily accessible to outsiders. Organizations with a non-comprehensive collective identity might consist of activists who have little in common, and who have little commitment to the organization besides, perhaps, an instrumental gain. Non-comprehensive collective identity and weak or non-existent solidarity within a movement organization is not necessarily a bad thing. Rather like Granovetter's (1973) concept of 'the strength of weak ties', non-comprehensive collective identities might result in a lack of solidarity between activists within a particular organization, but allow for bridges to be built between organizations and across movements with relative ease because of their weaker 'we-them' distinctions.

Although she frames it as a critique of my approach to collective identity, this is exactly what Flesher Fominaya (2010a) found in relation to three Madrid-based autonomous global justice groups that she researched ethnographically. Those three groups had weak group-level collective identities, allowing them to unite without conflict under their general anti-capitalist stance. The story may have been different were she to have included groups with encompassing collective identities in her study. What I show in this chapter is the corollary of, not a contradiction to, Flesher Fominaya's findings. Encompassing collective identities and strong solidarity (the opposite of Flesher Fominaya's 'weak' collective identity) can come at the expense of hostile relations with other movement organizations as part of the process of setting and affirming boundaries between the 'we' and the 'them'. In fact it appears that the greater the commitment and individual-identity shift involved in the effective participation within a movement organization, the greater the extent to which collective identities are defended at the expense of other movement organizations. At the extreme, this can result in committed activists fostering unintentional lies and misunderstandings about other organizations in an attempt to justify their own viewpoints and means of protesting.

Conceptualizing collective identity, movement culture and solidarity

There is so much discussion of identity in the social movements' literature that Snow and McAdam (2000: 41) claim that 'one could easily get the impression that identity is the key concept in social movement research today'. Nonetheless, identity remains a concept that is difficult to pin down, not least because of its nature as a process rather than an end product. Castells, for example, defines identity as nothing less than 'the *process* of construction of meaning on the basis of a cultural attribute, or a related set of cultural attributes that is given priority over other sources of meaning' (Castells 1997: 6).

For the rest of this chapter, I shall focus on both *individual* and *collective* identity. In analysing individual identity, I focus on how it can be defined and influenced by social movements through cultural influence. I review competing definitions of *collective identity* and its implications for solidarity within, and rivalry between, social movement organizations.

According to Johnston et al. (1994: 12) it is important to note that 'individual identities are brought to movement participation and changed in the process'. But different types of participation and types of movement organizations affect self-identity to varying degrees. Direct-debit supporters of protest-business type organizations have negligible changes to their identity. The furthest a participant's identity may be manipulated is through purchasing the tee shirt or affixing a car sticker (e.g. passive membership of Friends of the Earth and World Wide Fund for Nature (WWF)[2]). At the other extreme, a cult of personal transformation would have far-reaching effects on the individual, whose identity would become absorbed by their group's identity. Radical environmental organizations – as with radical social movement organizations generally – require a much greater degree of behavioural conformity, and a more significantly revised self-identity that is partly a result of a consensually defined collective identity (Snow and McAdam 2000: 55). Horton (2003: 65), for example, notes that

> At the 'radical' extreme . . . activists often favour highly mobile and 'close to nature' modes of dwelling, such as yurts and benders. 'Radical' activists also sometimes embody a 'counter-cultural' ethos through transgressive styles of hair and dress.

At the 'radical extreme', behaviours that are inconsistent from societal norms are consistently required, and, because individual behaviour change is essential for participation in such movement organizations, the collective identity will be more encompassing and the resultant solidarity stronger.

Although it is difficult to define an individual identity, because, as I have already stated, identity is a *process* under continuous reflexive revision, it is at least clear that it refers to the self-definition of an *individual* person; that is to say, it is about how the individual differentiates himself/herself from others. The definition of collective identity is much more complex. It too refers to a *process*, but this time one that results in differentiation of a particular collective from others, resulting in a sense of 'we-ness' (della Porta and Diani 1999: 85; Snow and McAdam 2000: 42). The added difficulty in the conceptualization of a collective identity is that it is often unclear whether the collective entity to which it refers is a group or a movement. Indeed, the complexity of the concept is probably one reason why 'there is no consensual definition' (Snow and McAdam 2000: 42).

Melucci (1989: 34), who can probably be credited with popularization of the term collective identity in social movement literature, defines it as an 'interactive and shared definition produced by several individuals (or groups at a more complex level)'. For him, collective identity is a reflexive, dynamic and never settled process, hence his insistence that it 'is *not a thing*, but a system of relations and representations' (Melucci 1995b: 50). By this, Melucci implies that collective identity is not static, but instead, consistently defined and redefined by actors involved.

Although Melucci insists that collective identity is not a 'thing', he does refer to outcomes of collective identity. In this sense, he merges the process and outcome approaches to collective identity. I am by no means the only scholar to consider that Melucci was concerned with both of these aspects. Karl-Dieter Opp's (2009: 210) careful 'disentanglement' of Melucci's work on collective identity suggests that Melucci believed that

A *collective identity* exists, by definition if there is a group (i.e. individuals with at least one common goal) with common beliefs, with common normative convictions, that is connected by social relationships (i.e. there is a social network) and by emotional bonds.

Common goals, beliefs and normative convictions are clearly stated in the above as products of the processes of social relationships and emotional bonds. The other thing to notice about Opp's (2009) disentanglement of Melucci's work is that he refers to a group, not to a movement. Even though Melucci suggests that collective identity can occur both between several individuals (in a *group*) and/or 'at a more complex level' between several organisations' (within a *movement*), much of his writing implicitly suggests that where it really takes place is at the *group* level. He suggests that it allows movement organizations to produce working definitions of themselves, to define their territory and scope. It 'determines the criteria by which members recognize themselves and are recognised' (Melucci 1996: 32). It does this through three processes – the setting of goals and strategies, the activation of relationships and shared decision-making, and emotional investments (Melucci 1989: 35). For Melucci, a collective identity results in 'unity of collective action', and yet he admits that 'social movements are not unified and homogenous realities' (Melucci 1996: 74–8). Therefore, perhaps, movements as a whole are too heterogeneous to share a collective identity even though activists within a particular movement organization might.

Indeed, Melucci is by no means the only author to regard collective identity as a feature of *groups* rather than movements. For Taylor (1989: 771), collective identity is 'the shared definition of a *group* that derives from members' common interests and solidarity'. According to Snow and Oliver (1995: 578–9), collective identity is something that evolves from the actions of *group* members. Klandermans and de Weerd (2000: 74) similarly suggest that 'collective identity concerns cognitions shared by members of a *single group*'. Owens and Aronson (2000: 195) stress the group dynamic of collective identity even more explicitly:

> Collective identity is a *distinctly group level* concept referring to how a group identifies itself . . . Consequently, collective identity is derived from the group's own self-identification. (Emphasis added to the word 'group' in all quotes given in this section)

It is probably correct to view collective identity as a group-level process rather than a movement-level one, not least for reasons given by Rootes, who, consequently, prefers to use the term 'shared concern'. He rightly suggests that collective identity is not a feature of entire movements because 'it appears to assume or require a degree of consensus which is unusual in the factious milieu of movement politics' (Rootes 1997b: 325). On reflection, it does not seem possible for an entire archetypal movement – which typically incorporates networks of organizations and individuals from a broad range of organizations and standpoints – to share those processes and procedures that trigger the process of collective identity formation. All organizations and activists within a broad movement certainly do not share identical definitions of their field, or agree on scope and territory, set and work to achieve shared goals, determine strategies collaboratively or engage in shared collective action. Neither do they all share a sense of 'we-ness' with other movement organizations working on different minutiae of a broader shared concern. This is especially true for environmental networks, which are broader than the 'green movement' (Doherty 2002). Furthermore, collective identity is believed to be shaped by the framing of opportunities and constraints, which will vary between organizations depending on their status and strategy (Chapter 5) and can never be shared by environmental networks that incorporate organizations and individuals with ideological and tactical differences. In short, the three components deemed essential in the formation of a movement's collective identity – a shared 'we', a common opponent, and a common view of those neutral to the problem (della Porta and Diani 1999: 87) – are unlikely to be ubiquitous across the broad range of organizations that make up the environmental networks that I focus on in this book.

Despite many claims that collective identity is something involving processes distinctly at the group level, and the concept's inapplicability at the movement level, many scholars make grand claims about the role of collective identity at the movement level. Melucci, for example, claims that collective identity leads to the formation of a social movement, and gives movements continuity and permanence (Melucci 1996: 74). For others (e.g. Diani 1992a) collective identity is a characteristic that all social movements share. However, there is clearly a mismatch between definitions of collective identity, which either specifically emphasize the group level or evoke processes that could only possibly take place within groups, and the grand claims of its role in binding movements together. Collective identity (in the singular) at the movement level does not always exist within broad ranging movements, like the environmental movement and global justice movement (GJM), but *collective identities* do. It might, however, be possible to talk of a single collective identity among more narrowly defined movements, such as 'the direct action movement' (Doherty et al. 2007), or the autonomous anti-capitalist movement that Flesher Fominaya (2010a) has researched. For broad ranging movements that include some organizations with encompassing collective identities and others without them, it would be more analytically useful when referring to the concept at movement level, to talk of either *collective identities*, in the plural, or, if we instead take the lowest common denominator of shared interests, to use the term 'shared concern'.

Scholars of what has become known as the GJM (della Porta 2007) could be said to have twisted the original meaning of collective identity by suggesting that the GJM's identity is heterogeneous, fluid and tolerant (della Porta 2005; Flesher Fominaya 2010b: 399). If this 'movement' is that heterogeneous, there is unlikely to be much interaction between the various parts of the movement, meaning that the affective bonds and sense of 'we-ness' required for collective identification may actually be missing. To defend against this charge, Flesher Fominaya (2010a) uses the argument that the activists she researched feel part of a global movement for justice. But who is to say that these individuals have the same idea of what this global movement is? If they do not, then it seems implausible for them to share a collective identity.

Because the three environmental organizations I focus on in this chapter are very different from one another, and because one of the three has an encompassing identity, it is necessary that we consider collective identification for the purposes of this chapter, at least, to be a *group-level process* within environmental networks. This is further justified with reference to Boström's (2004: 74) work on the Swedish environmental movement. Although he conflates ideology and identity, he concludes his account stating that

> it would seem irrelevant to speak of a 'green ideology' that is common for the environmental movement, even though its organizations share ideas and goals on the conceptual level. Instead, it is more relevant to consider a *broad range of green identities* and frames that are more or less related to each other and more or less workable in different arenas. (emphasis added)

The resultant group-level shared beliefs and a sense of 'we-ness' may shape individual participants' personal identity. If a group's collective identification encompasses the individuals involved they will more closely conform behaviourally with others in their group than they would with broader social norms, and the group's demands and beliefs will strongly resonate with them, resulting in solidarity. Shared concern, on the other hand, is considered to be a static and constant *movement-level belief*. Thus, while environmental organizations might have different collective identities from one another, which may change over time, all environmental organizations share the broader concern to protect or enhance the environment (Chapter 3). Castells (1997: 172) agrees, stating that the environmental movement's shared concern is 'about the relentless, multiform destruction of nature'. However, Castells is probably wrong to assume that this leads to 'a great deal of osmosis in the relationship between conservationists and radical ecologists' (ibid.) because of the role that intra-group solidarity can play in creating strong distinctions, and sometimes some animosity, between radicals and conservationists. The culture of movement organizations, to which the discussion now turns, contributes to the 'double-edged' outcome of solidarity. It is sometimes positive and sometimes negative. But first for a little conceptual clarity; if *collective identification* is the group-level process of defining a 'we', *collective identity* is the 'we', *culture* is the milieu out of which collective identification builds collective identity, and *solidarity* is one characteristic of collective identity.

A collective identity, then, emerges through the culture of movement organizations, defined by Williams (2004: 94) as 'the norms, beliefs, symbols, identities, stories and the like that produce solidarity, motivate participants and maintain collective actions'. Culture is incorporated into groups (not necessarily movements) by 'a given set of rituals, practices and cultural artefacts', and may be defined in a language that is unique to the group (Melucci 1995b: 44–5; Polletta and Jasper 2001: 284). It provides individuals with a sense of belonging, strengthened by ritualistic movement activity resulting in 'collective effervescence' (Durkheim [1984: 152] note here the relevance of interactionist collective behaviour approaches, see Chapter 1). A strong and binding communally negotiated collective identity (or, as I prefer to call it, an 'encompassing collective identity') fosters solidarity (Hunt and Benford 2004: 439). Activist groups that build and support their collective identity from the bottom up tend to have more solidarity than organizations that furnish activists with a preformed ideology that is filtered top-down. Instead of having a bureaucratic economy, radical environmental movement organizations have a '"libidinal economy" (Goodwin 2004) of friendship, solidarity or love that shapes the dynamics of the group' (Doherty 2002: 10).

Part of the process of manufacturing a movement organization's external image is concerned with marking boundaries around the organization and defining its unique niche within the social movement field (Chapter 4). This process of 'boundary demarcation' is widely recognized to be an important step in the formation of a social movement organization's collective identity (cf. Taylor and Whittier 1992). For rank-and-file activists, the result, when collective identity is encompassing, is for them to be able to easily make 'we-them' distinctions between adherents and non-adherents, and between organizations. As Jenkins (2008: 102) suggests:

> logically, *in*clusion entails *ex*clusion if only by default. To define criteria for membership, of any set of objects is, at the same time, also to create a boundary, everything beyond which does not belong.

While some regard collective identity and solidarity as synonymous, it is more useful to see collective identity as a process, and solidarity as a possible outcome. Unlike collective identity, solidarity is a rather stable characteristic of social groups. A high degree of solidarity is the result of the individuals involved having committed a large proportion of their private resources to 'collectively mandated ends' (Hechter 1987: 18).

Solidarity may be a positive thing for the activists involved, in terms of providing a sense of belonging, but the double-edged sword analogy is applicable to solidarity in practice. According to Misztal (1996: 34), it can lead to 'sectarian solidarity' that may have serious negative ramifications. She notes this because high levels of internal solidarity are often derived at the expense of developing intensely antagonistic relations with other groups through sharpening the 'we-them' distinction. At the extreme, this results in groups with high levels of internal solidarity regarding organizations with similar aims (shared concerns), but conflicting tactics, as the enemy within.

> How people come to distinguish between those with whom they have solidarity and others to whom they have no such obligations is a complex process of classification that has serious consequences, and it is in this light that Sennet's (1998) description of 'we' as the 'dangerous pronoun' makes sense. (Crow 2002: 28)[3]

Sennett (1998: 137) defines the 'dangerous we' as an often defensive demarcation of a community, which is likely to involve 'a rejection of . . . outsiders'. It is 'a false locution when used as a point of reference against the outside world'. The notions of 'sectarian solidarity' and '"we" as the dangerous pronoun' are, it seems, useful lenses through which to view conflict between organizations. The paradox is that a greater degree of internal solidarity within an organization may result in a proclivity for exclusivity and that the process of collective identity and resultant sectarian solidarity can actually divide rather than unite organizations in environmental networks.

The concept of sectarian solidarity is similar to inter-movement 'exclusive solidarity', which has been found to lead to divisions between social movements. Ferree and Roth (1998) found exclusive solidarity among West Berlin Labour activists and feminists. In this example, activists from the two different movements failed to collaborate in a women's workers strike because each group viewed the other as something distinct from their own 'we'. This 'can be seen as an indicator of the estrangement between the feminist avant-garde and the average unionized, working woman, the different worlds that at least one feminist thought unbridgeable' (Ferree and Roth 1998: 643). Very similar processes take place *within* environmental networks.

The exclusive identity of radical environmentalism

Radical environmental activist organizations do have a tendency to have an anti-capitalist ideology (Doherty 2000: 74), which Marangudakis (2001) suggests is an obstacle to making extensive movement alliances, amplified by their withdrawal from the social praxis. Many ex-road protesters have taken up lifestyle activism – living communally in almost independent eco-villages, and participating in pagan rituals – a personal politics that represents resistance to modernity and a preference for ancient traditions.

Paradoxically, many radical environmental organizations unsuccessfully attempt to be open and decentralized with the aim of being inclusive to all who wish to participate, hailing themselves exemplars of participatory democracy. Due to the processes behind the 'tyranny of structurelessness' (Freeman 1972), such a bold attempt at egalitarian politics often fails. These processes allow for experienced activists to become de facto leaders. It is especially prominent in groups that do not practice skill sharing and/or which have tight friendship groups. In practice, it can mean that the groups we would expect to be most egalitarian tend to have their meetings dominated by a small informal cadre (Saunders 2009b). George Monbiot (2000) explains the process in relation to the late Reclaim the Streets:

> The direct action movement insists that it is non-hierarchical – but this has never been true. Some people, inevitably, work harder than others, making things happen whether or not everyone else in the movement agrees. Consensus, often unwittingly, is manipulated or over-ridden, as people with a burning vision, with time and energy, drive the rest of the movement forward.

For the London Underground Collective, a radical environmentalist coalition that evolved out of Reclaim the Streets, attempts to be open and inclusive have resulted in poor organization and sometimes utter chaos. Similarly, within the Camp for Climate Action, there is a core of committed protesters who shape the Camp, exerting hegemony within an apparently non-hegemonic movement (Pursey 2009).

Furthermore, the strong subcultural currents in radical environmentalist circles along with negative media coverage make them relatively alienating in comparison to membership of more conventional environmental organizations, which, in just requiring a donation demands much less commitment and fewer changes in behaviour and therefore get more public support. Reclaim the Streets used to jest about the presence of the CID who take photographs and make random identity checks of attendees at their meetings – which is likely to make newcomers feel neither safe nor welcome. Reclaim the Streets and other radical environmental groups are paranoid (and justifiably so) of infiltration by agents of social control, which hardly makes for a welcome greeting, especially if you look too conventional. It is similarly off-putting to enter a Climate Camp. One is required to pass through a barrage of police who search participants from top to toe before permitting entrance (Saunders and Price 2009). Although less the case with the Climate Camps, to be made welcome at Earth First! gatherings and Reclaim the Streets type urban squatted social centres requires at least a minimal degree of subcultural capital.[4] As a key radical activist in Southwark told me in interview 'I think dreadlocks is a good start. But I mean, it's that ridiculous. If you went dressed up in certain [way] – maybe you need a certain type of personality as well'. Direct action camps especially,

> very often have an aggressive counter-cultural vibe, which most people will find alienating . . . You don't even need to visit a camp to feel alienated; the

spectacularisation of our movement has ensured that most TV viewers can now safely view eco-direct action as an alien 'phenomenon', rather than a challenge. (Anon 1999: 155)

As a Newbury bypass protester phrased it,

the cultural vanguardism of the campaign was alienating people from getting involved . . . although DIY culture has grown . . . it has become more and more of a clique because there seems to be a certain style one must conform to. (Anon 1996: 29)

The exclusivity of radical environmental organizations is heightened further by their tendency to develop (as predicted by new social movement theory, and cultural studies [see Chapter 6]) new and collective identities. These are patent in the form of lifestyle – dress, speech and rituals unique to the movement, as activists seek to fulfil their need for identity and belonging in a culturally impoverished social climate.

Earth First!ers share informal yet common lifestyle codes, for instance living in housing cooperatives or squats, rejecting car use, consuming soya milk, rejecting consumerism, and embracing 'drumming, drugs, dress and dreads' (Wall 1999b: 92–3), the last being a symbol of 'counter-hegemonic social resistance movements' (Kuumba and Ajanaku 1998: 227). The Dongas at Twyford even developed their own symbolic language, a particular favourite being shouting 'ayayayaya' at the top of their voices to provide a source of moral support and solidarity in the face of eviction from protest sites, undermining confidence of police and security guards in the process (Plows in McKay 1998: 138–9). Positive emotions and solidarity are further strengthened by rituals such as singing, dancing and consecrating protests sites sacred (Jasper 1997: 209; Szerszynsky 2002). Symbolism and expressivity are also widely used by radical environmentalists, with two of the most historically prominent artistic expressions of resistance being on the roads protest sites of the M11 – Wanstonia Free State (*Aufheben* 1998) and M77 – Pollock Free State. Seel (1997) compares the artwork within the Pollock Free State to the destruction caused by road building using the analogy of J. R. Tolkein's spiritually enlightening Lothlorien contrasted with the doom and gloom of Mordor. Throughout London, empty buildings are squatted by activists at every opportunity to form social centres and eco-art galleries, a prime example being the 1998–9 Cultures of Resistance and Cultures of Persistance (sic) exhibitions '. . . an art gallery, a café, a bar, a squatted space near Tower Bridge, a place to gather and socialize, a coming together of artists, activists, musicians, sound systems, film-makers, chefs, performers and different aspects of a creative culture' (Cultures of Persistance 2000: 1). Maffesoli

(1996: 77) suggests that such 'theatricality founds and reconfirms the [neo-tribal] community' and shows how activists, as Melucci suggested new social movements do generally, seek to control their own living conditions directly.

Collective identity and solidarity in three environmental organizations

Although it is not possible to accurately generalize the traits of conservationist, radical and reformist organizations from the three case studies of Chiswick Wildlife Group, Friends of the Earth and the Environmental Direct Action Group, they can at least give us some indication of the collective identity and solidarity forming processes that take place within different types of organizations in environmental networks. I shall assess whether there is a collective identity that these organizations share, or whether the term 'shared concern' might be more appropriate. I also discuss the extent to which solidarity is encompassing or non-comprehensive in different types of organizations, and whether strong intra-organizational solidarity seems to result in 'sectarian' behaviour.

Chiswick Wildlife Group

Overall, the shared goal of Chiswick Wildlife Group is to protect the nature reserve from development and manage it for biodiversity. Participants are mostly volunteers, who devote time to the cause either because they love nature, covet a job in conservation or both. If there is a collective identity in the group, it is defined by the committee, which is responsible for working out what the 'we' will do. To some extent, it is questionable whether Chiswick Wildlife Group volunteers share a collective identity at all. Rather than working out definitions of the collective and plans for action in an interactive manner, the committee devises the management plan which volunteers and staff follow, sergeant-major style. In other words, rather than there being a 'we shall do this . . .' and 'we believe that . . .' process of collective identity affirmation, there is instead a 'I will do this . . .' and 'you will do that. . .' and '. . . we will follow the management plan at all costs' process.

Although Chiswick Wildlife Group volunteers meet weekly and know each other well, their 'activism' does not permeate their lives beyond their collective conservation efforts at the reserve, and many of the skills they acquire are not used in their daily lives, nor govern their behaviour. All the volunteers I became acquainted with during 6 months of participation (every Tuesday) were very 'normal'. There were no vegetarians or vegans, no dreadlocks, all participants were retired or had jobs, drove cars, and happily used the conventional (rather than eco-friendly) hand wash and washing up liquid, non-organic milk and non-fair-trade tea and coffee available on site. One volunteer commented: 'I am not as green as I should be, although I do buy some organic food' (Karen Roberts, volunteer warden, interview, February 2004). The group is very inclusive and welcoming to any person genuinely wanting to help, and one immediately felt welcomed and a part of the loose-knit collective. As another volunteer told me 'we would always welcome anyone, and they could have a cup of tea and a biscuit!' (Emma Robertshaw, in interview, February 2004). No individual would be excluded on the grounds of their political views. Indeed, the ravers were the only sector of the public to which there was hostility. They had brought in sound equipment without permission and their communal fire had ruined the meadow.

It is therefore posited that the collective identity of Chiswick Wildlife Group is not so encompassing as in other types of environmentalism. This is because the conservationist identity is not often related to a broader set of values and has little impact on lifestyles and behaviours of its participants. Indeed, conservationism requires little more than a love of nature regardless of overarching political beliefs. Symbolic identifiers of conservationists, such as hiking boots and binoculars, are not indicators of a political ideology, just as pruning brambles or counting butterflies are behaviours that can easily be carried out by people with a wide range of values and beliefs.

Partly because of its local remit, Chiswick Wildlife Group has little contact with other environmental organizations locally or nationally, except its mother organization, London Wildlife Trust, and the Butterfly Conservation Trust that it liaises with for butterfly surveying. Its only criticism of London Wildlife Trust has been what Chiswick Wildlife Group volunteers believe to be a lack of appropriate support. Its non-comprehensive collective identity results in a lack of a coherent 'we'. This is partly the result of the lack of need to define themselves against opponents (that don't exist) or in line with adherents. It does not have strong views about wider environmental issues – 'we don't reach out much beyond conserving this patch' (Emma Roberts, volunteer warden, interview February 2004) – and there are environmental contradictions in some of the things it does. For example, it frequently accepts grants from companies despised by radicals, including British Airport Authorities and Shell. This allows these businesses to share in the glory of having done something positive for the environment when they are actually responsible for many environmental abuses. This is the kind of practice that organizations with a more encompassing collective identity like Friends of the Earth and the Environmental Direct Action Group, would abhor and stringently avoid. In this case, a non-comprehensive identity results in a weak solidarity, and little or no marking of boundaries between the group and others and individual participants and non-participants. Although its lack of relations with other groups is partly attributable to its narrow remit, there is a clear lack of sectarian solidarity, which could, at least partly, be a result of its non-encompassing collective identity.

Friends of the Earth

Although the 1980s was a prosperous decade for Friends of the Earth under the leadership of Des Wilson, many members of staff resented his leadership not least because of his preferred method of transport to work – the latest fashion sports car – because it was considered far from environmentally friendly and in stark contrast with the aims of the organization (Lamb 1996). Unlike in Chiswick Wildlife Group, participation in Friends of the Earth has generally permeated the lifestyles of its members of staff and activists, beyond their working day/group meetings. Nick Ferriday, Chair of West London Friends of the Earth, for example, commented in interview how his participation in Friends of the Earth changed his life. Although he has

> always been interested in wildlife . . . it was literally Friends of the Earth that made me change . . . I remember going to a Friends of the Earth meeting for the first time . . . it did actually change my life. (interview, June 2003).

His interest in nature spurred on an interest in broader issues, but it was Friends of the Earth that 'did actually change . . . [his] life'. This implies a shift in personal identity in order to fit in with the more demanding lifestyle changes and thought-provoking ideas that being a Friends of the Earth activist involves. Like other Friends of the Earth activists, he engages in a green lifestyle to the extent that he buys organic food, recycles his rubbish, avoids unnecessary consumerism and tries to reduce his energy use. Most members of staff in the Local Groups Department (now called the Capacity Building Team) appeared to get their take away lunches from Fresh and Wild, an organic health food shop close by, and Claudia Satori, then Local Group's Development Officer commented in interview that 'most people are pretty good, like you would never see anyone drinking a can of Coke' (in interview November, 2003). Indeed, the staff kitchen areas at Friends of the Earth's headquarters are very different from the Chiswick Wildlife Group kitchenette – not just in terms of their quantity and size, but also because they are stocked with organic and fair trade tea, coffee and soya milk. The detergents are eco-friendly, and there are even bleach-free organic sanitary wares in the ladies' toilets.

This type of reform environmentalism is different from conservationism in a number of ways, but one stark difference is the more encompassing collective identity noticeable through lifestyle changes or behaviours that staff and activists engage in to achieve greater consonance with their environmentalist identity. However, although there is a fair deal of solidarity among Friends of the Earth staff and activists, it is difficult for them to build strong affective bonds with one another because of the sheer size of the organization and the work demands placed upon them. There is also a qualitative difference with the radicals who live out their activism at their leisure. In Friends of the Earth, activism is staffers day-to-day work. Although staff may be able to build some solidarity through regular staff development away-breaks, and spending a lot of time in the same office space, these interactive moments usually fail to escape the confines of particular departments. As a volunteer, the culture of the organization feels more like a standard bureaucratic office space than a 'movement milieu' – with the exception of the ethical refreshments and detergents.

The bureaucratic nature of the organization, which Friends of the Earth is trying to make more participatory, is well illustrated by its decision-making style. The board ultimately decides the mission and targets of the organization, even though such decisions are increasingly based on broad consultation with all staff and local groups, and reports from external consultancies. Despite consultations, the idea of 'we' is rarely, if ever, defined consensually by the entire collective. The result is that the mission statement is fairly broad, allowing those with varying beliefs and campaign priorities to sign up to the principles, while providing scope for the adoption of different campaign styles between departments.

Similarly, local groups campaign on different issues and in varying styles depending on their expertise and local environments. Even though local groups have autonomy, they are often saved the bother of constructing their 'we' concept as the national Friends of the Earth stance on issues filters through to them. At Friends of the Earth's 5-year consultation plan meeting for local groups in September 2002, for example, local activists were presented with a rationale as to why Friends of the Earth's organizational campaigning priority is Corporate Globalisation. This was decided on the basis of bids put in from campaign staff and an internal decision (excluding local groups).[5] This provided local group members with a prefabricated ideology and strategy rather than a discursively agreed solidarity-building discussion. Friends of the Earth briefings fulfil a similar role by outlining the key issues, and are given to local group members on request and when a day of action is planned. Often, the packs sent out to local groups for days of action include a list of 'sticky questions' that amount to Friends of the Earth party-line answers provided for activists to learn pretty much by rote.

The fact that local groups spend less time working out their personal views on issues and campaigns gives them a weaker sense of 'we' than they would have should they have furnished their views independently of national Friends of the Earth. But local Friends of the Earth groups do also work on local issues, often using their own knowledge to work out their own fields of opportunities and constraints. It is probably therefore more accurate to suggest that Friends of the

Earth has a shared concern for environmental justice, but that local groups and departments each have their own collective identities. Nonetheless, the fact that they all work together as a broader collective, makes the overall organization fairly inclusive to outsiders, preventing cliques and strong solidarity. This is one reason why Friends of the Earth defines itself as the 'broad church' of environmentalism in Britain (Kenward, Friends of the Earth Local Groups Coordinator, personal correspondence 2002).

Despite disagreeing with radicals over campaign tactics, and the fact that Friends of the Earth's official stance is to not condemn or condone illegal direct action, it does regard radicals as important allies. Paul de Zylva (Head of England Regions at Friends of the Earth, interview February 2004) claimed that he has 'sympathy for them, even though he has suffered personally at the hands of a few'. In 2003, when direct activists occupied a crane on the site of Terminal Five at Heathrow airport, de Zylva (Head of Friends of the Earth England) had nothing but praise for the action because of the press coverage it generated. Friends of the Earth Climate Change Campaigner, Nick Rau, thought that the Environmental Direct Action Group's participation in office occupations gave diversity to the movement and worked to all environmental organizations' mutual benefit. Friends of the Earth has worked fairly extensively with the Environmental Direct Action Group on campaigns against the Baku Ceyhan pipeline, and in the No New Oil coalition (now called Peak Oil). Indeed, the only organizations that Friends of the Earth would seek to avoid cooperating with are those which have unclear motives. For example, Friends of the Earth has avoided working with the Countryside Alliance, which never had clear motives, and has now been exposed as primarily a blood-sports lobby (de Zylva, in interview, January 2004).

While 'moderate' organizations can benefit from the radical flank effect, as the campaigns of radicals serve to make their own demands more reasonable, radical organizations have less to gain from what they view to be the namby-pamby tinkering of reformists, and are often more overtly critical of their contemporaries.

Environmental Direct Action Group

Activists in the Environmental Direct Action Group commit a generous amount of personal time to it. The group strategizes via email (up to eight messages per day, with some requiring urgent response), and at weekly meetings in addition to attending social events and actions. This creates greater solidarity than what was present in both Friends of the Earth local groups that typically meet on a monthly basis and do little in between, and the weekly meetings of Chiswick Wildlife Group.

At its extreme, radical activists in London live, eat and breathe in the most environmentally and socially friendly manner possible to the extent of squatting, freeganism[6], sharing drugs, visiting social centres and attending culturally affirming parties, gigs and film nights. There are clear links between squatting culture and activism as the former coheres well with anarchistic principles that form the backbone of the belief structure of the Environmental Direct Action Group.

In the Environmental Direct Action Group, belief and behaviours reinforce one another to the extent that there is a degree of homology that coheres their environmentalism as a way of life. For instance, a belief that global capitalism is an underlying source of environmental and social problems tends to encourage certain types of behaviour, such as growing dreadlocks, attending counter-cultural festivals and engaging in direct action, as symbolic identifiers of beliefs. On engaging in these behaviours, beliefs are reinforced. For example, listening to protest music or attending festivals where there are like-minded people can make activists feel assured that others share their views, legitimizing and reinforcing them. Engagement in direct action is a behaviour stemming from beliefs that may, especially when deemed successful, increase an activist's passion. This is a reciprocal process whereby behaviours prop up beliefs and vice versa.

Unlike in Chiswick Wildlife Group and to a lesser extent in Friends of the Earth, there is evidence of a movement culture. Almost as many active members in the Environmental Direct Action Group had dreadlocks as did not, one meeting I participated in consisted entirely of vegans and at least two regular participants were squatters. At an all night 'Synergy' festival of grassroots resistance and alternative art, five dreadlocked activists manned the Environmental Direct Action Group stall. Many of the Environmental Direct Action Group protests are accompanied by a sound system that frequently plays political songs. During this process of homology where beliefs are expressed in behaviour and vice versa, the culture of radical protest is affirmed.

Besides linking belief systems and behaviours, direct action, especially sharing risks of arrest, or physical damage to oneself (Doherty 2000), serves to strengthen bonds between activists. Environmental Direct Action Groupers, like the radical activist quoted below see themselves as a 'family', almost to the extent of a lifelong bond:

> You know that if it came to it, that person would put their life at risk and lay down to protect you. You know that when the shit hits the fan that they'll be there. (Bongo interview, June 2001)

This process of homology that occurs through participation in movement culture leads to solidarity. The downside of this is that homology leads to strong solidarity and can create cliques of activists who know one another exceedingly well and share similar beliefs and behaviours at the expense of extra-group relations. Personally, I found the Environmental Direct Action Group cliquey (in its inaccessibility to newcomers rather than network terminology) because of the extent of knowledge activists had concerning their key campaigns, overuse of acronyms, occasional use of coded language, the location of meetings, and the intensive demands made upon participants. They are certainly closer to the 'exclusive' pole (Melucci 1996: 326–7) of movement affiliation than all of the other organizations discussed in this book.

The pace of the group is so fast that if a participant misses a couple of meetings and then turns up again, s/he will easily lose the thread of discussions. Newcomers are thrown in at the deep end and at their first meeting could easily be asked for their views on group literature, be persuaded to run a stall at a fete and help plan a direct action event. The group meets in a relatively rundown part of London that is decorated with 'Danger! Regular muggings are taking place' warnings, in an accessible but unwelcoming back street.

Despite these strong indications of a high level of intra-group solidarity, activists involved with the Environmental Direct Action Group are less happy to use the word clique to explain the nature of group relations:

> I don't know about cliquey, but I did find it quite hard in that they expect everyone to have the same beliefs as them. (Dorey [Greenpeace staff member and Environmental Direct Action Group campaigner], interview January 2004)

Freeman [Friends of the Earth/the Environmental Direct Action Group campaigner] argues:

> Maybe it is not as cliquey as it appears. It appears cliquey and they do have discussions about this but it doesn't seem to get very far. They do try to avoid this and not everybody wants to go to a meeting in a squatted old run down building. It was the same with living in camps. That in itself excludes a lot of people. (interview, February 2004)

But she does not doubt that it at least appears cliquey. This has important ramifications for environmental networks.

If the culture of the Environmental Direct Action Group has homologized and there is a degree of solidarity that has led to clique-type tendencies, this implies that it is easy to define who is and who is not part of the group. This definition could be rooted in appearance, behaviour, beliefs or all three. As discussed earlier in this chapter, a further corollary is that this can become dangerous in terms of resulting in limited or negative relations with the rest of the movement by creating 'sectarian solidarity' (Misztal 1996: 34), likely when solidarity is high. It can result in barriers to newcomers, exaggeration of the inadequacies of other groups and/or open hostility towards them.

The Environmental Direct Action Group's relentless anti-capitalist stance makes some conflict with national organizations that work with governing structures and businesses inevitable. Whereas the Environmental Direct Action Group argues that a company like BP (Beyond Petroleum) should not exist at all, Friends of the Earth, like Greenpeace, has been part of a 'trend over recent years to be advocating solutions . . . making the case for investment in renewables' (Juniper interview with Seel June 2000).

Unlike the Environmental Direct Action Group, Friends of the Earth are

not ideologically disposed to being anti-market. But . . . what can the market do? How can it work? What constraints need to be put on it? What kind of economic mechanisms can start bringing externalities into what the stock market does for instance? (Juniper interview with Seel, June 2000)

The debates over the efficacy of the Kyoto Protocol provide a good example of the conflict between the Environmental Direct Action Group and other more reformist environmental organizations. This issue demonstrates how differing identities can make collaboration difficult between radicals and reformists and how the process of sectarian solidarity plays out in practice and can be damaging for environmental networks.

For the Environmental Direct Action Group, scepticism about the Kyoto Protocol set in at COP6 in 2000 (the sixth United Nations Framework on Climate Change Conference to the Parties meeting). Since then, they have developed a comprehensive critique of Kyoto, believing that it will not lead to significant reductions in greenhouse gas emissions. The Intergovernmental Panel on Climate Change suggests that to avert dangerous climate change, a drop in the levels of carbon dioxide emissions by 60–90 per cent is required. In contrast, the

Kyoto Protocol was supposed to reduce greenhouse gas emissions by 5%, in the end it's 1% so not that great . . . and I just don't think the government are doing anything. I don't think they can. (Coleman [the Environmental Direct Action Group] interview, November 2003)

Environmental Direct Action Groupers consider the protocol dangerous as they believe it will lead to public complacency and misguided faith in international decision-makers' capacity to effectively deal with climate change. Aside from the objection to the 'minute' reductions in emissions that it entails, the Environmental Direct Action Group also say the protocol will bolster those very state-making institutions and power structures it so despises it [Kyoto] would entrench a new, 21st century version of colonialism in international law, whilst side stepping the core issue of our need to cut society's dangerous addiction to fossil fuels, not to mention economic growth. (the Environmental Direct Action Group literature, 2003)

As government representatives and corporate interests dominate the COP meetings, they are seen as holding little hope. Environmentalists did not design and negotiate the treaty, but it seems to radicals that oil executives, bankers, financiers, and co-opted NGOs were the main players. According to the Environmental Direct Action Group literature, what is required instead is 'international action . . . by individuals, communities and movements to challenge the power structures and create new ones'.

Their critique of the Joint Implementation and Clean Development Mechanism clauses echoes some of the concerns of academics (e.g. Grubb et al. 1999) and thus appears well founded. The text of a leaflet handed out during the solidarity action outside the UN offices at the time of COP9 (December 2003) that spells out the Environmental Direct Action Group's concerns is shown in Table 7.1.

The Campaign Against Climate Change agreed that the Kyoto Protocol has been betrayed and undermined, but rather than seeing it as a propagator of public complacency, it viewed it as a positive focal point around which public support could be built:

Kyoto is one of the things that we do that . . . [the Environmental Direct Action Group] don't do. Which I think is really important because I think that there is more scope for communication to the general public in making a campaign around Kyoto than anything else. I think that Kyoto has done more to raise awareness of climate change than anything else. (Thornhill [director of the Campaign Against Climate Change] interview, June 2003)

The Campaign Against Climate Change is also supportive of Kyoto because opposing it would undermine the work of Friends of the Earth and Greenpeace who are regarded by the Campaign Against Climate Change's director, Phil Thornhill, to be the most powerful players in the fight against climate change (interview, June 2003). Indeed, Greenpeace and Friends of the Earth have been campaigning to secure the enforcement of the Kyoto agreement since its inception; to abandon it now would mean wasting years of campaigning effort. The other reason Thornhill gives for focusing on Kyoto is because it relates specifically to climate change issues[7], whereas campaigning against oil pipelines can detract from a focus on climate change because of other environmental, social and human rights issues they encompass.

Table 7.1 The Environmental Direct Action Group's assessment of Kyoto: 'Why Kyoto is Pants'

NOW HERE'S WHY IT'S A TRAVESTY:

The targets are crap. The average reduction on 1990 levels is 5.2%, with 3 countries actually negotiating increases. The scientists say we need to reduce emissions by at least 60% on 1990 levels simply to stabilize things. Seeing that the rich world is responsible, we're going to have to cut emissions by up to 90%. 5.2% is a pretty pathetic start even without the loopholes.

Carbon Trading. The greatest weakness of the Protocol may be that it proposed an international commodity market in carbon. This allowed the talks to become dominated by the vested interests of financiers pushing for a new market opportunity on the back of vast creative accounting loopholes:

1. Joint Implementation allows countries to trade their emissions reductions – an accounting fiddle.

2. The Clean Development Mechanism allows rich countries to offset domestic emissions by funding dodgy projects in the third world which claim some vague climate change objective. It's a gift to the logging, nuclear and hydropower corporations.

3. Banking credits. Rich countries can 'bank' carbon credits and use them to offset future emissions after 2010. This is a recipe for corruption, future evasions, and rampant carbon speculation.

4. Land use changes and forestry. Countries can offset land use changes and tree planting against their reductions.

5. Air transport and shipping are excluded from the targets. On top of tax-free fuel, it's another huge incentive for international air transport. Planes are extremely polluting and the fastest growing source of emissions.

6. The Third World is not in it. Any long-term solution must be just and must involve everyone. At the moment it's a kind of carbon-based colonialism.

7. Who controls it and who polices it?

Implementation is still unresolved, but it's pretty certain that it will remain as it is now: controlled by a small group of powerful rich nations and administered to serve their economic interests.

If implemented, (a big 'if'), the actual reduction in emissions achieved over 20 years will be less than the increase in US emissions in just 1999 and 2000.

Source: Environmental Direct Action Group 2003

Environmental Direct Action Group activists frequently misread the Campaign Against Climate Change's, Friends of the Earth's and Greenpeace's support of Kyoto as an ineffective compromised approach and a willingness to accept small and inadequate carbon dioxide reductions. As one Environmental Direct Action Group activist expressed at a group meeting:

> I can't understand whey they [reformist groups] are promoting a toothless climate change treaty. Can't they see that it's nothing but hot air? The emissions reductions are too small, and I don't think supporting such a weak treaty can help, really.

However, in reality, Friends of the Earth was arguing that the Kyoto Protocol was far from perfect. But rather than agree with Kyoto's inadequate emissions reduction targets, Friends of the Earth continued to call for UK reductions of greenhouse gas emissions of 80–90 per cent by 2050, when the government was, in 2003–8, committed only to reductions of 60 per cent (Friends of the Earth 2003e).

Instead of taking the offensive with regard to emissions trading, Friends of the Earth accepts that it is part of the agreement and is working with the system to improve it. For example, the Emissions Trading Directive is seen as a potential vehicle for getting emission levels capped (Worthington, 2003). Despite its obvious inadequacies, Friends of the Earth conceives of Kyoto as an international decision-making process that can be strengthened and improved. As the 'only serious international framework for tackling the cause of climate change' (Friends of the Earth Media Advisory, 2003) and as the first sign of hope for an international treaty Friends of the Earth cannot refuse to promote and strengthen it.

The difference of opinion between the Environmental Direct Action Group and the reformist camp has implications for interaction between the organizations involved. There is a notable degree of animosity between the Campaign Against Climate Change and the Environmental Direct Action Group who not only have different principles of organization (the Campaign Against Climate Change has a hierarchical decision-making structure dominated by a single leader, whereas the Environmental Direct Action Group is run by consensus decision-making) but differing perspectives on the efficacy of Kyoto as a campaign target. The differences are great enough to warrant a strong 'we-them' distinction to such an extent that Freeman, who is involved in both organizations, referred to the Campaign Against Climate Change in an email to the Environmental Direct Action Group strategy list as 'the other group':

> I . . . you called the Campaign Against Climate Change 'the other group' . . .
>
> **SF** Did I, oh no!

I And I found that interesting

SF I was thinking that because it reminded me of the Houses of Parliament where the Lords are referred to as 'that other house', it is an old tradition that you don't mention the House of Lords . . . or maybe it's the Lords that don't mention the Commons, any way, whatever it is, one of them doesn't mention the other . . . there are some people, especially those who are heavily involved in the Environmental Direct Action Group that think 'our group is totally right and the other one is wrong'. (Freeman interview, February 2004)

The split between the Campaign Against Climate Change and the Environmental Direct Action Group may not be absolute, but there was certainly very visible tension. The Environmental Direct Action Group was very resistant to having its logo displayed on the Campaign Against Climate Change's annual climate change march leaflet (in 2003) and unanimously revoked the request. Environmental Direct Action Group activists were upset when activists involved with the national network of the Environmental Direct Action Group gave permission without securing consensus from the London group. This resulted in the logo being emblazoned on the bottom of the leaflet. One leading activist from the national Environmental Direct Action Group suggested that:

> Although he [Phil from Campaign Against Climate Change] is more supportive of Kyoto than we might be . . . I think that it is fair enough to bang on about the US pulling out of Kyoto as this was a serious problem for making international progress.

Speaking almost verbatim of the process of 'sectarian solidarity' he went on to suggest that

> It is a classic mistake of leftist political groups to obsess on small differences in ideology and ignore much larger commonalities. After all, 99.9% of people would not be able to spot the difference between us.

Both groups are passionate about the need to address the issue of climate change and share an antipathy towards the United States for the negative role it plays in global climate, oil and war politics. There certainly appears to be an element of sectarianism, but some participants in the Environmental Direct Action Group were disappointed that the facilitator of the national Environmental Direct Action Group implied that they were being 'needlessly sectarian and possibly competitive'. Despite being more distant in issue focus, ideology and tactics, the Environmental Direct Action Group appears to have a preference for working with Friends of the

Earth over Campaign Against Climate Change. Sectarian solidarity appears at least partially responsible.

Although Friends of the Earth and the Environmental Direct Action Group have a fairly constructive relationship, other organizations in the direct action wing of the environmental movement have remained hostile towards Friends of the Earth since it left the M3 protest site when threatened with an injunction in 1992. Within the Environmental Direct Action Group there are a wide variety of views, some activists feeling 'glad that they [Friends of the Earth] are there' and others seeing Friends of the Earth as part of the problem rather than the solution because, by dealing with the political establishment, it legitimizes state decision-making procedures. 'Bert' for instance claimed in an email discussion that

> I don't think there is an overall 'Friends of the Earth stinks' opinion amongst us. I got the feeling there was quite a range of opinions. To me, mostly I am glad they are there, but I'm also regularly frustrated by them, and do agree that when push comes to shove that their approach is part of an overall system that needs to be radically restructured. (email discussion list, February 2004).

It is the latter view that leads to the breeding of untrue rumours and contempt. For instance it is argued quite vehemently in *Do or Die* radical environmental journal that Friends of the Earth is a 'foe' to the direct action movement because of its reformist nature and cautious approach to direct action (Anon 2003: 9). Some the Environmental Direct Action Group participants have been critical of Friends of the Earth's apparently reformist approach on GM food, which involved the drafting of the GM Liability Bill. This was regarded as a reformist cop out that would allow GM crops to be planted under various conditions. However, the Bill was worded in such a manner as to make legal commercial growing of GM crops in Britain impossible. It could equally be argued by reformists that direct action is an ineffective means of preventing GM crops being grown as it does not make GM crop-growing illegal and is generally reactive – trashing crops after they have been planted and only where they can be found and identified. Yet reformist environmentalists rarely, if ever, voice such complaints about the efficacy of direct action, regarding it instead as another arrow for the bow of the environmental movement. Misunderstandings or simple ignorance like this serve to fuel animosity between radicals and reformists and sharpen further the 'we-them' distinction.

The more encompassing a collective identity, and behavioural adaptations, the more likely it will be that activists seek to justify the actions of their own group at the expense of downplaying the significance of others. This process of downplaying the positive role of other organizations can be based on unintentional misunderstandings about their goals and actions. These misunderstandings can be interpreted in part as a result of the 'we-them' boundaries that are drawn by activists within particular organizations. As one activist expressed:

> Some people think 'oh, Friends of the Earth, they are just so hierarchical and boring'. And some people from Friends of the Earth think 'these are just anarchists running around the street and doing something silly'. So there are misunderstandings all around. (Sheila Freeman, Post and Volunteers Coordinator, Friends of the Earth, February 2004)

Cat Dorey (Greenpeace Ocean's Campaigner) said with regard to criticisms that have been directed towards Greenpeace from the Environmental Direct Action Group that

> A lot of them . . . aren't legitimate, I mean, they don't know these things. Most of them have never worked with Greenpeace and have never done anything with them. It is all hearsay. (Cat Dorey, Greenpeace Oceans Campaigner in interview January 2004)

Perhaps as part of an attempt to place themselves on the moral pedestal and to justify the amount of personal and intellectual resources devoted to their cause, the Environmental Direct Action Group activists frequently criticize other organizations, sometimes only on the basis of misunderstandings. Reality is sometimes twisted to fit in with the overgeneralized idea that 'NGOs, political parties – these professional priests of assimilation are simply vampires . . .', which justifies their quest to '. . . do some staking' (Anon 2004: 9).

Concluding remarks

This chapter has focused mostly on the concept of collective identity, and argued that for environmental networks it is better regarded as a group-, rather than a movement-level process. The differing identities, issue foci and campaign actions of Chiswick Wildlife Group, Friends of the Earth and the Environmental Direct Action Group serve to demonstrate that it is not possible for these three organizations to share a collective identity, let alone for an entire set of environmental networks to do so; that is, unless I choose to water down my definition of a collective identity until it becomes virtually meaningless. Given that different organizations within a movement cannot and need not share a collective identity, it then becomes possible to conceive of collective identity as something with the potential to lead to rivalry between groups that are each competing to have their own views universally accepted.

Unlike in radical environmentalism and to a lesser extent in reform environmentalism, it is possible to be a conservationist without becoming immersed in movement culture. The cognitive praxis of conservationists is highly biased towards conservation issues, rather than broader environmentalism. In contrast, reform and radical environmentalism have more encompassing movement organization identities, require an attribution of the source of a problem and the choosing of a course of action based on opportunities and constraints, and are more often called upon to defend their beliefs to adversaries and mainstream culture.

Radical environmentalist organizations, more than other types of environmental organizations, are most prone to developing 'sectarian solidarity'. It is therefore harder for them to build up effective trust-benefit relations with other organizations, for it is likely that they will always be more sceptical of the work of 'them', which is constantly juxtaposed against their 'we'. They have a more encompassing collective identity than conservationists and reformists, are more likely than their contemporaries to view environmental problems as the result of systemic imbalances, tend to be motivated by sheer passion for the environment, commit generous amounts of personal time living the ethos of their political beliefs, and their identities are negotiated from the bottom up. Unlike conservation groups, both reformist and radical groups require some form of behaviour coherence. But while reformists have a collective identity that is often not systemically challenging, their activism shapes their lifestyles. In contrast, conservationists need not alter their lifestyles at all in order to work or volunteer in the conservation field, and they tend to learn their conservation knowledge from the more experienced in a top-down fashion. Whereas criticism from conservation and reformist organizations towards other environmental organizations might be attributed to organizational competition dynamics, the same cannot be said of non-competitive radical environmental organization networks. Therefore it seems that sectarian solidarity is a more apt means of explaining the conflict between radical environmental organizations and their contemporaries.

Clearly conservationists are closest to the direct-debit archetype, in which individual identity is hardly shaped at all by movement involvement, whereas radical environmental organizations are closer, but by no means synonymous to cults of personal transformation. Sheila Freeman, an activist who uncomfortably works with both Friends of the Earth and the Environmental Direct Action Group, effectively summed up the problems involved in becoming closely associated with one particular organization 'I can sort of see that if you are really committed you would begin to get the idea that the other groups are wasting their time'.

Although it is not universally problematic for environmental organizations within environmental networks to have differing collective identities – because these can give individual environmental organizations incentive to adapt, learn from one another, work in broad-based coalitions and take advantage of the radical flank effect – it can sometimes be problematic. The point at which it becomes problematic is when environmental organizations begin to work against the aims of others and become overly critical of them as a result of their immersion in and defence of their own organization. This is well demonstrated by campaigning for and against the Kyoto Protocol. While the Environmental Direct Action Group's critique of Kyoto reflects academic appraisals (Grubb et al. 1999), the overall stance it takes on the issue appears to be in direct contradiction to Friends of the Earth, Campaign Against Climate Change and Greenpeace. As such, the Environmental Direct Action Group's critique could serve to undermine the good progress that its contemporaries have made towards securing an albeit inadequate but groundbreaking international climate change protocol that they are seeking to strengthen.

We should therefore challenge the assumption that collective identity always has a binding effect on environmental networks. To the contrary, it has the potential to dangerously factionalize them. A similar conflict dynamic between radical and reformist social movement organizations has been reported to occur in several social movements (see e.g. Barkan (1986) on the civil rights movement; Downey (1986) on the anti-nuclear movement; and Strobel (1995) on the women's movement). The process of creating 'sectarian solidarity' via the formation of encompassing collective identities could be a convincing explanation of its cause.

But of course, collective identity cannot alone fully explain patterns of interaction in environmental networks. For that, we need to look at the political and social environment, organizations' strategies and status *and* their culture and identity. As we learned from Chapter 6, we also need to find a way to move away from the limits of a synchronic approach. I begin to step up to this challenge in Chapter 8.

8 Towards a Synthetic Analytical Framework for Understanding Interaction in Environmental Networks

T his chapter develops and applies a synthetic analytical framework for merging social movement theories in order to provide a more rounded explanation for interaction in environmental networks. To begin with, I recap on some of the strengths and weaknesses of previous theorizing. Next, I flesh out three key reasons for merging social movement theory to understand interaction in environmental networks: first, environmental networks include organizations that have formal and informal structures; second, many environmental organizations are hybrids that are neither pure pressure groups, as implied by some aspects of resource mobilization theory, nor informally organized cultural vanguards as anticipated by new social movement theory; and third, there is actually a good deal of complementarity. After that, I evaluate a significant attempt to unite the theories: *The Dynamics of Contention* research programme of McAdam et al. (2001). Although this programme can be commended for its attempt to create a dynamic model drawing on a broad range of theoretical insights, there remains a number of issues with the approach. In the context of this book, the most significant issue is the approach's attempt to understand the *conditions* that lead to particular forms of *contention*. The authors' emphasis on contention means that the underlying networking dynamics are underplayed, or, where they are discussed, that they are used as predictor variables for understanding contention. The purpose of this book, instead, has been to consider networks as the outcome variable to be explained. As I argued in the 'Introduction', a focus on contention at the expense of networks prioritizes the visible at the expense of important behind-the-scenes work that takes place among and between environmental organizations (Melucci 1989: 44).

To develop a new synthesis better suited to my research focus than the *Dynamics of Contention* approach, I draw on the concept of 'systemism' (see Chapter 1 and Bunge 1997), which considers interaction in environmental networks to be a product of a web of relations between and among environmental organizations, the polity, other campaign targets (if appropriate) and individuals. None of the theories discussed thus far – not excepting the *Dynamics of Contention* programme – merge all of these actors into a single analytical framework. This is despite the fact that, as illustrated by the sum of Chapters 4–7, each type of actor is clearly important in shaping environmental networks.

As well as bringing together all the different actors that shape environmental networks, I also emphasize the importance of considering two key forms of social action. Recall that resource mobilization theory has emphasized the strategic at the expense of the normative, and that new social movement theory does the opposite. Thus, as Habermas (1984) alludes to in his theory of social action, it is important in any synthetic analytical framework not only to consider the broader web of relations, but also to focus on both strategic and normative actions. I wind up the chapter by discussing campaigns against climate change and aviation expansion, which are illustrative of the framework's explanatory potential.

Limitations of social movement theories

There are three main types of limitations to the classic social movement theories that were discussed in Chapters 4–7. Some have limited scope, others generalize, and almost all of them adopt a synchronic and linear approach rather than a dynamic one. There are two types of limitations of scope, summarized in Table 8.1. One refers to the type of social action considered by the theories, the other to the actors included. With regard to social action, resource mobilization theory and political

Table 8.1 The scope of existing social movement theories

Theory	Social action		Actors involved			
	Strategic	Normative	Individuals	Organizations	Targets	Polity
Resource mobilization	Yes	No	Yes	Yes	No	No
Political opportunity/ process	Yes	No	No	Yes	No	Yes
New social movement theory	No	Yes	Yes	Yes	No	No

Note: A 'Yes' indicates that these forms of social action and actors are covered by the theory, a 'No' indicates that they are not.

opportunity theories prioritize the strategic over the normative; and new social movement theory ignores the strategic but lauds the normative.

With reference to the types of actors considered, many accounts of political opportunity/process theory can be charged with being overly statist. They focus purely on interactions between social movement organizations and the polity. By and large, they ignore political opportunities at the local or transnational level (with the exception of Van der Heijden 2006). Opportunities to challenge other actors like corporations or even to shape cultural frameworks are almost entirely overlooked. Resource mobilization theory gives some emphasis to relationships between organizations, and, at the micro-level, at how individuals can be motivated to participate in collective action. But it does not allow consideration of how environmental organizations interact with the broader polity.

The charge of overgeneralizing can be levelled at certain branches of new social movement theory and macro-political opportunity structure theorizing. Both have tended to assume that a set of very general characteristics of a society or polity (respectively) lead to homogenous social movements within nations. While new social movement theorists have assumed that general shifts in society result in culturally oriented movements across western democracies, broad-brush approaches to political opportunity theory have implied that structural conditions can lead to differences in movements between (but importantly not within) countries. Both, of course, do terrible injustice to the diversity of actors within movements, and also to the differences between different movements and organizations within a single country. When looking beyond what might be thought of as movements to broader environmental networks, these problems are more pronounced. Although new social movement theorists have done much work emphasizing that collective identity is a process, that process is often thought to arise in response to a set of relatively static variables that are actually themselves dynamic and interactive.

Learning lessons from previous theorizing, we need to search for an approach that is not confined in scope and does not overgeneralize. It should facilitate a dynamic approach, enabling explanation of how organizations in environmental networks interact during episodes (visible moments of contention) and during latency (the lulls between the visible moments). Most importantly, any attempt to merge the theories requires not only consideration of different types of social action (strategic and normative), but also the interactions between a variety of actors: the polity, other campaign targets, environmental organizations and individuals. This does not mean that we need to wipe the slate clean and start from scratch, for useful concepts abound in many of the theories that comprise the classic social movement agenda discussed in previous chapters. However, these useful concepts do need to be brought together into a more coherent framework to allow them to work for us. But why should concepts from different theories be integrated?

Why integrate social movement theories?

Environmental networks include new social movement(ish) organizations and pressure groups

Some studies of the environmental movement have claimed that new social movement theory is the most applicable theoretical lens through which to view radical environmental organizations like Earth First! (see e.g. Dalton 1994), and that resource mobilization theory is most useful for interpreting the actions of bureaucratically structured organizations or 'protest businesses', such as Friends of the Earth (Jordan and Maloney 1997). This is true to the extent that radical environmental organizations are more likely to pose a systemic challenge to the state and develop encompassing collective identities (Chapter 7), and 'protest businesses' are more likely to be concerned about organizational maintenance as they have offices and staff to pay for (Chapter 4). The evidence suggests that because these two types of environmental organizations exist within environmental networks, we need to draw on both resource mobilization and new social movement theories.

Environmental organizations diverge from ideal types

There is plenty of evidence that protest-business type organizations often act rationally (see e.g. Chapter 4). But the suggestion that organizational maintenance the only priority of formally organized campaign groups, as implied by Jordan and Maloney (1997), could be said to stretch the explanation too far in the direction of egotistical rationality. For instance, although Friends of the Earth and Greenpeace both have carefully crafted public images to consider (Chapter 4), they are not-for-profit initiatives increasingly making a conscious effort to become involved with and/or support local campaign initiatives (Saunders 2007b). Although Friends of the Earth's last Five-year plan (2003–8) contained details about how it wanted to improve its public profile through its campaign efforts, there was much more detail in the plan about how it was seeking to bring about environmental improvements than about its efforts to maintain itself and its reputation. Large environmental organizations, both reformist and conservationist, clearly have a priority to improve the environment. While organizational maintenance is necessary to sustain their efforts, it is clearly ancillary to the primary aim of protecting the environment.

In practice, environmental organizations combine formal and informal organizational structure and mix instrumental and cultural actions. For example, despite its best attempts to take a cultural approach, a This Land is Ours protest camp on the

Thames bank in Wandsworth was forced to take a course of instrumental action because its challenge was best directed towards the planning system (Halfacree 1999). Even the Climate Camp, which generally eschews challenging formal institutions of the state, has, against the wishes of its anti-authoritarian founders, engaged in lobbying activities as part of its attempt to broaden its participant base (Woodsworth 2008; Saunders 2012). Although cultural reproduction and freedom of expression are important within protest camps, some aspects of their actions are inevitably somewhat instrumentally oriented.

Complementarity of the theories

While resource mobilization and new social movement theories have commonly been juxtaposed against one another, they do actually share a number of key variables. This is particularly the case if we extend the definition of what it means to be 'rational' to include emotion and norms. While it is not always economically rational to become an environmental activist, it might be emotionally rational to do so. Furthermore, all environmental organizations require resources of some sort, and they employ a degree of rationality in their attempts to acquire such resources. While instrumentally oriented organizations may seek to build up and maintain financial resources, new social movement type organizations invoke solidarity to maintain affinity groups. It is evident that social movement theorists have made this link because of the frequently cited exposition that symbolic *and* solidaristic incentives can act as selective incentives that motivate social movement participation (see e.g. Johnston et al. 1994: 18). Resources – whether money, people or even ideas – play a significant role in both instrumental and cultural theories.

A related link between formal and new social movement agents is that both spend time on some form of maintenance. For radicals this might entail maintenance of a collective identity and sense of solidarity, and for formal organizations this may constitute maintenance of its staff base and office space. In practice, both types of maintenance are important to environmental organizations, even if variably. Even Melucci (1985: 729), in his theory heavily oriented towards new social movements, made links between different theoretical approaches. 'Action', of new social movements he wrote, 'has to be viewed as interplay of aims, *resources* and *obstacles*, as a purposive orientation which is set up within a systematic field of *possibilities and limits*' (emphasis added). 'Resources' clearly chimes with resource mobilization theory. And 'obstacles' and 'possibilities and limits' can be linked to political opportunity/process theory. Hence, it becomes difficult to disagree with Dalton's (1994: 10–11) point, in specific reference to the environmental movement, that an identity-oriented (new social movement) and resource mobilization approach are 'essentially complementary'. To this, we must add the political opportunity/

process approach, which complements new social movement and resource mobilization theories further. But political opportunity/process theory does need to some extent to be pulled away from its statist/structural bent to be of much help to us (Chapter 5).

As we discovered in Chapter 5, the political opportunity structure in the United Kingdom has been stable for a number of years. Neither the form of electoral representation nor the degree of centralization has changed significantly. Therefore structural political variables cannot be used to explain the changing nature of the British environmentalism (e.g. the dramatic rise in direct action in the early 1990s), or the configuration of relationships between environmental organizations. Neither can structural variables be used to explain variation in the relative openness of the polity depending on: (a) the issue at hand; and (b) the status of the environmental organization demanding the change. Therefore, the approach needs to be modified. It needs to be made more dynamic in order to improve its ability to understand interaction in environmental networks. In Chapter 5, I began to do this by suggesting that we consider also the more dynamic and contingent aspects of political opportunities by focusing on policy windows, democratic dead ends and organizations' location on the insider-outsider continuum.

Thus, each of the theories discussed in this book contributes something to our understanding of interaction in environmental networks. To fill in all the cells of Table 8.1 with yeses – that is to say something useful about strategic and normative actions and incorporate the influence of a range of social actors – such a merging is necessary. This means that theory bashing – at least to the point of entirely dismissing schools of thought – is mostly avoided in this book. Indeed, this discussion has not intended to overlook the contributions from collective behaviour theorists (Chapter 1). It is merely the case that many of the useful aspects of those theories – focusing on the receptiveness of government, the role of key movers and shakers, 'milling' and the development of a 'we-consciousness' – are taken up by political opportunity/process and new social movement scholars (Chapters 6, 7 and 8). Aspects of many extant social movement theories – including collective behaviour – are taken up by McAdam et al. (2001) in their *Dynamics of Contention* research programme. But how do they merge the theories? And what have been the strengths and weaknesses of their approach?

The *Dynamics of Contention*

In *Dynamics of Contention*, McAdam et al. (2001), criticized the classic social movement agenda for being too static, ignoring the interplay between actors, reducing complexity to framing or strategic calculation and compartmentalizing social movements.[1] While they may have come down a little too hard against existing theoretical work on social movements, including their own (Opp 2009: 312), they also share with me an insistence 'on the uselessness of choosing among culturalist, rationalist and structuralist approaches to contentious politics' (305). To address their criticisms of earlier social movement theorizing, they state that they 'adopted insights from all three where we found them useful' (ibid.). They used these insights to build a research programme they claimed had 'more dynamics, more relational analyses and more causal analogies' (ibid.). This is the key reason why appraising and building upon their research programme is a must for the study of environmental networks. At least on the surface, it seems ideally suited for addressing some of the limitations of theories discussed thus far. Another key aim of theirs – which is well beyond the scope of this book – was to try to generate causal mechanisms that work for a whole series of forms of political contention that they call 'contentious politics'. This took them beyond social movements to look also at democratization and revolutions. Their basic argument is that episodes – or spells of contention – result from two or more processes, which are comprized of mechanisms. Mechanisms are defined as 'a delimited class of events that alter relations among specified sets of elements in identical or closely similar ways over a variety of situations' (McAdam et al. 2001: 24). Such mechanisms, as they endeavour to show with their paired comparisons of very different episodes, appear evident across a broad range of forms of political contention. The concatenation of mechanisms in different combinations results in processes thought to give shape and form to contention. 'Processes' combine environmental, cognitive and relational mechanisms (McAdam and Tarrow 2010: 531) and are defined as 'regular sequences of . . . mechanisms that produce similar (generally more complex and contingent) transformations of those elements' (McAdam et al. 2001: 24). The process of polarization, for example, is defined as the 'widening of political and social space between claimants in a contentious episode and the gravitation of previously uncommitted or moderate actors towards one, the other, or both extremes' (322). This process, which quite closely resembles relations between different factions in US environmentalism (see Conclusion), 'combines mechanisms of opportunity/threat spirals, competition, category formation and the omnipresent brokerage' (ibid.). To spell out the jargon: *Opportunity/threat spirals* consist of sequences of political changes that are interpreted by challengers, resulting in collective action followed by the counteraction of members of the polity, causing future political changes and so on. In other words, it can be viewed as a dynamic way of interpreting political opportunities. *Competition* involves different factions trying to gain allies and outbid competitors, as presupposed by resource mobilization theory. *Category formation* creates divisions between a 'we' and a 'them'. This should ring a bell in relation to the new social movement theory I discussed in Chapter 7. And *brokerage* is the linking of two social sites that puts the previously disconnected into contact with one another, perhaps similar to the concept of 'milling' in collective behaviour theory (Turner and Killian 1957).

In short, then, mechanisms such as these are thought to join together in certain configurations to produce processes – like polarization – that shape episodes of contention. However, mechanisms sometimes seem work on their own without joining together to create processes. As I explore later, this has contributed to confusion over what the authors mean by 'mechanisms' and 'processes'. Let me first provide an example of the role of mechanisms in shaping a particular episode of collective action.

McAdam et al. (2001) use their mechanistic approach to uncover why contention led to civil war during the American Revolution in the 1800s, but to a peaceful transition to democracy in Spain in 1973, despite the assassination of dictatorial president Franco. They identify four mechanisms in the two cases: (1) brokerage (defined above); (2) identity shift, which involves the moving of identity markers; (3) radicalization, which they conceptualize as 'increasing contradictions at one or both extremes of a political continuum' that 'drive political actors between the extremes into clear alliance' (189); and (4) convergence, which is another label for the radical flank effect, whereby the more radical actors make the demands of the less radical appear increasingly acceptable to policymakers. They conclude that the relational mechanisms 'combined with very different environmental mechanisms to produce divergent outcomes' (162). In the US case, they identified brokerage only within the oppositional forces, whereas in Spain they found evidence of brokerage between challengers and members. They claim that identities of the US challengers and members were juxtaposed, whereas they find evidence of identity shifts among members in Spain. And while they found radicalization of views in the United States, they considered that in Spain, radicalization was tempered by convergence.

Evaluating the Dynamics of Contention

As McAdam and Tarrow (2010: 530) themselves admit, 'When it appeared in 2001, *Dynamics of Contention* was hardly greeted with universal acclaim by the fraternity of social movement scholars.' My critique centres on the book's apparent lack of focus, and charges the authors of having a structural bent and for, despite their best intentions, creating a somewhat linear theory. But the most damning criticisms point to the programme's lack of conceptual clarity and its sketchy guidance on how to apply the programme to one's own research. In accordance with what we would expect given the history of theory bashing in social movement studies, McAdam and

Tarrow (2010: 530) claim that 'scholars with sunk intellectual capital in a particular approach are always hard to convince'. Nevertheless, McAdam and Tarrow (2010: 350) have the modesty to accept that 'part of the fault was . . . our own'. They have admitted that the work was not theoretically specific, that they looked at too many case studies across a broad array of regime types and that they bombarded readers with 21 pages of references and over 20 mechanisms which they 'tossed off with little attempt at explanation or operationalization' (ibid.). Let us consider the criticisms raised against McAdam et al.'s work in a little more detail.

Broad but narrow: contentious politics restricted to state focused episodes

Regarding charges of a lack of focus, scholars have questioned the possibility of crafting a research programme to shape the entire field of contentious politics, with some seeing it as a blatant, if undesirable, attempt to dominate the field (Flacks 2003). A related worry is that the approach, rather like collective behaviour theory (Chapter 1), has become too 'grand' to effectively address social movements. It falls short of effectively addressing social movements because of its focus on contention. In terms of social movements, this boils down to emphasis on visible contention (read 'protest') directed only at the state. Thus, the approach ignores the underlying dynamics of social movements, their cultural elements and some of the more mundane actions that social movements engage in, such as trying to shift public opinion, organizing petitions or lobbying ministers. Anti-corporate campaigns, like those waged by the Environmental Direct Action Group consequently fall outside of McAdam et al.'s radar.

Although McAdam et al. attempt to reorient the study of contentious politics *away* from episodes to mechanisms and processes, they end up trying to understand only the mechanisms that (sometimes) lead to processes that (always it seems) result in episodes. Thus, their key focus remains episodes. This is not a problem per se, but it means that by trying to understand only the emergence of visible contention, the mechanisms at work in networks that sustain movements during periods of latency are lost. The lack of emphasis they give to periods of latency means also that they effectively lack a control group in which there is no contention with which to compare their cases of contention; in other words, who is to say if their mechanisms at work in the absence of contention? This is important because if their mechanisms are activated outside of periods of contention then their claim to have identified causality is exaggerated. Furthermore, their definition of contention – as interaction between challengers and members – means that they have restricted their focus to political actors and consequently overlook the cultural movements that new social movement scholars have been writing about for decades (Chapters 7 and 8).

The late Charles Tilly defended McAdam et al.'s apparent ignorance of contention targeting culture, corporations, public opinion, media and so on, by stating that he and his fellow authors needed to find a way to delineate the study. As Tilly said in interview with Anne Mische, 'The exposition would become unmanageable if we said we're looking at every form of contention everywhere' (Mische and Tilly 2003: 90). This is a good justification, but why did they not look at a range of forms of *social movement* instead of broadening out to include other forms of contention? Unfortunately, given that they ignore cultural movements, what really stands out here is that their attempt to merge aspects of the cultural approach has fallen well short of its aspirations. Furthermore, even though they claimed to build in cognitive mechanisms that speak to cultural elements of new social movement theory, their presentation of them has been criticized for being 'patently structural' (Platt 2004: 112), and for belittling human agency (Jasper 2010: 968). As Platt (2004: 113) explains:

> Having theoretically attributed cultural agency . . . to activists in theory . . . they cannot shut down their volition by tying them to structural networks or by capriciously reclaiming the structural determination of their thinking and consciousness.

New labels for old ideas: the problem of linearity remains

Their structural bent partly explains a tendency to continue to treat dynamic mechanisms as linear processes. Unfortunately, this also leads to the suspicion that they have done little more than apply new labels to old theoretical ideas. The move from 'certification' to 'decertification' – whereby challengers lose the validation of authorities – for example, is presented as straightforwardly linear. It assumes that decertification follows certification, precluding a change back the other way, or the possibility to be willingly never certified (what I elsewhere in this book call 'ideological outsiders' – see Chapter 5). There is also an assumption that an actor (or group of actors) will be certified on all of the issues that (s)he/it works on. Unfortunately, the concept of certification is not dynamic enough to deal with a group like Friends of the Earth, which could be said to be certified only on some of the issues it works on some of the time (Chapter 5). If we have things McAdam et al.'s way, contention is to be reduced to a single episode on a single issue, targeted at a single authority. Of course, the reality of contention is much more sophisticated than that. McAdam et al.'s concept of 'brokerage' seems even more linear, for there is no counter process of de-brokerage, and the possibility to reconnect latent links is ignored, for brokerage is, in McAdam et al.'s terms, used to refer to the linking of *previously disconnected* actors.

The concept of centralized brokerage, which is ill defined but seems to mean interaction with authorities, was used to explain why violence occurred in the Kenyan Mau Mau Rebellion, but not in the Filipino Yellow Revolution. In other words, in the Philippines – the case in which the state facilitated protest – the transition to democracy was peaceful. In Kenya, where the state actively repressed protest, violence erupted. In this case, as in many others throughout the book, it is hard to see how the mechanistic process gives us any added value from the standard structural approach to political opportunities (see Chapter 5). Similarly, the mechanism of category formation is little different from the 'we-them' distinctions that new social movement theorists have repeatedly discussed. And the mechanism of competition has been very clearly articulated by resource mobilization theorists.

Conceptual issues

Let us move on to look at more fundamental conceptual issues. According to Jasper (2010: 967), 'The main weakness was how the authors defined – or didn't define – mechanisms'. The authors themselves admit that calling mechanisms 'events' was confusing. In a subsequent rendition (McAdam and Tarrow [2011: 4], emphasis added), they replace 'a delimited class of *events* . . .' with 'delimited *changes* . . .' in their definition of a mechanism. This, however, does not solve a more fundamental set of problems. Nowhere is the difference between a mechanism and a process made explicit. Thus, processes and mechanisms are sometimes treated synonymously. Mechanisms sometimes coalesce into processes, and sometimes they seem to do their work alone (see the paired comparison of the American and Spanish revolutions that I briefly discussed above as an example). Furthermore, the score of mechanisms listed are not mutually exclusive; in the case of the Yellow Revolution, their discussion of what they call social appropriation (which seems to be a new label for mobilizing structures) appears to differ little from what they elsewhere call 'brokerage'. And the process of polarization seems almost indistinct from the mechanism they call category shift, which involves identities coalescing and the categorization of social groups into a distinct 'we' and 'them'. To add to the confusion, processes (rather than mechanisms) sometimes lead to other processes. For example, the *process* of scale-shift is thought to lead to the *process* of parliamentarization. This results in mixing of the structural and agential levels, not to mention the organizational level. As Welskopp (2004: 128) notes with reference to the process of 'identity shift':

it is by no means clear how, at which level, and when 'identity shift' occurs and how it can be wrought into a broad social movement. Are we facing micro-processes that accumulate into macro dynamics? Are we looking for macro-effects of micro-change? Do we explain macro-processes by micro-foundations?

McAdam et al. (2001) leave these as open questions.

Methodological issues

Another possible weakness is that McAdam et al. have reconstructed episodes of contention by relying on others' accounts of those episodes. The secondary accounts they refer to could have a peculiar historiographical bent that may miss allusion to mechanisms that did actually play a role in generating contention. The conceptual confusion combined with their reliance on secondary sources makes it difficult to understand how mechanisms were identified by McAdam et al., and nigh on impossible to apply the methodology to one's own research. As Flacks (2003: 101) suggests, 'Why and how these [mechanisms] have been selected and named is obscure.'

In a 2008 article, McAdam et al. seek to redress this by offering 'concrete demonstrations concerning how to identify coherent mechanisms' (309). However, their proposed methodology is disappointing. They give examples of three methodological processes and end up recommending triangulation. One of the three methods involves use of systematic event analysis to *understand* the process of scale-shift. Note the unhelpful shift here from trying to *identify* mechanisms expressed in the aims of their article, to the actual practice of trying to *understand* them. In this example, Tilly identified 1,500 verbs describing action in the process of parliamentarization in the United Kingdom. These were regrouped into 46 categories and also 8 very generic categories. McAdam et al. (2008) go on to state that

> With varying directness, the verbs serve as indicators for mechanisms of contention. In a given paired relationship, for example, an increase in the frequency of attack verbs indicates that 'polarization' is occurring, while an increase in the frequency of support verbs indicates that 'co-ordinated action' is gaining ground. (312)

Yet these are mechanisms that they derived from secondary research, meaning that they are doing little more than trying to fit existing models to examples of contention. There is nothing wrong with this, as such. However, this is exactly the sort of scholarship they are critical of in the *Dynamics* book. As Tilly stated in interview with Mische (Mische and Tilly 2003: 85), for example: 'People would match a set of events to the elements of a conceptual model . . . we say, this isn't supposed to be happening. We're supposed to be explaining these phenomena.' In any case, support verbs can indicate tacit support, which does not always manifest in coordinated action, as they presume. And the limitations of relying on press coverage to reconstruct protest are not even mentioned (see Rootes 2007: 17).

More fundamentally, McAdam et al. (2001) seem to come close to 'mechanism talk' (Norkus 2005), which involves using mechanisms as magic bullets to explain things that do not fit standard theories. Along these lines, Hedström and Ylikoski (2010: 56) had the following appraisal of Tilly's work:

> Despite his inspiring empirical work, his general discussions of mechanism-based explanation (e.g. Tilly 2001) left something to be desired. One gets the strong impression that he used the notion of mechanism as a label to refer to the kind of processes that he for other reasons was interested in.

It is probably fair to apply this appraisal to the McAdam et al. research programme at large. A follow-up book by Tilly and Tarrow (2007) does little to address the problems raised. A number of studies drawing on the *Dynamics* programme have similar or newly created weaknesses. Heany and Rojas (2011) and Karapin (2011), for example, look at (de)mobilization and opportunity threat spirals, respectively, but neither extend their theoretical framework and empirical insights far beyond what we might have learned from political process theories. Biessinger (2011) creates a new weakness. Although developing an account that brings the individual back into focus, it is one that can be critiqued for overplaying agential elements at the expense of the relational. Doubtless it is challenging to balance agency and structure.

Building on *the Dynamics of Contention*

So what can we learn from any of this? First, we can build on what McAdam et al. appear to have got right: the need for a dynamic and relational approach that brings in useful elements from all the strands of prior social movement theorizing. Second, we can seek to avoid their mistakes of 'mechanism talk', structural state-centric bias, unintended linearity and conceptual and methodological confusion.

For a number of reasons (see Chapter 1), I prefer not to adopt a mechanismic approach. In much mechanismic work, including McAdam et al.'s (2001) it is stressed that mechanisms are conditions that produce a constant effect within a particular sociopolitical environment. However, such an approach overlooks how organizational strategy and status – which are not themselves mechanisms – might lead to the same mechanism having different effects for different organizations even within the same sociopolitical environment. As we learn from the weak approach to political opportunities (Chapter 5), a polity deemed objectively open, will not ever be open to anti-state actors. Thus, the sociopolitical conditions that are conducive for a mechanism to lead to a given effect for one environmental organization can be expected to differ from those that are conducive for a different one. Drawing on the notion of systemism (Bunge 1997), a more convincing explanation for an environmental organization's choice of allies can be arrived at by drawing on a host of more dynamic variables. These include the nature of organizations' interactions with each of individuals, the polity (or other campaign targets) and its historical relations with other organizations. Moreover, it is necessary to consider both strategic *and* normative interactions between these different types of actors to derive an explanation for how environmental organizations select their allies. Put differently, I suggest that a synthetic approach which fills *all* of the cells of Table 8.1 is needed. I now illustrate the potential of a synthetic approach to social movement theory with reference to campaigns against climate change and aviation expansion.

A synthetic approach to campaigns against climate change and aviation expansion

As illustrated throughout the text, there is a host possible relationships that pairs or groups of environmental organizations can hold with one another. They might *collaborate*, through working together on a campaign or actions; they could *conflict* with one another, possibly resulting in open hostility;[2] they may *compete* for resources (whether for financial support or volunteers) without externally visible conflict; or they could *dissociate*, which involves passively ignoring one another in the absence of actual conflict. These four types of relationship give shape to environmental networks at large. Thus, in what follows, I discuss an example of an instance of each type of relationship. Collaboration is discussed in the context of the Baku Ceyhan Campaign. A clash between the Environmental Direct Action Group and WWF over oil pipelines is used to illustrate conflict. The interactions between the Environmental Direct Action Group and the Campaign Against Climate Change are used to illustrate how competition can develop. And non-conflictual dissociation between radicals and locals is discussed in relation to campaigns against a third runway at Heathrow. Here I shall tease out how organizational characteristics, coupled with the manner in which those organizations interact with individuals, the polity (and/or other campaign targets), and their previous relations with other organizations can be said to influence the nature of inter-organizational relationships. Emphasis is given to both strategic and normative forms of action. The account is peppered with theoretical insights gleaned from the contextualization of the theories, as discussed in previous chapters.

Collaboration in the Baku Ceyhan Campaign

The Baku Ceyhan Campaign was a collaborative effort between Cornerhouse, Friends of the Earth, the Ilusi Dam Campaign, Platform and (outside of environmental networks) the Kurdish Human Rights Project (see Chapter 3). The Environmental Direct Action Group unofficially worked with the coalition. The collaboration was fruitful despite major differences in the strategies deployed by organizational members. Ordinarily, we might expect organizations that engage in direct action to eschew collaboration with lobby groups (Chapter 4). Similarly, those with an established reputation in policymaking circles – like Friends of the Earth – might be expected to dissociate from a radical organization – like the Environmental Direct Action Group (Chapter 5). Organizations that have a similar degree of resources at their disposal, and comparable organizational structures and fields of action are usually the most likely contenders for cooperative relationships. This is especially the case when they are able to work on the basis of a division of labour (Chapter 4). However, in this example the organizations were very different from one another, and yet still collaborated. How then can we explain the collaboration drawing on the synthetic approach?

Looking first at historical relations between organizations, the coalition was built on the back of tried and tested relationships. Most of the organizations involved had previously worked together on the Ilusi Dam Campaign, thus facilitating trust-benefit relations (Chapter 4). Given that they had not worked together prior to the Ilusi Dam Campaign, their historical proclivity for collaboration rather than conflict or competition needs to be explained. Here we can draw on the concept of niches. The very different specialist remits of the partner organizations meant that each was able to contribute – in both the Baku Ceyhan and Illusi Dam Campaigns – to a productive division of labour, while preserving their niches. On the Baku Ceyhan Campaign, Platform brought a wealth of knowledge on oil issues, Cornerhouse had considerable expertise on international financial institutions, and Friends of the Earth, which brought credibility to the campaign, was able to mobilize its local groups. Needless to say, the Kurdish Human Rights Campaign, which has an entirely different ambit, could easily protect its niche among these coalition partners. The Environmental Direct Action Group, as unofficial partner, could also work its usual strategy of direct action. Its lack of a formal role in broader Campaign business meant that the other organizations involved in the Campaign could protect their reputations while the Environmental Direct Action Group itself was still free to engage in its usual radical actions. The Campaign's moderate strategy allowed it not only to avoid repression, but also made it possible for Friends of the Earth as an established organization concerned with resource maintenance, to be a partner. The selection of a wide range of targets – from government departments through to private lenders – also served to protect niche space. The Environmental Direct Action Group focused on shaming BP with audacious direct actions, as well as taking its share of the coordinated weekly street protests.

Moving beyond strategic insights gained from resource mobilization theory, it is also important to note that this particular campaign was not central to the construction of any of the organizations' sense of 'we' (Chapter 7). It did not fundamentally define or shape any of the individual organizations. The weak encompassing identity of the entire coalition allowed it to bear fruit without factions (Flesher Fominaya 2010a). In relation to interactions between individuals and organizations, it was certainly the case that individual identities were not heavily shaped by the Campaign in the way that the Environmental Direct Action Group moulds the identities of its individual participants. This allowed a more tolerant and flexible identity (della Porta 2005) to develop – not a group level collective identity in the sense implied by much of the social movements literature and applied in Chapter 7.

Regarding relationships with the polity, it was clear that all of the organizations involved in the Campaign viewed the political opportunities for influencing the polity to be closed. This was because the Export Credit Guarantee Department had promised to underwrite a substantial portion of the finance for the pipeline (see Chapter 3). All of the organizations involved agreed that there was a need to pull out all the stops to encourage the ECGD to alter its decision and prevent other banks from funding the scheme. Hence, as on the anti-roads protests (Wall 1999a, b) and campaigns against the multiplex entertainment complex at Crystal Palace (Chapter 5, Saunders 2007c), a critical campaign moment facilitated networking across a broad range of organizations. Similarly, none of the organizations directly involved in the campaign had a facilitative or constructive relationship with the large banks (European Bank for Reconstruction and Development, the International Finance Corporation and smaller private banks) they were targeting. As with the ECGD, these banks seemed committed to funding the oil pipeline, leaving the way open for a more frontal campaign attack that overtly welcomed the contribution of radicals.

Conflict over oil pipelines

Although relations between the Baku Ceyhan Campaign members and the Environmental Direct Action Group were cordial, even productive, relations between the Environmental Direct Action Group and World Wildlife Fund (WWF) were tense and conflictual. The situation became so dire that the Environmental Direct Action Group even held a protest *against* WWF. The Environmental Direct Action Group was motivated to protest against WWF because WWF was working in close partnership with BP on the Tanguhh gas pipeline project. The protest consisted of a mock wedding between WWF and BP held during a BP-organized conference meeting that sought to mitigate the worst effects of the pipeline (see Table 8.2 for the script). Leaflets were handed out to prospective attendees urging them to

Table 8.2 The wedding of BP to WWF

Minister: Dearly beloved, we are gathered here in the presence of the devil to join together BP and WWF; to signify the union between the corrupt and the corruptible; which capitalism dost adorn. Let us be reminded that marriage is not to be entered into unadvisedly or lightly; but reverently, discreetly and after considerable thought. If any person knows any just cause why this couple may not lawfully be joined together, let him now speak, or forever hold his peace. If either of you know why you should not be joined in Holy Matrimony, you should now confess it.

Minister: BP will you take WWF as thy wedded wife, to corrupt her? Will you exploit her, weaken her, ignore her and use her for green wash PR spin? Will you have flings with other NGOs and divorce her when you feel like abusing the environment? Will you love her when your relationship causes her early retirement due to loss of public support?

BP: I will

Minister: WWF, will you take BP to be thy wedded husband, to honour and obey his commands? Will you love him, comfort him, honour and keep him regardless of how he abuses you and breaks environmental laws? Will you forgive him for the loss of public support you will receive as a result of your marriage? Will you love him in floods, droughts, heat waves, hurricanes and typhoons so long as you both shall live?

WWF: I will

Minister: BP repeat after me: 'I BP take thee WWF to be my wedded Wife . . .

'To use and abuse for as long as I feel like it . . .

'So long as the world isn't flooded and I can continue to make money out of oil. . .

'And as long as it is useful for me, we shall be united . . .

'And this is my solemn vow.'

Minister: WWF, repeat after me: 'I WWF take thee BP to be my wedded Husband . . .

'To have and to hold from this day forward . . .

'For better, for worse, for richer, for poorer . . .

'Whatever the weather, till death us do part . . .

'I promise to help BP convince the public that it has the interests of the environment at heart even though this is a blatant lie . . .

'And this is my solemn vow.'

Minister: Capitalism dost preserve and keep you and will look upon you with merciful favour; that ye may allow the oil industry to flourish. You will help suppress information on climate change, pipeline spillages and general environmental destruction and make climate change threats and human rights abuses everlasting. Amen.

Source: EDAG 2003d

boycott the event and stating that 'collaborations between NGOs and corporations result in the manipulation of those NGOs as pawns, disguising those corporations' profit-above-all-else mind set and thus giving them unwarranted credibility'. The leaflet incorporated one activist's rebranding of the WWF logo as a devil (Figure 8.1). While the Environmental Direct Action Group was able to work with Baku Ceyhan Campaign members in relative harmony, why was it not able to work with WWF?

Unlike the Baku Ceyhan Campaign members, WWF and the Environmental Direct Action group had no previous track record of collaboration. The lack of historical collaboration coupled with the encompassing identity of the Environmental Direct Action Group (Chapter 7) makes it somewhat easier for WWF to be placed, by radical activists, under the banner of an archetypal 'namby-pamby' NGO that needs to be 'staked' (Anon 2004, see Chapter 8). From the Environmental Direct Action

Figure 8.1 Environmental Direct Action Group's rebranding of the WWF logo

Group's perspective, BP's invitation of stakeholders to their meeting amounted to little more than a BP public relations exercise. In contrast, WWF felt it was making progress building on its previous engagement with BP. Previously, WWF had limited success in improving the company's poor environmental performance. But the lack of any fundamental change in BP's overall approach led to the Environmental Direct Action Group's trenchant critique of WWF's approach. Thus, not only were different strategies deployed, but the overall objectives of their campaigns were different: WWF, with its constructive relationship with BP, was happy to moderate the impact of BP's actions. In contrast, the Environmental Direct Action Group had an antagonistic relationship and wanted the Tanguhh project halted, point blank. Halting the project entirely might require that individuals reduce their overall demand for energy, whereas WWF's approach allows for a society as usual scenario. This identity-based chasm seems impossible to bridge given intense differences between the organizations. It is therefore more likely to lead to conflict than more minor identity-based differences. When coupled with the two organizations' very different relationships with campaign targets, conflict became inevitable.

While this account resembles many other descriptions of conflict between radicals and reformists across many different social movements (see e.g. Downey 1986), it is important to note that reducing the cause of conflict to an ideological clash masks over several strategic and normative processes taking place at multiple levels. In this case, WWF was working strategically to build on what it considered to be historically successful relations with BP at the same time at which the Environmental Direct Action Group was working on a frontal attack of BP as an informal partner in the Baku Ceyhan Campaign. Thus, they had very different relationships with their campaign targets. Coupled with these varying strategic priorities, the organizations did not have any experience of working together in the past, allowing the cultural process of sectarian solidarity to come fully into play (Chapter 7). Thus, individuals with identities bound to the Environmental Direct Action Group were primed for lambasting a more moderate group.

Competition between Campaign Against Climate change and others

In Chapter 4, the awkward relationship between the Campaign Against Climate Change and the Environmental Direct Action Group was deemed to be due to them being in direct competition for supporters at their actions. Despite different strategies, their similarities have made it relatively more difficult for these single-issue groups to carve out a niche for themselves. To make matters more serious, Environmental Direct Action Group members considered that the Campaign Against Climate Change had not returned the favour of offering support to its actions, leaving an unfavourable trust-benefit balance (Chapter 4).

In relation to interactions with the polity, both groups had very different perceptions of the potential of the global climate change regime to halt dangerous climate change. The Campaign Against Climate Change was in favour of strengthening the Kyoto agreement, seeing it a useful stepping stone towards a more robust framework. But the Environmental Direct Action Group considered the whole United Nations Framework Convention on Climate Change process to be fundamentally flawed and toothless to bring about positive change. Instead, it preferred grass-roots solutions and directed its campaigns at multifarious targets – not just at the global climate regime. But given differences in campaign strategies, niche overlap is clearly not the key explanandum in this instance of competition.

The Environmental Direct Action Group found it harder to appeal to individuals for support, routinely attracting a dozen or fewer participants to its actions. Its lack of popular support could be said to have sharpened its negative reaction to the lack of reciprocity from the Campaign Against Climate Change. A boost in numbers from Campaign Against Climate Change activists would have increased its capacity enormously. Able to attract hundreds, sometimes even thousands, of supporters to its actions, the Campaign Against Climate Change would not be hit so hard by losing a handful of supporters to the Environmental Direct Action Group.

The Environmental Direct Action Group also encouraged among its participants an encompassing collective identity that resulted in a high degree of intra-group behavioural conformance. This increased the emotional stakes, thus making it more likely to be defensive of its own approach and critical of others' (Chapter 7). Its encompassing identity alone is not enough to set the Environmental Direct Action Group at a distance from all other environmental groups – it worked in collaboration with Friends of the Earth and others on the Baku Ceyhan Campaign. But, in combination with vastly different perceptions of political opportunities, failure to build trust-benefit relations with the Campaign Against Climate Change and its own inability to attract a broader campaign base, competition resulted.

Dissociation of radicals and niche protection in the campaign against the third runway

In the case of the No Third Runway Action Group facilitation and funding of the campaign by the local authority did not result in conflict with radicals, but instead in passive dissociation. The No Third Runway Action Group took advantage of the funding it had received because it was invaluable for enabling it to manage the resources it required to wage its campaign. At the same time, the campaign was careful to protect its reputation with both the local authority and the campaign target – British Airports Authority. Although the campaign was challenging its opponents – its involvement with British Airports Authority could by no means be demoted to the status of co-option – campaigners were careful not to jeopardize the possibility of having a facilitative relationship with the Airports Authority in the event of the campaign failing. Despite this, No Third Runway Action Group members – as individuals – had offered support to radical activists who had scaled a crane associated with construction of Terminal 5, allowing trust-benefit relations to develop.

Furthermore, organizations within the broader anti-aviation expansion network have been able to work on the basis of a successful division of labour. Local groups are in a unique position to challenge local governance structures. And a number of others fill unique niches, reducing the scope for conflict. Heathrow And Communities Against Noise specializes in noise effects of living under flight paths around Heathrow Airport. The Campaign for the Protection of Rural England brought respectability to the campaign and focused upon the threat to areas of tranquillity and the English countryside. Friends of the Earth used broad-based campaigning and supported its local groups and thereby effectively disseminated information through the network. London Friends of the Earth groups mostly played the role of supporting West London Friends of the Earth that offered a more regional perspective on Heathrow airport and wrote the inquiry submissions and consultation responses on behalf of national Friends of the Earth. The Aviation Environment Federation produced the background research and policy arguments that other organizations were able to draw upon. The Royal Society for the Protection of Birds (RSPB) was particularly active in the campaign against an airport at Cliffe and is continuing to work on policy arguments. London Wildlife Trust has been involved in mitigating the wildlife impacts of Terminal 5. And Hounslow Against New Terminals, Earth First! and the Environmental Direct Action Group have engaged in more spontaneous direct action to raise the profile of the issue. Airport Watch loosely holds the network of aviation campaigners together. Greenpeace came late to anti-aviation campaigning, but the groundswell of popular discontent meant that it had to contribute in order to protect its reputation and ensure continued support.

All individuals involved in these campaigns shared the key aim of preventing the building of a third runway at Heathrow. As the government had, at the time of field research, given a green light for the proposal providing air quality standards were maintained, all involved perceived the opportunities for influencing policy using conventional means to be closed. If the No Third Runway Action Group was not supported by the local authority, more open collaboration between radicals and reformists, as in the Baku Ceyhan Campaign, would be likely to have developed. A positive trust-benefit balance, coupled with a division of labour and a set of political opportunities perceived as closed usually leads to more open collaboration rather than dissociation.

Concluding remarks

This chapter has pulled out the aspects of social movement theory useful for understanding interaction between environmental groups. Drawing on McAdam et al.'s (2001) *Dynamics of Contention* research programme, it has proposed a synthetic analytical framework for understanding patterns of interaction in environmental networks. This framework emphasizes the importance organizational characteristics in the context of a host of relationships with the polity, campaign targets, individuals and previous relations with other environmental organizations for explaining interaction in environmental networks. It helps begin to overcome some limitations social movement theories. In particular, it addresses their static nature, the structure/agency gap and the chasm between rational and cultural approaches. The approach goes some way to explaining the different configurations of relationships among organizations campaigning against climate change and aviation expansion.

At the very least, this chapter has shown that each of the theories discussed in earlier chapters of this book is required, in an integrated manner, to explain interaction in environmental networks. Thus, rather than viewing social movement theories as competing paradigms, this chapter confirms that it is useful to embrace them eclectically in order to advance understanding of a complex reality. Can this synthetic analytical framework help us understand environmental movements in other countries? And what are the broader questions that it raises for social movement studies? I address these remaining questions in the concluding chapter.

Conclusion

This book has explored environmental movement networks in London through the lens of social movement theory. It has sought to make an empirical *and* a theoretical contribution to the literature on environmentalism specifically, and social movements, more generally. The chapters have located the results of the survey of London's environmental organizations in the broader social movement literature. Empirically, the book has shown that there are links across London-based environmental networks' ideological strands and spatial dimensions, especially during critical campaigns. Generally, local environmental organizations are pleased with the support they receive from national environmental organizations, although they ask for support much less intensely and frequently than anticipated. National environmental organizations are unable to support all campaign initiatives, so they make decisions about where their resources can best be placed. Inevitably, instrumental factors, including there being a high chance of there being some kind of campaign success, play a key role in shaping those decisions. Environmental organizations within the same niche have a tendency to compete, and competition can be heightened by sectarian solidarity. A lack of resources appears to constrain rather than encourage network links, and a wealth of resources does not necessarily mean broad-ranging linkages (Chapter 4). I also found that national and community groups do, as expected, publicly shun the actions of radicals. Instead, there are private links that are not publicly apparent, even if these links only manifest themselves as tacit support (Chapter 5). Radical environmental organizations' strong collective identity encourages a systemic critique of capitalism that results in a radical ideology that sits uncomfortably with reformism and conservationism. The solidarity that results from their collective identity further decreases their accessibility for collaborative campaigning as their 'we' can be defined partly at the expense of other environmental organizations (Chapter 7).

The findings of the study are, of course, likely to be shaped by the choice of location, and I cannot claim to be able to generalize about environmentalism in other countries, or even within the United Kingdom. However, before drawing this book to a close, I will examine the usefulness of the analytical framework developed in Chapter 8 in understanding environmentalism in other parts of the world, especially in southern European countries and the United States. But it needs to be stated that it would also be a mistake to assume that interactions between environmental organizations in London are typical of relations between organizations within Britain at large. London is unique, as a centre of government, commerce and finance, and as an international metropolis. As such, the number of campaign targets concentrated in a relatively small geographic area is second to none. While this provides a unique opportunity to study the interactions between different types of environmental organizations, it also raises questions about generalizability. No other city houses the offices of so many purported environmental villains, as well as the headquarters of banks, Parliament and the home of the prime minister. This provides London-based environmental organizations with more opportunities for collaborative ventures by comparison with those in more peripheral locations. It is also the case that high-profile environmental protests in London are much more likely to be widely advertised and broadly attended than their counterpart protests held elsewhere in the country. Therefore, they are all the more likely to attract collaboration. Furthermore, London has the highest density of national (mostly reformist) environmental organizations of any area in Britain, with the result that a similar study elsewhere would be less likely to pick up so much detail on interaction between types of environmentalism (local to national, and conservationist to radical).

While London has many characteristics that might lead us suggest that patterns of environmentalist interaction are exaggerated in comparison to the United Kingdom at large, there are also some characteristics that can be said to constrain network links. London is the largest city in the country, and it can take up to 3 hours to travel across it using public transport links. One radical activist told me that it regularly took her over 2 hours to travel from her home in north London to the meeting place of the Environmental Direct Action Group – almost as long as my journey there from Canterbury, Kent. Furthermore, radical social centres are mostly many miles apart. This means that the radical part of the movement is likely to be much more fragmented than it is in smaller cities. My impression is that, as a result of geographical distance, London's radicals are quite specialized, and tend to associate with a particular preferred social centre or pet issue, unlike in smaller towns and cities where fewer activists muscle in on a wider range of projects via a smaller number of more centralized social centres (see, e.g. Doherty et al. 2007 on direct action networks in Manchester, Oxford and Wales). The infrastructure of London may stifle collaboration not just between radicals, but throughout the whole movement as geographical distance can create social barriers. In their study of environmental groups in Alabama, Lhotka et al. (2008) found that physical proximity remains an important factor in effective communication, despite e-communication. Thus, it would be interesting to carry out similar studies in other parts of the country to allow for a proper investigation of the effects of locality on the research. Indeed, instead of selecting two localities within London (southeast and northwest), a future study could focus on two similarly sized localities *outside* of London (see e.g. Diani and Bison 2004, but note that they looked beyond environmentalism to a variety of kinds of civic action). Perhaps local chapters of national environmental organizations outside of London feel more distanced from their national headquarters than the research participants in my study. Similarly, it would be interesting to apply this type of research to other movements to see whether configurations of relationships between national, regional and local, and reformist and radical social movement organizations can be generalized across movements.

Regardless of these peculiarities, it can be said that London's environmental network represents a dynamic mix of collaborative, competitive and occasionally conflictual relations. It remains open to question whether the extent of collaboration is sufficient to justify labelling London's environmentalism a 'movement'. It remains open because *some* definitions insist on a conflictual element among those who form part of a movement (Chapter 2). Some of the organizations researched in this book refrain from conflictual action, and yet, are still engaged in environmental campaigning. To avoid confusing use of the term 'movement', I prefer to include non-conflictual organizations and to refer to the object of study using the alternative concept of 'environmental networks'. This book has illustrated that 'environmental networks' is a term that can safely be used to incorporate nature lovers, political ecologists and green anarchists. It also allows us to include campaigns that are sometimes dismissed as 'not in my back yard' (NIMBY). The diversity of environmental networks is what makes them so potent: they attract the support of different sectors of the population, and constitute a force difficult for decision-makers to ignore. The success of the broad-ranging 2011 campaigns against the coalition government's plans to sell off public forests is a case in point.

Theoretically, the book has sought to develop an analytical framework for understanding interaction in environmental networks. In so doing, it has evaluated several strands of social movement theories, taking useful elements from each. The framework was built both inductively and deductively. Starting from theoretical and empirical insights of others, it sought to discover which variables might shape relations between environmental organizations. It then used results of a survey and qualitative research to inductively piece together the analytical framework. The result is an attempt to understand interaction in environmental organizations in the context of environmental organizations' broader relationships to the polity, their campaign targets, individuals and their historical relations with other environmental organizations. But to what extent can this framework help us explain environmental networks in a different context? Can my approach illuminate our understanding of environmentalism in different countries? Reflection on existing secondary sources can usefully illustrate the general appeal of my analytical framework even if the empirical insights are not especially rich.

In the United States, environmental networks are strongly segmented. It is common to think of US environmentalism as consisting of conservationists (such as the Wilderness Society and the Sierra Club), 'new' environmental campaigning organizations (like Friends of the Earth and Greenpeace), radical networks (Sea Shepherd and Earth First!) and grass-roots/environmental health networks (Citizen's Clearing House) (Connelly et al. 2012, Chapter 3). Interactions among these different segments of what is called the 'environmental movement' are few. Similarly, in southern Europe, there exists a 'rich local network of environmental groups that are not supported by strong formal environmental organizations' (Kousis et al. 2008: 1636). How can we explain the apparent lack of interaction across spatial scales and ideological streams?

Central to any explanation of the lack of interaction between different types of environmental group in the United States is the role of an influential group of environmental organizations known as the G-10 and the political context in which it emerged. G-10 was established as a coalition of politically oriented and reputable US environmental organizations in the early 1980s, in response to then President Reagan's attack on environmental policy. It consisted only of organizations with access to Congress or corporate decision-making structures. As such, it excluded apolitical organizations (like World Wildlife Fund [WWF] and the Nature Conservancy) and radical groups distrustful of central government (Greenpeace and Environmental Action) and/or engaged in direct action (Earth First!). G-10's formal policy document, *Environmental Agenda for the Future,* was derided by many environmentalists as a weak compromise overlooking corporate power and social justice. Never a huge success, the group lost cohesion when it rebranded as the Green Group in the late 1990s and invited more radical members, including Friends of the Earth US and Greenpeace US. Although the Green Group no longer formally exists, the 'Group of Ten' is still used as a disparaging label for what are taken to be bureaucratized, institutionalized, white and middle-class American environmental organizations. Such labelling sets the established groups miles apart from environmental justice campaigners and radicals.

Thus, established environmental organizations in the United States are considered to be 'old, fat and unimaginative' (Sierra Club renegade, cited in Bosso 2005: 148). But why is this? Bosso argues that it is because they had little choice given prevailing political circumstances. Political opportunity structure scholars have long suggested that movements in the United States are kept moderate as a function of the 'strong position of the Congress, the lack of tightly integrated political parties, [and] the relative openness of a deeply fragmented administration' (Kitschelt 1986: 66). Moderate environmental groups in the United States also had to survive a particularly unfavourable political climate and felt obliged to follow through on gains they had won in Congress in to the court rooms. The seemingly more favourable political climate under Clinton and Gore looked promising, yet arguably resulted in the environmental organizations making yet more compromises. Although environmentalist and one-time Vice President Gore ensured that national environmental organizations could gain access to the president, environmental organizations' elevated status and reputation had meant that compromise was the order of the day if they were to maintain access. As Bosso (2005: 91) states, 'The imperatives of organizational maintenance and the need to establish a permanent advocacy presence in national politics typically outweighed ideological purity.'

It was against a backdrop of compromises that Earth First! emerged in the United States – a full decade before it appeared in the United Kingdom. In 1979, the US Forest Service Roadless Area Review Evaluation was launched, designating 65 million of 80 million acres of wilderness for logging, mineral development and recreation. Half the remaining protected area was 'rock and ice' (Dowie 1995: 210). The Wilderness Society claimed success for the 15 million acres that were saved and staffer Dave Foreman consequently left in disgust to establish Earth First!. Seeking to avoid oligarchy and organizational maintenance issues, Earth First! activists set themselves up as a 'nomadic action group' immune to the self-preservation that was shaping the mainstream organizations (Dowie: 1996: 210). As Scarce (1990: 62) states: 'EF! was to be like a Plains Indian tribe, existing in autonomous groups which shared the same beliefs'. Unfortunately for them, Earth First! has never gained much public sympathy in the United States, and their leaders have been actively repressed.

Local groups campaigning for environmental justice emerged because the large national groups were apparently becoming increasingly distanced from the grassroots, and found guilty of institutional racism. A 1992 study by the US Environmental Careers Organization, for example, found that one-third of the mainstream US environmental organizations had no people of colour on their staff. Consequently, a number of civil rights organizations wrote to them charging them with 'racist hiring practices' (Dowie 1996: 47). At the same time, *environmental racism* – that is the disproportionate siting of sources of pollution in neighbourhoods dominated by ethnic minorities – was continuing apace (Bullard 1990).

Despite existing in drastically different political structures and having contrasting historical trajectories, the story in southern Europe is not so different. There, environmental organizations have been subject to a mix of liberal and neo-corporatist political structures, in which movements have, historically, been actively repressed (Kousis et al. 2008: 1640). This means that mainstream southern European environmental organizations are generally much younger and less well-resourced than their north European counterparts. Nonetheless, the mainstream environmental organizations there have come to develop close relationships with the state in some countries, such as Italy, as they have taken on contractual relations following the retrenchment of public services. Consequently, they have become distanced from grass-roots and community-based campaigns. As with Western European environmental organizations (van der Heijden 1999), their professionalization has tamed their action repertoires, leading to compromises rather than all out success.

How can we understand the lack of interaction between distinct types of environmentalism in the United States and in southern Europe? In both geographical areas, the combination of a lack of historically successful interactions across factions, the drastically contrasting assessments of the value of compromising with the state, and the different emphasis given to individual level biographical characteristics of class and race have driven a wedge between the radicals and the reformists. Thus, as my synthetic analytical framework would predict, organizations' historical lack of relationships, the factions' differing relationships (from cooperative to hostile) to their campaign targets and the interactions between individuals and organizations matter deeply. Large environmental organizations apparent preoccupation with organizational maintenance appears to strengthen the gulf still further.

Thus, the key point of my analytical framework – that the shaping of environmental networks is a dynamic process, which builds on historical interaction between environmental organizations as well as past and current interactions with individuals, the polity and/or other campaign targets – appears to help us understand patterns of interaction between environmental organizations in other places, too. Of course a much more detailed empirical study of environmental networks across the world – and even across countries – is required before the synthetic approach I apply can be deemed a general theory. Moreover, it would be useful to conduct similar empirical studies of other social movements to see whether the analytic framework is equally useful across different social movement industries. I imagine that a number of other variables might come into play during such a cross-national and cross-movement study. It would be especially interesting to begin to understand how the degree of heterogeneity of particular movements influences the applicability of my analytical framework. Environmental networks are relatively large and heterogeneous compared to the anti-psychiatry movement (Crossley 2007), but relatively small and homogeneous when set against what has been called the global justice movement (GJM), of which ecology movements are considered to be just a small part (della Porta 2007). At the very least, I hope to have avoided the worst excesses of theory bashing, while developing an analytical framework that allows very different theories to talk to one another. I look forward to seeing the synthetic approach applied in future studies concerned with the configuration of social movement networks within and across different social movements.

Appendix 1

List of interviewees

nterviews followed with '(TEA)', were carried out while I was working as a research assistant on the Transformation of Environmental Activism project (Autumn 2000–Autumn 2001).

'Bongo' (TEA), Alternative media eco-activist (Pirate TV), 23 June 2001.

'Dave', 56a-goer 29 September 2003.

'Rooby too Good' (TEA), eco-activist at Crystal Palace, 23 June 2001.

Bates, Jennifer, (TEA), Greenwich & Lewisham FoE, 6 February 2001.

Bates, Jennifer, Coordinator London FoE and Greenwich FoE, 31 October 2003 and 6 November 2003.

Coleman, Matthew, eco-activist, EDAG, 8 November 2003.

Collins, Shane (TEA), Ecotrip, EF!, RTS, Green Party, 11 July 2001.

Connolly, Philip (TEA), Coordinator GASP, Living Streets Coordinator, 8 February 2001.

Cowdell, Julia (TEA) PCEG, 6 June 2001.

Cowdell, Julia, Chair, PCEG, 20 September 2003.

de Zylva, Paul, Head of England Team, FoE, 16 January 2004.

Dorey, Cat, Greenpeace Marine Campaigner and North West London Area Networker, 17 January 2004.

Ferriday, Nic, Coordinator West London FoE, 10 June 2003.

Freeman, Sheila, FoE Post Room and Volunteers coordinator and EDAG activist, 19 February 2004.

Gaines, Ralph (TEA), Director, London Wildlife Trust, 12 July 2001.

Gray, Barry (TEA), People Against the River Crossing, 2 August 2001.

Hammond, Marie, (TEA), Greenwich Greenpeace, 12 February 2001.

Hanton, Alisdair (TEA), Committee member South Circular ALERT (1992), vice chair of Pedestrians Association, committee member of Transport 2000, London Transport Activist's Round Table attendee, 26 April 2001.

Hill, Edward (TEA), Greenwich Town Centre Campaign and MILNET, 28 May 2001.

Hollemby, Peter (TEA), BETTER, 26 April 2001.

Juniper, Tony (TEA), Campaigns and Policy Director (now Director), Friends of the Earth, interview with Ben Seel, 2000 (month unknown).

Livingston, John & Joanna (TEA), BADAIR, 22 February 2001.

Pearce, Rita, Longford Residents Association, 30 January 2004.

Poruun, Storm (TEA), eco-activist, Environment Office, various local conservation groups, 22 February 2001.

Rau, Nic, Climate / Corporates Campaigner, FoE, 19 January 2004.

Rear, David, Voluntary Warden, Chiswick Wildlife Trust, 15 January 2004.

Redding, Sam, Campaigner, CPRE, 22 December 2003.

Roberts, Karen, Voluntary Warden, Chiswick Wildlife Trust, 17 February 2004.

Robertshaw, Emma, Voluntary Warden, Chiswick Wildlife Trust, 17 February 2004.

Sartori, Claudia, Local Groups Development Officer, FoE, 24 November 2003.

Sauven, John (TEA), Greenpeace, interviewed by Ben Seel, 2000 (month unknown).

Schofield, Richard, Head of Regions, CPRE, 20 October 2003.

Sobey, Bryan, NoTRAG, Harmondsworth & Sipson Residents Association, 7 February 2004.

Spencer, Patrick, (TEA), Secretary, Dulwich Society, 13 February 2001.

Stewart, John (TEA), Chair ALARM-UK and Lambeth Public Transport Group, 25 February 2001.

Stewart, John, HACAN, Airport Watch, 31 January 2004.

Sweeting, Susan, Coordinator Hillingdon FoE, 20 February 2004.

Thornhill, Phil, Coordinator Campaign Against Climate Change, 18 June 2003.

Torrance, Jason, Greenpeace Network Coordinator, 1 July 2003.

Vincent, Stan (TEA), Logistics Director, Greenpeace, interview with Debbie Adams, 2000 (month unknown).

Watson, Anna, Waste Campaigner, FoE, 19 January 2004.

Waugh, Miranda, Volunteer Coordinator, London Wildlife Trust, 10 June 2003.

White, Rosy, Senior Development Officer, CPRE, 20 October 2003.

Appendix 2

Survey

QUESTIONNAIRE

ORGANIZATION NAME...
(Please Note: *If you wish to remain anonymous, just the name of your organization and a contact number will suffice. All data will be held on a secure database and will not be passed on to any third parties*)

Name of Contact .... **Position of Contact** ....

Address of Organization ....

Postcode...................... **Email**..

Website...

Phone Number............................. **Fax**...

Please answer the questionnaire from the point of view of **your** organization, even if it is a local or regional branch of a national organization.

1. Do you consider your organization to be part of the environmental movement?
    Yes ☐   No ☐

2. What are the aims of your organization? *(please paraphrase the relevant section of your organization's constitution if it has one)*

....

3. Is one of your organization's *main* aims to protect or preserve the environment?
    Yes ☐   No ☐

4. Is your organization part of a *network* of environmental organizations? *That is, is your organization in regular contact with at least one other organization that you consider to be part of the environmental movement?*

    Yes ☐   No ☐

If No, there are no further questions, please return questionnaire.

5. At which *one* of the following levels does your organization most often operate?
Please tick only one box.

i.   Very local (e.g. specific to a single road or park)   ☐
ii.   Local (at the borough level)   ☐
iii.   Regional (greater than one borough, or London-wide)   ☐
iv.   National (throughout the UK)   ☐
v.   International (the UK and beyond)   ☐

6. Which *one* of the following most accurately describes the primary function of your organization?
Please tick only one box.

i.   Single Issue Environmental Organization   ☐
ii.   Multi-Issue Environmental Organization   ☐
iii.   A Community Development Organization   ☐
iv.   A Countryside Management / Wildlife Conservation Organization   ☐
v.   A Recreational Organization   ☐
vi.   An Environmental Education Organization   ☐
vii.   An Urban Conservation Organization (concerned with built heritage)   ☐
viii.   An Amenity Society   ☐
ix.   A Tenants or Residents Association   ☐

7. Which of the following activities has your group engaged in within the last 12 months?
Please tick *as appropriate*; you may tick *more than one* box.

i.   Social Events   ☐
ii.   Petitions   ☐
iii.   Leafleting   ☐
iv.   Media Work (press releases or radio/TV interviews)   ☐
v.   Press Conference   ☐
vi.   Letter Writing   ☐
vii.   Researching and Reporting   ☐
viii.   Education or Training   ☐
ix.   Lobbying   ☐
x.   Practical Conservation   ☐
xi.   Government Consultee   ☐
xii.   LA21 or similar Council-ran Local Environment Committee Involvement   ☐
xiii.   Procedural Complaints (e.g. planning objection)   ☐
xiv.   Litigation   ☐
xv.   Marches   ☐
xvi.   Public Meetings   ☐

xvii.	Rallies	☐
xviii.	Demonstrations	☐
xix.	Cultural Performance	☐
xx.	Boycotts	☐
xxi.	Disruption of Events	☐
xxii.	Blockades / Occupations	☐
xxiii.	Ethical Shoplifting	☐
xxiv.	Ecotage	☐
xxv.	Adbusting	☐

8. Which *one or two* categories best represent the underlying source of the environmental problem(s) that your organization works to resolve?
Please tick no more than 2 boxes.

i.	Erosion of nature / wilderness	☐
ii.	Urban growth	☐
iii.	Poor planning decisions	☐
iv.	Failure to cost environmental goods	☐
v.	Over-consumption in consumerist society	☐
vi.	Unequal distribution of resources	☐
vii.	Domination of nature under capitalism	☐
viii.	Globalization	☐

9. Which *one or two* categories best represent the overall solution to the environmental problem(s) that your organization works to resolve?
Please tick no more than 2 boxes.

i.	Practical conservation / management of reserves	☐
ii.	Halting building on Greenfield sites	☐
iii.	Improved planning decisions	☐
iv.	Technological innovation	☐
v.	Participatory democracy	☐
vi.	Reallocation of resources	☐
vii.	Reduction of consumption	☐
viii.	Self-sufficient communities (e.g. bioregions)	☐
ix.	Anarchy	☐
x.	Revolution	☐

10. Which *single* statement best characterizes your organization's relationship with each of national, regional and local government?

Please tick one box per column	National	Regional (GLA)	Local (Borough Council)
a) The government/council frequently seeks the advice of our organization	☐	☐	☐
b) The government/council is friendly to our organization, but our organization initiates most of the contact	☐	☐	☐
c) The government/council sometimes receives our organization with hostility and other times is welcoming depending on the issue/s or department/s involved	☐	☐	☐
d) The government/council never listens to our organization although our organization does try to influence them	☐	☐	☐
e) Our organization prefers to campaign in other ways	☐	☐	☐

11. QUESTION 11 ASKS YOU ABOUT THE *ENVIRONMENTAL ORGANIZATIONS* FROM WHICH YOUR ORGANIZATION *RECEIVES* INFORMATION OR ADVICE ON ENVIRONMENTAL ISSUES, OR CAMPAIGNING MATTERS. Please include local branches of your own organization if appropriate. *If your organization does not receive any information or advice from other environmental organizations, please tick this box and go to question 12* ☐.

a. Please list the 5 most important local environmental organizations in southeast London (within the boroughs of Greenwich, Lewisham, Southwark and Lambeth) from which you have received information or advice in the last 12 months and approximate how frequent these occurrences have been.

Please list the organizations here and tick one box for each row	Daily	Weekly	Monthly	Quarterly	6-monthly	Annually
i.	☐	☐	☐	☐	☐	☐
ii.	☐	☐	☐	☐	☐	☐
iii.	☐	☐	☐	☐	☐	☐
iv.	☐	☐	☐	☐	☐	☐
v.	☐	☐	☐	☐	☐	☐

b. Please list the 5 most important local environmental organizations in northwest London (within the boroughs of Hillingdon, Hounslow and Ealing) from which you have received information or advice in the last 12 months and approximate how frequent these occurrences have been.

Please list the organizations here and tick one box for each row	Daily	Weekly	Monthly	Quarterly	6-monthly	Annually
i.	☐	☐	☐	☐	☐	☐
ii.	☐	☐	☐	☐	☐	☐
iii.	☐	☐	☐	☐	☐	☐
iv.	☐	☐	☐	☐	☐	☐
v.	☐	☐	☐	☐	☐	☐

c. Please list the 5 most important regional (London-based) environmental organizations from which you have received information or advice in the last 12 months and approximate how frequent these occurrences have been.

Please list the organizations here and tick one box for each row	Daily	Weekly	Monthly	Quarterly	6-monthly	Annually
i.	☐	☐	☐	☐	☐	☐
ii.	☐	☐	☐	☐	☐	☐
iii.	☐	☐	☐	☐	☐	☐
iv.	☐	☐	☐	☐	☐	☐
v.	☐	☐	☐	☐	☐	☐

d. Please list the 5 most important national (London-based) environmental organizations from which you have received information or advice in the last 12 months and approximate how frequent these occurrences have been.

Please list the organizations here and tick one box for each row	Daily	Weekly	Monthly	Quarterly	6-monthly	Annually
i.	☐	☐	☐	☐	☐	☐
ii.	☐	☐	☐	☐	☐	☐
iii.	☐	☐	☐	☐	☐	☐
iv.	☐	☐	☐	☐	☐	☐
v.	☐	☐	☐	☐	☐	☐

12. QUESTION 12 ASKS YOU ABOUT THE ENVIRONMENTAL ORGANIZATIONS
TO WHICH YOUR ORGANIZATION PROVIDES INFORMATION OR ADVICE ON
ENVIRONMENTAL ISSUES, OR CAMPAIGNING MATTERS. *If your organization* does
not *provide any information or advice for other environmental organizations,*
please tick this box and go to question 13 ☐

a. Please list the 5 most important local environmental organizations in
southeast London (within the boroughs of Greenwich, Lewisham, Southwark and
Lambeth) to which your organization has provided information or advice in the
last 12 months and approximate how frequent these occurrences have been.

Please list the organizations here and tick one box for each row	Daily	Weekly	Monthly	Quarterly	6-monthly	Annually
i.	☐	☐	☐	☐	☐	☐
ii.	☐	☐	☐	☐	☐	☐
iii.	☐	☐	☐	☐	☐	☐
iv.	☐	☐	☐	☐	☐	☐
v.	☐	☐	☐	☐	☐	☐

b. Please list the 5 most important local environmental organizations in
northwest London (within the boroughs of Hillingdon, Hounslow and Ealing) to
which your organization has provided information or advice in the last 12 months
and approximate how frequent these occurrences have been.

Please list the organizations here and tick one box for each row	Daily	Weekly	Monthly	Quarterly	6-monthly	Annually
i.	☐	☐	☐	☐	☐	☐
ii.	☐	☐	☐	☐	☐	☐
iii.	☐	☐	☐	☐	☐	☐
iv.	☐	☐	☐	☐	☐	☐
v.	☐	☐	☐	☐	☐	☐

c. Please list the 5 most important regional (London-based) environmental organizations to which your organization has provided information or advice in the last 12 months and approximate how frequent these occurrences have been.

Please list the organizations here and tick one box for each row	Daily	Weekly	Monthly	Quarterly	6-monthly	Annually
i.	☐	☐	☐	☐	☐	☐
ii.	☐	☐	☐	☐	☐	☐
iii.	☐	☐	☐	☐	☐	☐
iv.	☐	☐	☐	☐	☐	☐
v.	☐	☐	☐	☐	☐	☐

d. Please list the 5 most important national (London-based) environmental organizations to which your organization has provided information or advice in the last 12 months and approximate how frequent these occurrences have been.

Please list the organizations here and tick one box for each row	Daily	Weekly	Monthly	Quarterly	6-monthly	Annually
i.	☐	☐	☐	☐	☐	☐
ii.	☐	☐	☐	☐	☐	☐
iii.	☐	☐	☐	☐	☐	☐
iv.	☐	☐	☐	☐	☐	☐
v.	☐	☐	☐	☐	☐	☐

13. QUESTION 13 ASKS YOU ABOUT THE ENVIRONMENTAL ORGANIZATIONS WITH WHICH YOUR ORGANIZATION COLLABORATES ON CAMPAIGNS AND OTHER ENVIRONMENTAL ACTIVITY. *If your organization does not collaborate with other environmental organizations, please tick this box and go to question 14* ☐

a. Please list the 5 most important local environmental organizations in south east London (within the boroughs of Greenwich, Lewisham, Southwark and Lambeth) with which your organization has collaborated on a campaign or other environmental activity in the last 12 months and approximate how frequent these occurrences have been.

Please list the organizations here and tick one box for each row	Daily	Weekly	Monthly	Quarterly	6-monthly	Annually
i.	☐	☐	☐	☐	☐	☐
ii.	☐	☐	☐	☐	☐	☐
iii.	☐	☐	☐	☐	☐	☐
iv.	☐	☐	☐	☐	☐	☐
v.	☐	☐	☐	☐	☐	☐

b. Please list the 5 most important local environmental organizations in northwest London (within the boroughs of Hillingdon, Hounslow and Ealing) with which your organization has collaborated information or advice in the last 12 months and approximate how frequent these occurrences have been.

Please list the organizations here and tick one box for each row	Daily	Weekly	Monthly	Quarterly	6-monthly	Annually
i.	☐	☐	☐	☐	☐	☐
ii.	☐	☐	☐	☐	☐	☐
iii.	☐	☐	☐	☐	☐	☐
iv.	☐	☐	☐	☐	☐	☐
v.	☐	☐	☐	☐	☐	☐

c. Please list the 5 most important regional (London-based) environmental organizations with which your organization has collaborated on a campaign or other environmental activity in the last 12 months and approximate how frequent these occurrences have been.

Please list the organizations here and tick one box for each row	Daily	Weekly	Monthly	Quarterly	6-monthly	Annually
i.	☐	☐	☐	☐	☐	☐
ii.	☐	☐	☐	☐	☐	☐
iii.	☐	☐	☐	☐	☐	☐
iv.	☐	☐	☐	☐	☐	☐
v.	☐	☐	☐	☐	☐	☐

d. Please list the 5 most important national (London-based) environmental organizations with which your organization has collaborated on a campaign or other environmental activity in the last 12 months and approximate how frequent these occurrences have been.

Please list the organizations here and tick one box for each row	Daily	Weekly	Monthly	Quarterly	6-monthly	Annually
i.	☐	☐	☐	☐	☐	☐
ii.	☐	☐	☐	☐	☐	☐
iii.	☐	☐	☐	☐	☐	☐
iv.	☐	☐	☐	☐	☐	☐
v.	☐	☐	☐	☐	☐	☐

14. QUESTION 14 ASKS YOU ABOUT THOSE ENVIRONMENTAL ORGANIZATIONS WITH WHICH YOUR ORGANIZATION IS IN COMPETITION. *If your organization does not compete with other environmental organizations, please tick this box and go to question 15* ☐

Please list those 5 environmental organizations with which your organization most competes, and indicate what you compete for.

Please list the organizations here and tick the appropriate boxes. You may tick more than 1 per row if applicable	Members	Activists	Finances	Publicity	Influence	Other (specify)
i.	☐	☐	☐	☐	☐	....
ii.	☐	☐	☐	☐	☐	....
iii.	☐	☐	☐	☐	☐	....
iv.	☐	☐	☐	☐	☐	....
v.	☐	☐	☐	☐	☐	....

15. Please list those 5 environmental organizations that you consider to be the most similar to your own organization (in terms of scale of influence, membership base, organizational size and structure, issues and strategies). *Local organizations, please ensure that the groups you list are local and within your locality. National and regional groups, please list organizations in London only.*

Please list similar organizations here

Please rank them here. Give them a number between 1 and 5, with 1 being the most similar and 5 the least

i. ....

ii. ....

iii. ....

iv. ....

v. ....

Thank you for Completing this Questionnaire

Appendix 3

List of survey respondents

Southeast

Badair
Blackheath Group of Ramblers Association*
The Brixton Society
The Camberwell Society*
Catford Resident's Association*
Crystal Palace Campaign*
Dulwich Society
East Dulwich Society
Friends of Beckenham Palace Park
Friends of Nunhead Cemetery
Friends of Greenwich Park
Friends of Jubilee Gardens
Green Party Lambeth
Greenwich Action to Stop Pollution
Greenwich and Bromley Greenpeace
Greenwich Conservation Group
Greenwich Grinpeace*
Hernehill Society
Groundwork Southwark
Ladywell Fields User Group*
Lee Manor Society*
Lettsom Gardens Association*
Opposition to the Destruction of Open Green Spaces*
Nunhead Residents' Association
Peckham Society
Plumstead Common Environment Group
Rockingham Estate Play Association*
Roots and Shoots
RSPB Wildlife Explorers – Bermondsey
RSBP Bromley

Southbank Ramblers*
Southwark Heritage Association
Southwark Social Investment Forum
Sydenham Society
Use Your Loaf Social Centre*
Vauxhall Society
Woodlands Farm Trust

Northeast

Bedford Park Society
Chiltern Society
Chiswick House Friends
Cranford and Staines Area Conservation Group*
Chiswick Protection Group
Culpepper Community Garden
Ealing Aircraft Noise Action Group
Ealing Allotments and Gardens Society
Ealing Civic Society
Ealing Green Party
Ealing Local Agenda 21 Allotments Group
Ealing Local Agenda 21 Pollution and Public Health Project Group
Ealing Local Agenda 21 Transport Group
Ealing Wildlife Network
Earthworks Conservation Volunteers
Federation of Heathrow Airport Noise Groups
Ferndale Area Residents' Association
Friends of Blondin Park
Friends of Dukes Meadows*
Friends of Horsenden Hill
Friends of Osterley Park
Gatehill (Northwood) Residents' Association*
HACAN Clearskies
Harefield Tenants' and Residents' Association
Harmondworth and Sipson Residents' Association
Harrow National Trust
Hayes End Garden and Allotments Association*
Groundwork Thames Valley
Heston Residents' Association

Hillingdon Friends of the Earth

Hillingdon Natural History Society

Ickenham Residents' Association

Isleworth Society

Iver Nature Study Centre

The Larches Residents Association

London and West Middlesex National Trust Volunteers*

London Wildlife Trust, Chiswick Group

Long Lane Community Association Hillingdon*

Middlesex Campaign for Open Spaces

Northolt and Greenford Country Park Society

No Third Runway Action Group

Peachey Lane Gardens Association*

Ruislip Residents' Association

South Ruislip Residents' Association

Southside Action Group Ealing

The Strand-on-the-Green Association

Uxbridge Moor Residents' Association*

Uxbridge Rovers Angling and Conservation Society

Watch Ealing

West London Friends of the Earth

West London Organic and Wildlife Gardening Association

West London Group of the Ramblers

West Ruislip Commuters' Association*

Windsor Lines Passengers Association

Regional

Bioregional Development Group

CAPITAL Transport Campaign

Emmaz

Friends of the Earth London

Green Events

London Greenpeace (but responses were vague – i.e. 'various')

London Community Recycling Network

London Forum of Civic and Amenity Societies

London SCARE

London Natural History Society

London Walking Forum

London Wildlife Trust
River Thames Society
Street Tree
Thames Explorer Trust
Woodland Trust London

National

Anarchist Federation
UK Association of Preservation Trusts
Aviation Environment Federation
British Herpetological Society
British Union for the Abolition of Vivisection*
Campaign Against Climate Change
Campaign for the Abolition of Angling
Civic Trust
Christian CND*
Commonwealth Human Ecology Council*
Class War*
Communities Empowerment Network*
Campaign to Protect Rural England
Environmental Law Foundation
Forests Forever*
Friends of Conservation
Environmental Justice Foundation*
Federation of City Farms and Community Gardens
Freshwater Action Network
Friends of the Earth
Global Action Plan
Green Anarchist
Greenpeace UK
International Primate Protection League*
Justice*
League Against Cruel Sports
Living Earth Foundation*
National Federation of Badger Groups
Mammal Society
No Sweat*
One World Action*

Orangutan Foundation
Platform
Rainforest Concern
Ramblers' Association
Real Nappy Association
Save the Rhino Association
Survival*
Waste Watch
Wildlife and Countryside Link
Women's Environmental Network
Year Zero*

Total of 149 organizations that responded to the questionnaire. Out of this, 35 (asterixed) were not part of a network of environmental organizations and were excluded from the analysis.

Appendix 4

Key to Figures 6.2 and 6.3

Figure 6.2

1. 56a
2. Alarm
3. Anti-Terrorism Act
4. Archway Alert
5. Association for Monetary Reform
6. Bexley and District Against Incineration Risk
7. Barrydale Allotments Association
8. British Horse Society
9. Blackheath Society
10. Boycott UCI
11. Brixton Greenpeace
12. Brockley Society
13. Brockley Cross Action Group
14. Bromley Greenpeace
15. British Trust for Conservation Volunteers
16. Camberwell Society
17. CAST
18. Centre for Alternative Technology
19. Charlton Society
20. Chernobyl Children
21. Christian Ecology Link
22. Civic Trust
23. Campaign for Nuclear Disarmament (CND)
24. Corporate Watch
25. Countryside Agency
26. Crystal Palace Campaign
27. Crystal Palace Foundation
28. Crystal Palace Protest
29. Cyclists Tourist Club
30. Dog Kennel Hill Society

31. Dulwich Society
32. East Dulwich Society
33. Ecotrip
34. Earth First!
35. Eltham Society
36. English Heritage
37. Environment Office
38. Fareshares
39. Friends of Burgess Park
40. Friends of Camberwell Park
41. Friends of Dawson's Hill
42. Friends of Dulwich Park
43. Federation of City Farms
44. Friends of Great North Wood
45. Flora and Fauna
46. Friends of Nunhead Cemetery
47. Friends of the Earth
48. Forum for the Future
49. Friends of Peckham Rye Park
50. Friends of Beckenham Park
51. Greenwich Action Plan
52. Greenwich Action to Stop Pollution
53. Gene Concern
54. Georgian Group
55. Green Party
56. Green Anarchist
57. Green Lanes
58. Greenpeace
59. Greenwich Conservation Group
60. Greenwich Cyclists
61. Greenwich Environment Forum
62. Greenwich Friends of the Earth
63. Greenwich Green Party
64. Greenwich Greenpeace
65. Greenwich Local History Society
66. Greenwich Local Agenda 21
67. Greenwich Society
68. Greenwich Wildlife Advisory Group
69. Hastings Bypass Campaign

70. Hillyfields Action Group
71. Huntington Life Sciences Campaign
72. Justice?
73. Lambeth Cyclists
74. Lambeth Environment Forum
75. Lambeth Green Party
76. Lambethians Society
77. Lambeth Transport Users Group
78. Lambeth Walk First
79. Lambeth Local History Society
80. London Cycling Campaign
81. Legal Defence and Monitoring Group
82. Lee Manor Society
83. Lettsom Gardens Association
84. Lewisham Cyclists
85. Lewisham Environment Trust
86. Lewisham Green Party
87. Lewisham Pedestrians Association
88. Lewisham Wildlife Trust
89. London Forum of Amenity Societies
90. London Forum of Green Parties
91. Liberty
92. London Natural History Society
93. London Anarchy
94. London SCARE
95. London Walking Forum
96. London RSPB
97. London Wildlife Trust
98. May Day Collective
99. MedACT
100. Greenwich Sustainable Millenium Network
101. Minet Conservation Association
102. Monetary Justice
103. New Economics Foundation
104. Norwood Society
105. People Against the River Crossing
106. Plumstead Common Environment Group
107. Peace camps
108. Peckham Society

109. Pedestrians Association (now Living Streets)
110. Pirate TV
111. Plant Life
112. Primal Seeds
113. Quaggy Waterways Action Group
114. Residents Association [unspecified]
115. Rail Passengers and Commuters Association (SE)
116. Ridge Wildlife Group
117. Road Peace
118. Rockingham Estates Play Area
119. Royal Society for Nature Conservation
120. Royal Society for the Protection of Birds
121. Reclaim the Streets
122. SAVE
123. *SchNEWS*
124. South East London World Development Movement
125. South Greenwich Forum
126. Simon Wolfe Charitable Foundation
127. Siren Sound System
128. Socialist Alliance
129. Sounds of Dissent
130. South Bank Ramblers
131. South London Collective
132. South London Link
133. Southwark Cyclists
134. Southwark Open Spaces Society
135. spc.org
136. Stonehenge Campaign
137. Sustrans
138. Socialist Worker
139. Southwark Animal Rights
140. Southwark Environmental Forum
141. Southwark Friends of the Earth
142. Southwark Green Party
143. Southwark Groundwork
144. Southwark Heritage Association
145. Southwark LA21
146. Southwark Park Rangers
147. Southwark Social Investment

148. Southwark Wildlife Trust
149. Sydenham CND
150. Sydenham Society
151. Sydenham UN Association
152. Transport for London
153. Tidy Blackheath
154. Tidy Britain (now ENCAMS)
155. Transport 2000
156. UN Association
157. Undercurrents
158. Urban 75
159. Victorian Society
160. World Development Movement
161. Wildlife Gardening Initiative
162. Wombles
163. Woodlands Farm Trust

Figure 6.3

1. Bankside Open Spaces Trust
2. British Trust for Conservation Volunteers
3. Bexley and District Against Incineration Risk
4. Bromley Royal Society for the Protection of Birds
5. Crystal Palace Campagin
6. Campaign to Protect Rural England
7. Camberwell Society
8. Centre for Wildlife Gardening
9. Creekside Forum
10. Dog Kennel Hill Campaign
11. Dulwich Society
12. East Dulwich Society
13. Encams (previously Tidy Britain)
14. Forum of Conservation and Amenity Societies
15. Friends of the Earth
16. Federation of City Farms
17. Forum for Stable Currencies
18. Friends of Belair Park
19. Friends of Burgess Park
20. Friends of Dulwich Park

21. Friends of Greenwich Park
22. Friends of Jubilee Gardens
23. Greenwich Action to Stop Pollution
24. Greenwich Wildlife Advisory Group
25. Greenwich Conservation Group
26. Greenwich Friends of the Earth
27. Greenwich Greenpeace
28. Greenwich Wildlife Trust
29. Groundwork
30. Groundwork London
31. Groundwork Southwark
32. London Wildlife Trust
33. Learning Through Landscapes
34. Lee Manor Society
35. People Against the River Crossing
36. Plumstead Common Environment Group
37. Peckham Society
38. Bromley Royal Society for the Protection of Birds
39. Roots and Shoots
40. Southwark Friends of the Earth
41. Sustainable Energy Action
42. Southwark Social Investment Forum
43. Vauxhall Society
44. Vision for Vauxhall
45. Walk First
46. Walworth Garden Farm
47. Waste Watch
48. Woodlands Farm Trust

Notes

Chapter 1 Introduction

1   Some radical groups call themselves 'disorganizations' to reflect their non-hierarchical and participatory structure. Despite this, the term 'organization' is used throughout to refer to all types of groupings of environmentalists whether formally organized or not.

2   See the appendices of the DANGO Project's *NGOs in Britain Handbook* for recent poll results www.ngo.bham.ac.uk/appendix/Green_Membership.htm. The World Values Survey finds 16 per cent of the British claim to be members of environmental organizations, with a population of 50,431,700 this would amount to over 8 million. The British Social Attitudes Survey (2005) found that 5.4 million British people were members of local or national conservation/environmental groups.

3   The importance of networks in mobilization is not to be overlooked. Diani (1995) found that 72 per cent of the environmental activists he surveyed in Milan joined environmental organizations through their social networks.

4   Chapter 2 opens with further clarification of the woolly and variably used term 'social movement', comparing it with definitions of pressure groups, interest groups, protests, political movements and social movement organizations.

5   There is, of course, the more recent trend towards seeing the theories as complementary. This is discussed later in the book.

6   Neff Gurney and Tierney (1982) suggest that other responses such as withdrawal, or lowering one's expectations are more likely to be the outcome of frustration than aggression. Others, including Dalton (1996), show evidence which suggests that protest is no more likely among the dissatisfied than those content with the political system.

7   To highlight the emphasis that collective behaviour theorists placed on interaction, I have italicized the word 'interaction' in my account.

8   According to Mayntz (2004: 237) 'a survey of the relevant empirical and methodological literature soon bogs down in a mire of loose talk and semantic confusion about what "mechanisms" are' (see also Gerring 2007). For some, mechanisms amount to mid-range laws (Bunge 1997). For others, they are less law-like because irregularities in outcomes are thought explainable by diversity in the initial conditions (Darden 2002: 356; Mayntz 2004: 241; Falletti and Lynch 2009) and the ways in which mechanisms can combine (Tilly 2001). For others still, mechanisms are theoretical constructs that allow us to postulate causes (Hedström and Swedburg 1996: 290).

9   'Environmental Direct Action Group' is a pseudonym because group participants preferred their organization to remain anonymous.

10   Of the surveys, 6 per cent were returned unanswered, some informing me that the organization had folded, others claiming that the organization did not exist at the address to which I mailed surveys. This is expected, given the nature of collective action. As Knoke (1990) suggests, the environmental movement, especially at the grassroots level, is known to experience periodic attrition and renewal as organizations fold when issues are resolved or activists burn out, and new ones take their place. Although it seems low, this response rate

is not drastically lower than the expected average response rate of 50 per cent for surveys of social movement organizations (Klandermans and Smith 2002). If we add to the response rate those organizations that had folded/were not contactable, this does not compare unfavourably with Ansell's (2003) response rate for a similar survey of US environmental organizations (40%). However, not all respondents provided data on their network links. In all, 114 listed their 5 most important links with other environmental organizations at each of the national, London-wide and local (borough) levels.

Chapter 2 Environmental Movements and Networks

1 I recognize that generalization does some violence to the particularities of particular accounts. Indeed within schools of thought there is variation within definitions as much as between them.

2 See Chapter 4 for a discussion of the meaning of rationality.

3 Coxall (2001) for instance notes the important differences between sectional (also known as interest) groups and cause groups. 'A sectional pressure group represents the self-interest of a particular economic or social group in society: examples are the confederation of British Industry, the TUC . . . A cause group is formed to promote a particular cause based on a shared set of attitudes or beliefs' (Coxall 2001: 5). Environmental groups generally fall into the latter category, although NIMBY groups could be conceived of as interest groups.

4 WWF is not based in London and therefore is not discussed in depth in this book. However, it did come into conflict with the Environmental Direct Action Group during my period of field research. A conflictual episode is discussed in Chapter 8.

5 Do-it-yourself groups seek to bring about social change by themselves and for themselves.

6 The debate is a result of a failure to establish a coherent theoretical argument about the characteristics that feminist and women's campaigning should have in order to be called a movement (Nash 2002b). Bashevkin's (1996: 542) interviews with 43 feminists representing the movement in the early 1990s revealed that one-quarter of them 'insisted there *was no* British women's movement, just a multitude of separate fragments working on individual issue campaigns'. However, others strongly argue that 'something that looks like a women's movement does still exist', and although it cannot any longer be called a 'mass movement', there are a 'large collection of single-issue organisations that press for feminist aims in many different accents' (Walter 1998: 44).

7 There is still a clash of values in conservationism, especially between pro- and anti-hunting, and urban and rural conservationists. For rural conservationists, brown field sites are a way to save green field sites. For urban conservationists, developing brown field sites precludes their chance of reverting to green space.

8 Dalton concluded that the environmental movement is an example of ideologically structured action in practice, but that the effects of ideology on courses of action were much less pronounced than he expected given the overriding influence of political structures and other contingent factors.

9 The labels (emboldened) were not displayed in the questionnaire.

10 This was recoded from a list of types of action given in question 7 of the questionnaire – see Appendix 2.

Chapter 3 Key Organizations and Campaigns in London's Environmental Network

1   Environmental campaigners argue that the planning system is biased in favour of developers. Although planning inspectors can withhold development approval, developers can appeal to the secretary of state. However, should the planning inspector grant outline or full planning permission, objecting members of the public, local authorities, interest groups and statutory agencies have no opportunity for appeal, even if they have a strong case.

2   The government proposed in a Green Paper (a consultation document) to remove the rights of local people to attend public inquiries to question the need for large-scale developments such as airports and motorways and to abolish County Structure Plans – two key planning processes the Campaign uses to restrict abuse to the countryside. While the former was revoked, Campaign to Protect Rural England is dismayed to see that County Structure Plans have been scrapped and that energy infrastructure is exempt from planning scrutiny.

3   www.greenpeace.org.uk/about/our-vision, last accessed 5 January 2011.

4   Note that Rucht (1995) writes about Greenpeace in Germany. Greenpeace UK is very similar in this regard.

5   www.wildlondon.org.uk/, last accessed 6 Jan 2011.

6   The Capacity Building team worked to integrate national and local campaigning, and to help local groups reach their full potential.

7   See Guenther (2009) for a discussion of the ethical controversies around naming or anonymizing research participants.

8   NB. The legally binding targets were conditional on their being a minimum number of nations ratifying the protocol. To come into force, enough industrialized countries needed to ratify to account for a total of 55 per cent of their emissions. As Russia has now ratified, the protocol is now legally binding.

9   Mr Putin's advisor on Kyoto, Andrei Illarionov claimed that Kyoto would have 'deadly economic consequences' for Russia and that it was 'a death treaty, no matter how strange that seems, because its main purpose is to stifle economic growth and economic activity in countries which assume its responsibilities' (Osborn and Castle 2004).

10   Reimann (2000) discusses the 1997 protests in Kyoto.

11   This involves choosing a politically motivated target and administering a custard pie to their face.

12   The Global Climate Coalition was an industry-based group that opposed action on climate change. In 1997, it sponsored a series of television adverts designed to sway public opinion against the Kyoto agreement. By 2000, most of the heavy-weight corporations that had supported the Coalition had withdrawn.

13   A critical mass is an event where a large number of cyclists, skate boarders and roller skaters converge at a given meeting point and move slowly about the streets, blocking traffic and spreading a political message.

14   www.yes2wind.com/, last accessed 26 Aug 2011.

15   www.cpre.org.uk/campaigns/transport/airport-expansion, last accessed 5 Jan 2011.

16   This is not to be confused with the Labour Environment Campaign (SERA) which played a role in drawing to public attention some of the weaknesses of the economic arguments

made in the SERAS report nor with the Southeast Regional Assembly (SERA) which also supported the case for no airport expansion in the Southeast.

17 Although the response focused especially on their local airport at Heathrow, many of the points raised were relevant to the overall consultation and a broad approach was taken where possible.

18 In the context of Friends of the Earth, arm-chair activists are people who sign up to Campaign Express, which involves receiving a small pack with a short briefing about the issues, pre-written letters/postcards to sign and post, and ideas for quick and simple actions three times a year.

19 Greenpeace website, 2011, at www.greenpeace.org.uk/climate/airplot, last accessed 27 Jan 2011.

Chapter 4 The Role of Resources in Relationships

1 The work of Oberschall (1973) and some of the work of Zald and his colleagues (Zald and Ash 1966; Zald 1976) placed the approach on the starting blocks prior to Gamson.

2 Olson's original theses sought to explain participation in the trade union movement. Others have regarded it as a more general theory about participation in collective action.

3 'Rational' organizations prioritize on the basis of instrumental rationality.

4 Oberschall's (1973) emphasis on components of solidarity (e.g. 'moral commitment, trust, friendships . . .') in his definition of a resource features little if at all in the work of most resource mobilization theorists including his own.

5 Rosenthal et al. (1985) found this in the New York women's movement.

6 Bosso (1995: 107) suggests that the word 'member' is a misnomer for many professional or semi-professional environmental organizations because 'members' frequently do little more than pay an annual subscription. Instead, he prefers to use the term 'supporter'. It is also a misnomer because some environmental organizations do not have mass memberships.

7 Rawcliffe (1998) shows how environmental organization budgets have increased, for example Friends of the Earth's budget rose from £306,285 in 1985 to £3,839,325 by 1995.

8 This statement cannot be said with such conviction since 2002, because Greenpeace has reinvigorated its connection with the grassroots and now has a busy 'active supporters unit' (Torrance in interview 2003).

9 Barkan [1986] found reformists had similar complaints about radicals in the southern civil rights movement.

10 Similarly, in the 1980s, Greenpeace was accused of stealing the limelight from Friends of the Earth on whales, and the seal pelt issue from International Federation for Animal Welfare (Pearce 1991: 25, 28).

11 There are many other similar examples of conflict between radical activists and local campaigners, including that which North (1998) found on the Save Our Solsbury roads protest and the case of Crystal Palace; there the local campaigners proclaimed that they would not condone illegal protest (Saunders 2007c). Yet on other protests, good relations were established with locals, as suggested by Cathles (2000). Locals may have given their support in some cases out of desperation – in which case perceived political opportunity structures is potentially a more applicable theory than resource mobilization theory.

12 Although some may view the League Against Cruel Sports to be an animal rights organization, it answered all the boundary questions in the affirmative. It was considered to be an environmental organization because of its emphasis on the protection of animals in their natural setting as part of its campaign against blood sports.

13 While it would have been a more rigorous exercise to have listed all pairs of potentially competitive organizations and to have compared this list with cases where competition actually exists in order to determine whether niche overlap led to competition, this approach could not be used because only 8 of 114 organizations listed their competitive relationships in the questionnaire.

14 A DL list is a text-based format for entering network data in UCINet. Essentially, it is a list of organizations and the network links that they mention. For instance if Campaign to Protect Rural England lists Friends of the Earth, Greenpeace, Wildlife and Countryside Link and WWF as four out of five top links, the following partnerships would be listed:

Campaign to Protect Rural England Friends of the Earth
Campaign to Protect Rural England Greenpeace
Campaign to Protect Rural England WildlifeCountrysideLink
Campaign to Protect Rural England WWF

The same would be done for each organization's elected choices. UCINet converts data inputted in this format into a socio-matrix (Borgatti et al. 1999).

15 It may be that the lists of local collaborators or information providers/receivers are too numerous or too difficult to rank. Anheier (1987: 579), for example, warns of the bias that 'power and size differentials' are likely to yield as 'smaller organisations tend to be well aware of informal and cooperative relations with larger organizations, but not vice versa'.

16 Three network relations are combined for this analysis (information provided, information received and collaboration) for each local, regional and national organization with a maximum of five organizations listed for each spatial dimension. National organizations could list local organizations from the southeast and the northwest, whereas local environmental organizations were only given the opportunity to list network relations to others in the same locale.

17 National and regional organizations could list a maximum of 20 organizations – 5 each of local (southeast), local (northwest), regional and national. Local organizations could only list 15 because they were not asked about their links to local organizations in a different locality. Thus, southeast organizations listed a maximum of five each of local (southeast), regional and national organizations. To make them equally weighted to local organizations scores, the total number of regional and national ties were each multiplied by 0.75.

18 London Wildlife Trust has in the past been routinely awarded £125,000 per year by the Association of London Grants. In June 2003, this support was withdrawn partly because the new grant application process required organizations to apply for funding whereas in the past applications were renewed annually. This fact was reportedly poorly communicated to civil society groups. Apparently money had still been set aside for London Wildlife Trust in July 2003, but by December, no money was available. Thus it appears likely that there was no Association of London Grants money available for London Wildlife Trust between 2003 and 2007.

Chapter 5 Political Structures, Political Contingencies and Environmental Networks

1 The questionnaire also asked about relationships with the Greater London Authority, however it was rarely noted as a foci for environmental campaigns.

2   By British exceptionalism, Rootes (1992) was referring to the (then) exceptionally
    moderate character of British environmental organizations in comparison to other Western
    democracies.

3   The Carbon Plan suggests that emissions from travel can be reduced by a shift to electric
    cars rather than by reducing demand for private motor car travel.

4   The language they all spoke was that of sustainable development, a term sufficiently flexible
    to allow for it to be twisted in favour of economic development by business and government
    (cf. Sachs 1991).

5   For reference, a more recent MORI poll asking this question – in December 2010 –
    found a reduction to 64 per cent. See www.ipsos-mori.com/researchpublications/
    researcharchive/poll.aspx?oItemId=2442 for the trend data. Website last accessed
    23 August 2011.

6   Note that Poloni-Staudinger (2009) looked at only 33 UK groups and excluded radical
    organizations.

7   www.ipsos-mori.com/researchpublications/researcharchive/2773/ReutersIpsos-MORI-April-2
    011-Political-Monitor.aspx, last accessed 5 August 2011.

8   Note that these results also mix environmental organizations from across London boroughs.
    Therefore, it matters little for networking how many of the organizations get on with their own
    borough because it is frequently a different borough from their alters'. Overall, it appears that
    relationships with local borough councils only seem to make a difference for organizations
    that campaign at a purely local level.

9   By 2003, 12 local authorities had signed up. These are Cornwall, Somerset, South Somerset,
    South Gloucestershire, Shropshire, Cumbria, Warwickshire, Rydale, South Hams, York, East
    Riding and the Lake District National Parks Authority

10 Zero Waste is the idea that all rubbish be ultimately reused, recycled or composted so that
    landfill sites and incinerators along with their associated environmental problems become
    a thing of the past. The Green Party suggest a target of 2020 for Zero Waste to become a
    reality.

11 Note that this quote was given before the Department of Energy and Climate Change was
    constituted.

Chapter 6 Environmental Networks and New Social Movement Theory

1   By anti-progress, I mean expressing aversion to the illusion of 'progress', which is a belief
    in the benefits of ever-increasing consumption, regardless of its social and environmental
    consequences.

2   Tarrow's notion of the demise of movements is perhaps overly pessimistic. Also, it is by
    no means inevitable that all movements will tread the institutional path. Many movement
    organizations form with the explicit aim of remaining a-institutional. Some movements have
    parts that fully institutionalize, while other components remain or even become increasingly
    independent from formal political institutions.

3   Protest event analysis – using data from the mainstream media as an indicator of the extent
    and type of protest – is not a very reliable tool for understanding environmental protest.
    This is especially the case because newspapers no longer routinely report on protest. For

example, in the six weeks preceding and six weeks following the December 2009 National Climate Change march there was no reportage of that demonstration in the *Guardian*, *Telegraph*, *Mirror* and *Sun* combined.

4   One could also argue that Rucht's inclusion of strategic/instrumental ends-oriented NIMBY groups meant that he found weak proof of NSM dynamics by virtue of casting the net too widely.

5   Rochon's (1990: 118) empirical work on the peace movement – a supposed new social movement – also demonstrates the gap between theory and practice. He shows how the peace movement chose to engage in political negotiations having the effect of suppressing the movement's broader cultural critique.

6   For consistency, this type of society will be referred to as 'contemporary society'.

7   This figure comes from data collected as part of the Caught in the Act of protest project, coordinated by Bert Klandermans, VU University, Amsterdam. See www.protestsurvey.eu datastore for more information. Last accessed 21 October 2012.

8   This reference used to be on the RTS homepage,www.rts.gn.apc.org/. It no longer appears there.

9   See www.artnotoil.org.uk/bpweekofaction for details. Last accessed 21 May 2012.

10 Crossley (2003) calls these types of protests 'anti-corporate'.

11 Brokerage was calculated using Freeman's (1979) concept of betweenness. The top seven normalized betweenness scores all exceed 10, setting them apart as the most important brokers; the next highest score was less than four.

Chapter 7 Collective Identity and Solidarity: Unity or Factionalism?

1   I even took a survey along to a group meeting at which there was consensus to refuse to complete it.

2   These organizations can have activist or fund-raising groups but the majority of 'subscribers' are just 'cheque-book' supporters – that is, they do nothing beyond making a direct debit donation.

3   Sennett (1998, chapter 7), for example, notes how people actively seek a community in response to the pressures of contemporary society (that he calls 'new capitalism').

4   This is a term appropriated by Thornton (1995) in the context of subcultural youth movements – but most especially the dance culture. It refers to being 'hip' and 'in the know' as well as conforming to a certain lifestyle code, and is equally applicable to the environmentalist subculture.

5   This type of hierarchical decision-making is being phased out in an attempt to make Friends of the Earth more accountable to local groups.

6   This involves not only purchasing goods free of animal products, but striving to survive for free by reclaiming food from supermarket skips and other outlets. One activist I met acquired a sack full of cold baked potatoes that formed a squatted household's staple diet for nearly a week.

7   In reality, even Kyoto involves other a multitude of other issues – social justice, development, equity and genetically modified organisms to name a few.

Chapter 8 Towards a Synthetic Analytical Framework for Understanding Interaction in Environmental Networks

1   While they avoid compartmentalization of social movements by looking beyond them to contentious politics more broadly, I avoid it by talking not of environmental movements, but of broader environmental networks.

2   Note that conflict could also be latent rather than visible and open. Political organizations often develop a 'mobilisation of bias', which involves 'exploitation of certain kinds of conflict and the suppression of others' (Schattschneider 1960: 71). Environmental organizations are not immune to this as they each favour certain forms of knowledge over others. Radicals, for example, are more likely to draw on anarchist principles, whereas more reformist groups will rely more heavily on rational scientific arguments.

References

Airport Watch (2002). Flying into Trouble: The Threat of Airport Growth. London, Airport Watch.

Aitken, M. (2002). 'Terminal velocity'. *Green Events* January–December 2001: 5–6.

Aldrich, H. (1999). *Organizations Evolving*. London, Sage.

Almanzar, P. N. A., H. Sulivan-Catlin, et al. (1998). 'Is the political personal? Everyday behaviours as forms of political participation'. *Mobilization* 3(2): 185–205.

Anheier, H. K. (1987). 'Structural analysis and strategic research design: Studying politicised interorganiastional networks'. *Sociological Forum* 2(3): 562–82.

Anon. (1996). 'A critique of Newbury'. *Do or Die* 6: 27–32.

— (1999). 'Comments on camps'. *Do or Die* 8: 155–8.

— (2000). 'Rebelling against our domestication'. *Do or Die* 9: 171–2.

— (2003). 'Down with the empire! Up with the spring!' *Do or Die* 10: 1–101.

Ansell, C. (2003), 'Community embeddedness and collaborative governance in the San Franscisco Bay area environmental movement'. In M. Diani and D. McAdam (eds) *Social Movements and Networks: Relational Approaches to Collective Action*. Oxford, Oxford University Press: 122–44.

Ash-Garner, R. and M. Zald (1987). 'The political economy of social movements'. In M. Zald and J. D. McCarthy (eds) *Social Movements in an Organizational Society*. New Brunswick, NJ, Transaction Books. 119–45.

Atkinson, A. (1991). *Principles of Political Ecology*. London, Belhaven Press.

Baggott, R. (1995). *Pressure Groups Today*. Manchester, Manchester University Press.

Bagguley, P. (1992). 'Social change, the middle class and the emergence of new social movements: A critical analysis'. *Sociological Review* 40(1): 26–47.

Bandy, J. and J. Smith (2005). Coalitions Across Borders: Transnational Protest and the Neoliberal Order. Lanham, MD, Rowman and Littlefield.

Barbone, C. (2004). *Stop Stansted!* Post White Paper Airport Watch Conference, London School of Economics.

Barcena, I. and P. Ibarra (2001). 'The ecologist movement in the Basque Country'. In K. Eder and M. Kousis (eds) *Environmental Politics in Southern Europe*. Kluwer, Dordrecht: 175–96.

Barkan, S. E. (1986). 'Interorganisational conflict in the southern civil rights movement'. *Sociological Inquiry* 56(2): 109–209.

Barker, C. (2000). Cultural Studies: Theory and Practice. London, Sage.

Barman, E. A. (2002). 'Asserting difference: The strategic response of nonprofit organizations to competition'. *Social Forces* 80(4): 1191–222.

Barvoso-Carter, E. (2001). 'Multiple identity and coalition building: How identity differences within us allow radical differences among us'. In J. M. Bystydzienski and S. P. Schacht (eds) *Forging Radical Alliance Across Difference*. London, Rowman and Littlefield: 21–34.

Bashevkin, S. (1996). 'Tough times in review: The British women's movement during the Thatcher years'. *Comparative Political Studies* 28: 525–52.

Bennett, A. (1999). 'Subcultures or neo-tribes? Rethinking the relationship bewteen youth, style and musical taste'. *Sociology* 33(3): 599–617.

Biessinger, M. (2011). 'Mechanisms of Maidan: The structure of contingency in the making of the Orange Revolution'. *Mobilization* 16(1): 25–43.

Biliouri, D. (1999). 'Environmental NGOs in Brussels: How powerful are their lobbying activities?' *Environmental Politics* 8(2): 173–82.

Blumer, H. (1986). *Symbolic Interactionism*. Berkeley, University of California Press.

Bookchin, M. (1994). *Deep Ecology and Anarchism: A Polemic*. London, Freedom Press.

Borgatti, S. P., M. G. Everett and L. C. Freeman (1999). *UCINET 5.0*. Natick, Analytic Technologies.

Bosso, C. (1995). 'The colour of money: Environmental groups and the pathologies of fundraising'. In A. J. Cigler and B. A. Loomis (eds) *Interest Group Politics*. Washington, QC Press: 101–30.

— (2005). *Environment, Inc: From Grassroots to Beltway*. Lawrence, University Press of Kansas.

Boström, M. (2004). 'Cognitive practices and collective identities within a heterogeneous social movement: The Swedish environmental movement'. *Social Movement Studies* 3(1): 73–88.

Boudreau, V. (1996). 'Northern theory, Southern protest: Opportunity structure analysis in cross-national perspective'. *Mobilization* 1(2): 175–89.

Brand, K. W. (1990). 'Cyclical aspects of new social movements: Waves of cultural criticism and mobilization cycles of new middle class radicalism'. In R. J. Dalton and M. Kuechler (eds) *Challenging the Political Order*. Cambridge, Polity: 23–42.

Brower, D. (1990). 'Foreword'. In R. Scarce (ed.) *Understanding the Radical Environmental Movement*. Chicago, Nobel Press.

Brown, M. and J. May (1991). *The Greenpeace Story, Greenpeace Books*. New York, Dorling Kindersley.

Bryant, B. (1996) *Twyford Down, Roads, Campaigning and Environmental Law*. London: E. and F.N. Spon: 297–309.

Buechler, S. M. (2004). 'The strange career of strain and breakdown theories of collective action'. In D. A. Snow, S. A. Soule and H. Kriesi (eds) *The Blackwell Companion to Social Movements*. Oxford, Blackwell: 47–66.

Bullard, R. (1990). *Dumping in Dixie: Race, Class and Environmental Quality*. Boulder, CO, Westview Press.

Bunge, M. (1997). 'Mechanisms and explanation'. *Philosophy of the Social Sciences* 27(4): 410–65.

— (2004). 'How does it work? The search for exploratory mechanisms'. *Philosophy of the Social Sciences* 34(2): 182–210.

Burstein, P. and A. Linton (2002). 'The impact of political parties, interest groups, and social movement organisations on public policy: Some recent evidence and theoretical concerns'. *Social Forces* 81(2): 380–408.

Burstein, P., R. L. Einwohner and J. A. Hollander (1995). 'The success of political movements: A bargaining perspective'. In J. C. Jenkins and B. Klandermans (eds) *The Politics of Social Protest: Comparative Perspectives on States and Social Movements*. London, UCL Press: 275–96.

Byrne, P. (1997). *Social Movements in Britain*. London, Routledge.

Bystydzienski, J. M. and S. P. Schacht (2001). *Forging Radical Alliances Across Difference: Coalition Politics for a New Millenium*. London, Rowman and Littlefield.

Calhoun, C. (1994). *Social Theory and the Politics of Identity*. Oxford, Blackwell.

Carmin, J. and D. B. Balser (2002). 'Selecting repertoires of action in environmental movement organizations: An interpretive approach'. *Organization and Environment* 15(4): 365–88.

Carson, R. (1962). *Silent Spring*. Boston, Houghton Mifflin.

Carter, N. (2001). *The Politics of the Environment: Ideas, Activism, Policy*. Cambridge, Cambridge University Press.

Castells, M. (1997). *The Power of Identity: Volume II of the Information Age, Economy, Culture and Society*. Oxford, Blackwell.

Cathles, G. (2000). 'Friends and allies: The role of local campaign groups'. In B. Seel, M. Paterson and B. Doherty (eds) *Direct Action in British Environmentalism*. London, Routledge: 167–82.

Catton, W. R. and R. E. Dunlap (1978). 'Environmental sociology-New paradigm'. *American Sociologist* 13(1): 41–9.

— (1980). 'A new ecological paradigm for post-exuberant sociology'. *American Behavioral Scientist* 24(1): 15–47.

Christoff, P. (2008). 'The Bali roadmap: Climate change, COP 13 and beyond'. *Environmental Politics* 17(3): 466–72.

Clapp, B. W. (1994). *An Environmental History of Britain since the Industrial Revolution*. London; New York, Longman.

Clark, A. (2004). 'Campaigners challenge airports plan'. *The Guardian* 8 March 2004. Available at http://www.guardian.co.uk/uk/2004/mar/08/environment.transport, last accessed 17 September 2009.

Clark, W. (1990). *Activism in the Public Sphere: Exploring the Discourse of Political Participation*. London, Ashgate.

Cohen, J. (1983). 'Rethinking social movements'. *Berkeley Journal of Sociology* XXVIII: 97–113.

Connelly, J., G. Smith, D. Benson and C. Saunders (2012). *Politics and the Environment: From Theory to Practice. Third Edition*. London, Routledge.

Corrigal Brown, C. and D. S. Meyer (2010). 'The pre-history of a coalition: The role of social ties in win without war'. In N. Van Dyke and H. J. McCammon (eds) *Strategic Alliances: Coalition Building and Social Movements*. Minnesota, University of Minnesota Press: 3–21.

Cotgrove, S. and A. Duff (1980). 'Environmentalism, middle-class radicalism and politics'. *The Sociological Review* 28(2): 333–51.

Coxall, W. N. (2001). *Pressure Groups in British Politics*. London, Longman.

CPRE (1993). *Sense and Sustainability: Land Use Planning and Environmentally Sustainable Development*. London, CPRE.

— (2000). *70 Years of Achievement*. London, CPRE.

— (2003a). *Transport, Policy Position Statement*. London, CPRE.

— (2003b). *New Roads and Bypasses, Policy Position Statement*. London, CPRE.

— (2003c). *Energy, Policy Position Statement*. London, CPRE.

— (2003d). *Expanding Airports Destroy the Countryside*. London, CPRE.

— (2003e). *The Future Development of Air Transport in the United Kingdom, A Submission by CPRE*. London, CPRE.

Cress, D. M. and D. A. Snow (1996). 'Mobilization at the margins: Resources, benefactors, and the viability of homeless social movement organizations'. *American Sociological Review* 61(6): 1089–109.

Crook, S., J. Pakulski, and M. Waters (1992). *Postmodernism: Changes in Advanced Society*. London, Sage.

Crossley, N. (2002). *Making Sense of Social Movements*. Buckingham; Philadelphia, Open University Press.

— (2003). 'Even newer social movements? Anti-corporate protests, capitalist crises and the remaking of society'. *Organization* 10(2): 287–305.

— (2007). *Contesting Psychiatry: Social Movements in Mental Health*. London: Routledge.

Crow, G. (2002). *Social Solidarities: Theories, Identities and Social Change*. Buckingham, Open University Press.

Cultures of Persistence (2000). *Cultures of Resistance: Cultures of Resistance*. London, The Book Factory.

Dale, S. (1996). McLuhan's Children: The Greenpeace Message and the Media. Ontario, Canada, Between the Lines.

Dalton, R. J. (1994). *The Green Rainbow: Environmental Groups in Western Europe*. New Haven CT, Yale University Press.

— (1996) *Citizen Politics*, London: Chatham house

Dalton, R, J., M. Kuechler and W. Burklin (1990). 'The challenge of new movements'. In R. J. Dalton and M. Kuechler (eds) *Challenging the Political Order*. Cambridge, Polity Press: 3–20.

Darden, L. (2002). 'Strategies for discovering mechanisms: Schema instantiation, modular subassembly, forward/backward chaining'. *Philosophy of Science* 69(S3): 354–65.

Davies, J. (1969). 'The J-curve of rising and declining satisfactions as cause of some great revolutions and a contained rebellion'. In H. D. Graham and T. R. Gurr (eds) *Violence in America*. New York, Praeger: 690–730.

della Porta, D. (1995). *Social Movements, Political Violence and the State*. Cambridge, Cambridge University Press.

— (2005). 'Making the polis: Social forms and democracy in the global justice movement'. *Mobilization* 10(1): 73–94.

— (ed) (2007). The Global Justice Movement: Cross-National and Transnational Perspectives. Boulder, Paradigm Press.

della Porta, D. and M. Diani (1999). *Social Movements: An Introduction*. London, Blackwell.

della Porta, D. and O. Fillieule (2004). 'Policing social protest'. In D. A. Snow, S. Soule and H. P. Kreisi (eds) *The Blackwell Companion to Social Movements*. London, Blackwell: 217–41.

della Porta, D. and Rucht, D. (2002). 'The dynamics of environmental campaigns'. *Mobilization* 7(1): 1–14.

Department for Transport (2003). *The Future of Aviation, White Paper*. London, Department for Transport.

Department for Transport Environment and Regions (2000). *Ten Year Transport Plan*. London, Department for Transport.

Department of Energy and Climate Change (2011). *The Carbon Plan: Delivering our Low Carbon Future*. London, Department of Energy and Climate Change.

Department of Environment Transport and the Regions (2000). *Southeast and East of England Regionlal Air Service Study*. London, DETR.

DeShallit, A. (2001). 'Ten Commandments of how to fail in an environmental campaign'. *Environmental Politics* 10(1): 111–37.

Devall, B. (1991). 'Deep ecology and radical environmentalism'. *Society and Natural Resources* 4: 247–58.

Devall, B. and G. Sessions (1985). *Deep Ecology, Living as Nature Intended*. Salt Lake City, Gibbs Smith.

Diani, M. (1992a). 'The concept of social movement'. *Sociological Review* 40(1): 1–25.

— (1992b). 'Analysing social movement networks'. In M. Diani and R. Eyerman (eds) *Studying Collective Action*. London, Sage: 107–35.

— (1995). *Green Networks: A Structural Analysis of the Italian Environmental Movement*. Edinburgh, Edinburgh University Press.

— (2003). 'Networks and social movements: A research programme'. In M. Diani and D. McAdam (eds) *Social Movements and Networks: Relational Approaches to Collective Action*. Oxford, Oxford University Press: 299–319.

Diani, M. and I. Bison (2004). 'Organizations, coalitions and movements'. *Theory and Society* 33(3–4): 281–309.

Diani, M. and P. R. Donati (1999). 'Organisational change in West European environmental groups: A framework for analysis'. In C. Rootes (ed) *Environmental Movements: Local, National and Global*. London, Frank Cass: 13–34.

Diani, M. and R. Eyerman (1992). 'The study of collective action: Introductory remarks'. In M. Diani and R. Eyerman (eds) *Studying Collective Action*. London, Sage: 1–21.

Diani, M. and E. Rambaldo (2007). 'Still the time of environmental movements? A local perspective'. *Environmental Politics* 16(5): 765–84.

Dimitrov, R. S. (2010). 'Inside UN climate negotiations: The Copenhagen Conference'. *Review of Policy Research* 27(6): 795–821.

Dobson, A. (1990). *Green Political Thought*. London, Routledge.

Doherty, B. (1998). 'Opposition to road building'. *Parliamentary Affairs* 51(3): 371–85.

— (1999). 'Paving the way: The rise of direct action against road-building and the changing character of british environmentalism'. *Political Studies* XLVII: 275–91.

— (2000). 'Manufactured vulnerability: Protest camp tactics'. In B. Seel, M. Paterson and B. Doherty (eds) *Direct Action in British Environmentalism*. London, Routledge: 62–78.

— (2002). *Ideas and Actions in the Green Movement*. London, Routledge.

Doherty, B., A. Plows and D. Wall (2007). 'Environmental direct action in Manchester, Oxford and North Wales: A protest event analysis'. *Environmental Politics* 16(5): 805–25.

Dowie, H. (1996). *Losing Ground: American Environmentalism at the Close of the Twentieth Century.* Cambridge, MIT Press.

Downey, G. L. (1986). 'Ideology and the clamshell identity: Organizational dilemmas in the anti-nuclear power movement'. *Social Problems* 33(5): 357–73.

Doyle, T. and A. Kellow (2006). *Environmental Politics and Policy-making in Australia*. Melbourne, MacMillan.

Doyle, T. and D. McEachern (1998). *Environment and Politics*. London, Routledge.

Dryzek, J. S., D. Downes, C. Hunold, D. Scholsberg and H. Hernes (2003). *Green States and Social Movements: Environmentalism in the United States, United Kingdon, Germany and Norway.* Oxford, Oxford University Press.

Durkheim, E. (1984). *The Division of Labour in Society*. New York, The Free Press.

Dwyer, J. and I. Hodge (1996). Countryside in Trust: Land Management by Conservation, Recreation and Amenity Organisations. Basingstoke, Wiley Blackwell.

Edwards, B. and J. D. McCarthy (2004). 'Resources and social movement mobilization'. In D. A. Snow, S. Soule and H. Kriesi (eds) *The Blackwell Companion to Social Movements*. London, Blackwell: 116–52.

Edwards, G. (2004). 'Habermas and social movements: What's 'new'?' *The Sociological Review* 52(s1): 113–30.

— (2007). 'Habermas, activism and acquiescence: Reactions to "colonization" in UK trade unions'. *Social Movement Studies* 6(2): 111–30.

Ehrlich, P. (1968). *The Population Time Bomb*. New York, Ballantine.

Eisinger, P. (1973). 'The conditions of protest behaviour in American cities'. *American Political Science Review* 81: 11–28.

Elster, J. (2002). Explaining Social Behaviour: More Nuts and Bolts for the Social Sciences. Cambridge, Cambridge University Press.

Environment Council (1999). *Who's Who in the Environment*. London, Environment Council.

Environmental Direct Action Group (2003). 'Why Kyoto is Pants'. Group leaflet.

Epstein, B. (2001). 'Anarchism and the Anti-Globalisation Movement'. *Monthly Review* 53(4): 1–14.

Eyerman, R. and A. Jamison (1991). *Social Movements: A Cognitive Approach*. London, Polity.

Falletti, T. G. and J. Lynch (2009). 'Context and causal mechanisms in political analysis'. *Comparative Political Studies* 42(9): 1143–66.

Ferree, M. M. and F. Miller (1985). 'Towards integration of social-psychological and resource perspective on social movements'. *Sociological Inquiry* 55(1): 38–61.

Ferree, M. M. and S. Roth (1998). 'Gender, class, and the interaction between social movements: A strike of West Berlin day care workers'. *Gender and Society* 12(6): 626–48.

Fillieule, O. (2002). 'Local environmental politics in France: The case of the Louron valley, 1884–1996'. *French Politics* 1: 1–26.

Fireman, B. and W. A. Gamson (1979). 'Utilitarian logic in the resource mobilization perspective'. In M. Zald and J. D. McCarthy (eds) *The Dynamics of Social Movements: Resource Mobilization, Social Control and Tactics*. Cambridge, MA, Winthrop: 8–44.

Flacks, R. (2003). 'Review of The dynamics of contention'. *Social Movement Studies* 2(1): 103–9.

Flesher Fominaya, C. (2010a). 'Creating cohesion from diversity: The challenge of collective identity formation in the global justice movement'. *Sociological Inquiry* 80(3): 377–404.

— (2010b). 'Collective identity in social movements: Central concepts and debates'. *Sociology Compass* 4(6): 393–404.

Forder, J. E. (1996). 'Can campaigning be evaluated'. *Non Profit and Voluntary Sector Quarterly* 25(2): 225–47.

Foss, D. A. and R. W. Larkin (1986). *Beyond Revolution: A New Theory of Social Movements*. Westport, Connecticut, Bergin and Garvey.

Freeman, J. (1972). 'The tyranny of structurelessness'. In A. Koedt, E. Levine and A. Rapone (eds) *Radical Feminism*. New York, Quadrangle.

Freeman, L. C. (1979). 'Centrality in social networks: Conceptual clarification'. *Social Networks* 1: 215–239.

Friends of the Earth (2002a). *Campaigners Unite to Oppose Planning Reforms*. Press Release, London, Friends of the Earth.

— (2002b). *Strategic Plan 2003–2008*. London, Friends of the Earth.
— (2002c). *Partnership Agreement*. London, Friends of the Earth.
— (2002d). *Help stop BP's Baku Ceyhan pipeline*. London, Friends of the Earth.
— (2002e). Stop the UK funding climate change! Oppose UK support for the UK Baku Ceyhan Oil Pipeline. Friends of the Earth Majordomo list for local climate campaigners, 11 November.
— (2003a). *Carbon Dinosaurs, A Report Highlighting The Role Of Coal-Fired Power Stations In UK Climate And Energy Policy*. London, Friends of the Earth.
— (2003b). 'Baku pipeline update'. *Change Your World* Oct/Nov (43): 6.
— (2003c). *Climate Changing Pollution from Aircraft set to Soar, Friends of the Earth Press Release*. London, Friends of the Earth.
— (2003d). *Press Release: Airport Expansion will Wreck UK's Climate Change Targets*. London, Friends of the Earth.
— (2003e). 'Climate Action Plan'. *Friends of the Earth Strategy document,* London, Friends of the Earth.
— (2004). *Green Energy League Table*. London, Friends of the Earth.
Friends of the Earth International (2003). *Kyoto Agreement on Climate Change gets nearer*. Friends of the Earth Media Advisory London, Friends of the Earth.
Gaines, R. (2003). '21 years of the London wildlife trust'. *Wild London* Winter 2002–3: 8–9.
Gamson, W. (1975). *The Strategy of Social Protest*. London, Dorsey.
— (1990). *The Strategy of Social Protest: 2nd Edition*. Belmont, CA, Wadsworth.
Gerber, L. (2002). 'What is so bad about misanthropy?' *Environmental Ethics* 24(1): 41–55.
Gerlach, L. (1983). 'Movements of revolutionary change: Some structural characteristics'. In J. Freeman (ed.) *Social movements of the 1960s and 1970s*. London, Longman: 1363–147.
Gerring, J. (2007). 'Review article: The mechanismic worldview: Thinking inside the box'. *British Journal of Political Science* 38: 161–79.
— (2010). 'Causal mechanisms: Yes, but . . . ' *Comparative Political Studies* 43(11): 1499–526.
Glidewell, I., QC (2004). *Heathrow Terminal 4 Inquiry*. London, Department for Transport Environment and the Regions.
Goldstone, J. A. (2003). 'Bridging institutionalised and non-institutionalised politics'. In J. A. Goldstone (ed.) *States, Parties and Social Movements*. Cambridge, Cambridge University Press: 1–24.
Goodwin, J. and J. M. Jasper (1999) 'Caught in a winding, snarling vine: The structural bias of political process theory', *Sociological Forum*, 14(1): 27–54.
Goodwin, J. and J. M. Jasper (2004) *Rethinking Social Movements: Structure, Meaning and Emotion*. Oxford, Rowman and Littlefield.
Gordon, C. and J. Jasper (1996). 'Overcoming the 'NIMBY' label: Rhetorical and organizational links for protesters'. *Research in Social Movements Conflict and Change* 19: 159–81.
Gordon, M. (1994). 'Thames Gateway – sustainable development, or more of the same?' *Town & Country Planning* 63(12): 332–3.
Gould, R. (2000). 'Why do networks matter? Rationalist and structuralist approaches'. *Social Movement Analysis: The Network Approach Conference*. Ross Priory, Loch Lomond.
Graeber, D. (2009). *Direct Action: An Ethnography*. London, AK Press.
Granovetter, M. S. (1973). 'The strength of weak ties'. *American Journal of Sociology* 78(6): 1360–80.
Grant, H. (2003). 'Heathrow protest march'. *Hillingdon Times*. 13 June 2002.
Grant, W. (1995). *Pressure Groups, Politics and Democracy in Britain*. New York, Harvester Wheatsheaf.
Green, B. (1981). *Countryside Conservation*. London, George Allen and Unwin.
Greenpeace (2000). *Nature's bottom line: Climate Protection and the Carbon Logic*. London, Greenpeace.
— (2001). *Zero Waste Strategy*. London, Greenpeace.
— (2002a). *Exporting Pollution: Double Standards in UK Energy Exports*. London, Greenpeace.
— (2002b). *Exxon's Weapons of Mass Destruction: The Assessment of Greenpeace International*. London, Greenpeace.

Grove, R. (1990). 'The origins of environmentalism'. *Nature* 345: 11–14.

Grubb, M., C. Vrolijk and D. Brack (1999). *The Kyoto Protocol: A Guide and Assessment.* London, Earthscan.

Guenther, K. M. (2009). 'The politics of names: Rethinking the methodological and ethical significance of naming people, organizations and places'. *Qualitative Research* 9(4): 411–21.

Gurr, T. R. (1970). *Why Men Rebel.* New Jersey, Princeton University Press.

Habermas, J. (1981). 'New social movements'. *Telos* 49: 33–47.

— (1984). *Theory of Comunicative Action, Vol.1: Reason and the Rationalisation of Society.* Cambridge, Policy.

— (1987). *Theory of Communicative Action, Vol.2; System and Lifeworld.* Cambridge, Polity.

— (1992). *Post Metaphysical Thinking.* Cambridge, Polity.

Haenfler, R., B. Johnston, et al. (2012). 'Lifestyle movements: Exploring the intersection of lifestyle and social movements'. *Social Movement Studies* 11(1): 1–20.

Haines, H. H. (1988). *Black Radicals and the Civil Rights Mainstream 1954–1970.* Knoxville, University of Tennesee Press.

Halfacree, K. (1999). 'Anarchy doesn't work unless you think about it: Intellectual interpreation and DIY culture'. *Area* 31(3): 209–20.

Hannan, K. and J. Freeman (1977). 'The population ecology of organisations'. *American Journal of Sociology* 82: 929–64.

— (1989). *Organizational Ecology.* Cambridge, Cambridge University Press.

Hannigan, J. A. (1985). 'Alian Touraine, Manuel Castells, and social movement theory: A critical appraisal'. *The Sociological Quarterly* 26(4): 435–54.

— (1995). *Environmental Sociology: A Social Constructionist Perspective.* London, Routledge.

Hare, R. (1997). *The Carbon Logic.* London, Greenpeace.

Harper, T. (2010). 'Poor, disadvantaged? Pull the other one . . . The rich rioting students are unmasked'. Mail online. www.dailymail.co.uk/news/article-1329510/Poor-Disadvantaged-Pull – the-rich-rioting-students,html, last accessed 14 November 2011.

Hartley, S. (1997). *Working Together for Wildlife, Local Group Development in the London Wildlife Trust.* London, LWT.

Heany, M. T. and F. Rojas (2011). 'The partisan dynamics of contention: Demobilization in the antiwar movement in the U.S., 2007–2009'. *Mobilization* 16(1): 44–64.

Hebdige, D. (1979). 'Subculture and the meaning of society'. Reprinted in K. Gelder and S. Thornton (eds) (1997). *The Subculture Reader.* Routledge, London.

Heberle, R. (1951). *Social Movements: An Introduction to Political Science.* New York, Appleton Century.

Hechter, M. (1987). *Principles of Group Solidarity.* Berkeley, University of California Press.

Hedström, P. and R. Swedberg (1996). 'Social mechanisms'. *Acta Sociologica* 39: 281–308.

Hedström, P. and P. Ylikoski (2010). 'Causal mechanisms in the social sciences'. *Annual Review of Sociology* 36: 49–67.

Her Majesty The Queen (2006). 'Queen's speech'. www.publications.parliament.uk/pa/ld200607/ldhansrd/text/61115–0001.htm, last accessed 10 March 2012.

Hetherington, K. (1998). *Expressions of Identity.* London, Sage.

Horton, D. (2003). 'Green distinctions: The performance of identity among environmental activists'. *The Sociological Review* 51: 63–77.

— (2011). 'Environmentalism and the bicycle'. *Environmental Politics* 15(1): 41–58.

Hunt, S. A. and R. D. Benford (2004). 'Collective identity, solidarity and commitment'. In D. A. Sow, S. A. Soule and H. Kriesi (eds) *The Blackwell Companion to Social Movements.* Oxford, Wiley-Blackwell: 433–57.

Inglehart, R. (1971). 'The silent revolution in europe: Intergenerational change in post-industrial societies'. *American Political Science Review* 64(4): 991–1017.

— (1987). 'Generational replacement and the future of post-materialist values'. *The Journal of Politics* 49: 231–41.

— (1990). *Culture Shift in Advanced Industrial Society.* Princeton, NJ, Princeton University Press.

IPCC (2007). 'Summary for policymakers'. In S. Solomon, D. Qin, M. Manning, Z. Chen, M. Marquis, K. B. Averyt, M. Tignor and H. L. Miller (eds) *Climate Change 2007: The Physical Science Basis. Contribution of Working Group 1 to the Fourth Assessment Report of the Intergovernmental panel on Cilmate Change*. Cambridge, Cambridge University Press.

Ipsos MORI (1998). 'Political attitudes in Great Britain for April 1998' available at www.ipsos-mori. com/researchpublications/researcharchive/poll.aspx?oItemId=2099, last accessed 20 May 2012.

Jasper, J. M. (1997). *The Art of Moral Protest*. Chicago, University of Chicago Press.

— (2010). 'Social movement theory today: Toward a theory of action?' *Sociological Compass* 4(11): 965–76.

Jenkins, J. C. (1983). 'Resource mobilization theory & the study of social movements'. *Annual Review of Sociology* 9: 527–53.

— (1985). The Politics of Insurgency: The Farm Workers' Movement in the 1960s. Columbia, Columbia University Press.

Jenkins, R. (2008). *Social Identity. Third Edition*. Abingdon, Routledge.

Johnston, H., E. Laraña and J. R. Gusfield (1994). 'Identities, grievances and new social movements'. In E. Laraña, H. Johnston and J. R. Gusfield (eds) *New Social Movements: From Ideology to Identity*. Philadelphia, Temple University Press: 3–35.

Jordan, G. (1999). 'Politics without parties: A growing trend?' *Parliamentary Affairs* 51(3): 314–28.

Jordan, G. and W. Maloney (1997). *The Protest Business: Mobilizing Campaign Groups*. Manchester, Manchester University Press.

Jung, J. K. (2010). 'Disentangling protest cycles: An event-history analysis of new social movements in Western Europe'. *Mobilization* 15(1): 25–44.

Juniper, T. (2000). 'Supping with the devil'. *Earth Matters* June 2000: 34.

Juris, J. S. (2008). 'Performing politics: Image, embodiment and affective solidarity during anti-corporate globalization protests'. *Ethnography* 9(1): 61–97.

Kalberg, S. (1980). 'Max Weber's types of rationality: Cornerstones for the analysis of rationalization processes in history'. *American Journal of Sociology* 85(5): 1145–79.

Karapin, R. (2011). 'Opportunity/threat spirals in the U.S. women's suffrage and German anti-immigration movements'. *Mobilization* 16(1): 65–80.

Kempton, W., D. C. Holland, et al. (2001). 'Local environmental groups: A systematic enumeration in two geographical areas'. *Rural Sociology* 66(4): 557–78.

Kenward, T. (2002). Friends of the Earth's position on population control policies. Personal email, 24 November.

Killian, L. M. (1983). 'Review of Doug McAdam: Political process and the development of black insurgency, 1930–1970'. *Critical Mass Bulletin* 8(2): 1–5.

Kitschelt, H. (1986). 'Political opportunity structures and political protest: Anti-nuclear movements in four democracies'. *British Journal of Political Science* 16(1): 57–86

— (1991). 'Resource mobilization theory: A critique'. In D. Rucht (ed.) *Research on Social Movements: The State of the Art in Western Europe*. Frankfurt/M Boulder, Campus Verlag: 17–44.

Klandermans, B. (1987). 'Potentials, networks, motivations and barriers: Steps towards participation in social movements'. *Americal Sociological Review* 52(4): 519–31.

— (1994). 'Mobilization and participation: Social psychological explanations of resource mobilization theory'. *American Sociological Review* 49: 583–600.

— (2000). 'Must we redefine social movements as ideologically structured action?' *Mobilization* 5(1): 25–30.

Klandermans, B. and M. De Weerd (2000). 'Group identification and political process'. In S. Stryker, T. J. Owens and R. W. White (eds) *Self, Identity and Social Movements*. Minneapolis: University of Minnesota Press: 68–91.

Klandermans, B. and D. Oegma (1987) 'Potentials, networks, motivations and barriers: Steops towards participation in social movements, *American Sociological Review*, 52(4): 519–31.

Klandermans, B. and J. Smith (2002). 'Survey research: A case for comparative designs'. In B. Klandermans and S. Staggenborg (eds) *Methods of Social Movement Research*. Minneapolis, University of Minnesota Press: 3–31.

Klein, N. (2000). *No Logo*. London: Flamingo.

Knoke, D. (1990). *Political Networks: The Structural Perspective*. Cambridge, Cambridge University Press.

Kousis, M., D. della Porta and M. Jiménez (2008). 'Southern European environmental movements in comparative perspective'. *American Behavioral Scientist* 51(11): 1627–47.

Krissi, H. (1995). 'The political opportunity structure of new social movements'. In J. C. Jenkins and B. Klandermans (eds) *The Politics of Social Protest: Comparative Perspectives on States and Social Movements*. London, UCL Press: 167–98.

Kriesi, H., R. Koopmans, J. W. Duyvendak and M. G. Guigni (1995) *New Social Movements in Western European: A Comparative Analysis*, Minneapolis, University of Minnesota Press.

Kuumba, B. M. and F. Ajanuku (1998). 'Dreadlocks: The hair and aesthetics of cultural resistance and collective identity'. *Mobilization* 3(2): 227–43.

Lamb, R. (1996). *Promising the Earth*. London, Routledge.

Laraña, E. (1996). Convergence and continuties in theories on social movements. *2nd European Conference on Social Movements*. Vitoria: 2–6 October.

Laraña, E. and J. R. Gusfield (eds) (1992) *New Social Movements: From Ideology to Identity*, Philadelphia, Temple University Press.

Lash, S. and J. Urry (1987). *The End of Organized Capitalism*. Madison, University of Wisconsin.

Le Bon, G. (1969). *The Crowd: A Study of the Popular Mind*. Chicago, University of Chicago Press.

Lentin, A. (1999). 'Structure, strategy, sustainability: What future for new social movement theory?' *Sociological Research Online* 4(3): www.socresonline.org.uk/4/3/lentin.html, last accessed 17 September 2012.

Levitsky, S. R. (2008). 'Niche activism: Constructing a unified movement identity in a heterogenous organizational field'. *Mobilization* 12(3): 271–86.

Lhotka, L., C. Bailey, et al. (2008). 'Ideologically structured information exchange among environmental groups'. *Rural Sociology* 72(2): 230–49.

Lichbach, M. I. (2008). 'Modelling mechanisms of contention: MTT's positivist constructivism'. *Qualitative Sociology* 31: 345–54.

Lipsky, M. (1970). *Protest in City Politics*. Chicago, Rand-McNally.

Lofland, J. (1993). 'Theory-bashing and answer improving in the study of social movements'. *American Sociologist* 24: 37–58.

— (1996). *Social Movement Organisations: Guide to Research on Insurgent Realities*. New York, Aldine de Gruyter.

London Wildlife Trust (2002). 'Champion of wasteland'. *Wild London* Autumn 2002: 5.

Lowe, P. D. (1983). 'Values and Institutions in the History of British Nature Conservation', in Warren A & Goldsmith FB, *Conservation in Perspective*, London: John Wiley & Sons: 329–52.

Lowe, P. and J. Goyder (1983). *Environmental Groups in Politics*. London, George Allen and Unwin.

Lucas, C. (2002). Introducing the Airport Watch Conference. *Options, Alternatives and Opportunities for Campaigning*. Airport Watch Conference, City Hall, London.

Maffesoli, M. (1996). *The Time of the Tribes: The Decline of Individualism in Mass Society.* London, Sage.

Maguire, D. (1995). 'Opposition movements and opposition parties: Equal partners or dependent relations in the struggle for power and reform'. In J. C. Jenkins and B. Klandermans (eds) *The Politics of Social Protest: Comparative Perspectives on States and Social Movements*. London, UCL Press: 199–229.

Mahoney, J. (2001). 'Beyond correlational analysis: Recent Innovations in theory and method'. *Sociological Forum* 16(3): 575–93.

Marangudakis, M. (2001). 'Rationalism and irrationalism in the environmental movements: The case of Earth First!', *Democracy and Nature* 7(3): 457–67.

Martin, P. Y. (1990). 'Rethinking feminist organizations'. *Gender and Society* 4: 182–206.

Maynz, R. (2004). 'Mechanisms in the analysis of social macro-phenomena'. *Philosophy of the Social Sciences* 34: 237–58.

McAdam, D. (1982). *Political Process and the Development of Black Insurgency 1930–1970*. Chicago, Chicago University Press.

— (1989). 'The biographic consequences of activism'. *American Sociological Review* 54(5): 744–60.

— (2002). 'Beyond structural analysis: Towards a more dynamic understanding of social movements'. In M. Diani and D. McAdam (eds) *Social Movements and Networks: Relational Approaches to Collective Action*. Oxford, Oxford University Press: 281–98.

McAdam, D., J. D. McCarthy and M. Zald (1988). 'Social movements'. In N. J. Smelser (ed.) *Handbook of Sociology*. London, Sage: 695–793.

McAdam, D. and S. Tarrow (2010). 'Ballots and barricades: On the reciprocal relationship between elections and social movements'. *Perspectives on Politics* 8(2): 529–42.

— (2011). 'Introduction: *Dynamics of Contention* Ten years on'. *Mobilization* 16(1): 1–10.

McAdam, D., S. Tarrow and C. Tilly (2001). *The Dynamics of Contention*. Cambridge, Cambridge University Press.

— (2008). 'Methods for measuring mechanisms of contention'. *Qualitative Sociology* 31: 307–31.

McCammon, H. J. and K. E. Campbell (2002). 'Allies on the road to victory: Coalition formation between the suffragists and Woman's Christian Temperance Union'. *Mobilization* 7: 231–51.

McCarthy, J. D. and M. Zald (1977). 'Resource mobilization and social movements: A partial theory'. *American Journal of Sociology* 82(6): 1212–41.

McCormick, J. (1991). *British Politics and the Environment*. London, Earthscan.

McKay, G. (1998). *Party and Protest in Nineties Britain*. London, Verso.

McNaughten, P. and J. Urry (1998). *Contested Natures*. London, Sage.

McPhail, C. (1991). The Myth of the Maddening Crowd (Social Institutions and Social Change). New York, Walter de Gruyter.

Meadows, D. H., D. L. Meadows, J. Randers and W. W. Behrens III (1972). *Limits to Growth*. Bungay, Suffolk, Chaucer Press.

Medley, G. J. (1992). 'WWF UK creates a new mission'. *Long Range Planning* 25(2): 63–8.

Melucci, A. (1980). 'The new social movements: A theoretical approach'. *Social Science Information* 19(2): 199–226.

— (1984). 'An end to social movements? Introductory paper to the sessions on "New movements and change in organisational forms'." *Social Science Information* 23: 819–35.

— (1985). 'The symbolic challenge of contemporary movements'. *Social Research* 52(4): 789–816.

— (1989). *Nomads of the Present*. Philadelphia, Temple University Press.

— (1994). 'A strange kind of newness: What's "new" in new social movements?' In E. Laraña, H. Johnson and J. R. Gusfield (eds) *New Social Movements: From Ideology to Identity*. Philadelphia, Temple University Press, 101–30.

— (1995a). 'The new social movements revisited: Reflections on a sociological misunderstanding'. In L. Maheu (ed.) *Social Movements and Social Classes: The Future of Collective Action*. London, Sage: 107–19.

— (1995b). 'The process of collective identity'. In H. Johnston and B. Klandermans (eds) *Social Movements and Culture*. London, UCL Press: 41–63.

— (1996). *Challenging Codes: Collective Action in the Information Age*. Cambridge, Cambridge University Press.

Merton, R. (1968). *Social Theory and Social Structure*. New York, Free Press.

Meyer, D. (2004). 'Protest and political opportunities'. *Annual Review of Sociology* 30: 125–45.

Meyer, D. and S. Staggenborg (1996). 'Movements, countermovements, and the structure of political opportunity'. *American Journal of Sociology* 101(6): 1628–60.

Milton, K. (1996). *Environmentalism and Cultural Theory: Explaining the Role of Anthropology in Environmental Discourse*. London, Routledge.

Mische, A. (2003). 'Cross talk in movements: Reconceiving the culture-network link'. In M. Diani and D. McAdam (eds) *Social Movements and Networks: Relational Approaches to Collective Action*. Oxford, Oxford University Press: 25–280.

Mische. A. and Tilly, C. (2003). 'Interventions: dynamics of contention'. *Social Movement Studies* 2(1): 85–96.

Misztal, B. A. (1996). *Trust in Modern Societies*. Cambridge, Polity Press.

Monbiot, G. (2000). 'No way to run a revolution' available at www.monbiot.com/2000/05/10/no-way-to-run-a-revolution/, last accessed 21 May 2012.

Mooers, C. and A. Sears (2003). 'The new social movements and the withering away of state theory'. In W. K. Carrol (ed.) *Organizing Dissent: Contemporary Social Movements in Theory and Practice*. Toronto, Garamond Press: 52–6.

Moore, R. (2004). 'Postmodernism and punk subculture: Cultures of authenticity and deconstruction'. *The Communication Review* 7(3): 305–27.

Mueller, T. (2009). 'The movement is dead, long live the movement!' *Turbulence* 4 at http://turbulence.org.uk/turbulence-4/the-movement-is-dead-long-live-the-movement/, last accessed 20 May 2012.

Muggleton, D. (2000). *Inside Subculture: The Postmodern Meaning of Style*. Oxford, Berg.

Muttitt, G. and J. Marriot (2002). *Some Common Concerns: Imagining BP's Azerbaijan-Georgia-Turkey Pipelines System*, CEE Bankwatch, The Corner House, Friends of the Earth International, The Kurdish Human Rights Project, Platform.

Nash, K. (2002a). Contemporary Political Sociology: Globalization, Politics and Power. London, Wiley Blackwell.

— (2002b). 'A movement moves . . . Is there a women's movement in England today?' *European Journal of Women's Studies* 9(3): 311–28.

Nedelmann, B. (1984). 'New political movements and changes in processes of intermediation'. *Social Science Information* 23(6): 1029–48.

Neff Gurney, J. and K. J. Tierney (1982). 'Relative deprivation and social movements : A critical look at 20 years of theory and research'. *Sociological Quarterly* 23 (Winter): 33–47.

Norkus, K. (2005). 'Mechanisms as miracle makers: The rise and inconsistencies of the "mechanismic approach".' *History and Theory* 44(3): 348–72.

North, P. (1998). 'Save Our Solsbury! The anatomy of an anti-roads protest'. *Environmental Politics* 7(3): 1–25.

O'Riordan, T. (1981 [1976]). *Environmentalism*. London, Pion.

Oberschall, A. (1973). *Social Conflicts and Social Movements*. London, Prentice Hall.

Offe, C. (1985). 'New social movements: Challenging the boundaries of Institutional politics'. *Social Research* 52(4): 817–68.

Olson, M. (1965). *The Logic of Collective Action*. Cambridge, Harvard University Press.

Opp, K. (1989). *The Rationality of Protest*. Boulder CO, Westview Press.

— (2009). *Theories of Political Protest and Social Movements: A Multi-Disciplinary Introduction, Critique and Synthesis*. London, Routledge.

Osbourne, A. and S. Castle (2004). Russia may be ready to ratify Kyoto treaty on climate change. *Independent*. 24 April 2004.

Owens, T. J. and P. J. Aronson (2000) 'Self-concept as a force in social movement involvement', in S. Stryker, T. J. Owens and R. W. White (eds) *Self, Identity and Social Movements*, Minneapolis, University of Minnesota Press: 191–214.

Pakulski, J. (1991). *Social Movements: The Politics of Moral Protest*. Melbourne, Australia, Longman Cheshire.

Parisi, D., M. Taquino, et al. (2004). 'Civic responsibility and the environment: Linking local conditions to community environmental activeness'. *Society and Natural Resources* 17(2): 97–112.

Park, R. and E. Burgess (1924). *Introduction to the Science of Sociology*. Chicago, University of Chicago Press.

Passy, F. (2003). 'Social networks matter: But how?' In M. Diani and R. Eyerman (eds) *Social Movements and Networks: Relational Approaches to Collective Action*. Oxford, Oxford University Press: 21–48.

Pearce, F. (1991). *Green Warriors: The People and the Politics behind the Environmental Revolution*. Chatham, MacKays.

Pepper, D. (1983). *Eco-Socialism: From Deep Ecology to Social Justice*. London, Routledge.

— (1996). *Modern Environmentalism: An Introduction*. London, Routledge.

Perrow, C. (1973). *Complex Organizations: A Critical Essay*. New York, Random House.

Pharr, S. (1996). *In the Time of the Right: Reflections on Liberation*. Berkeley, California, Chardon Press.

Pickel, A. (2004). 'Systems and mechanisms: A symposium on Mario Bunge's Philosophy of social science'. *Philosophy of the Social Sciences* 34(2): 169–81.

Piven, F. F. and R. Cloward (1977). *Poor People's Movements: Why they Succeed, how they Fail*. New York, Panthean.

Platt, G. M. (2004). 'Review essay: Unifying social movement theories'. *Qualitative Sociology* 27(1): 107–16.

Plows, A. (2006). 'Blackwood 2004: An emerging (re)cycle of UK eco-action?' *Environmental Politics* 15(3): 474–84.

Polletta, F. and J. M. Jasper (2001). 'Collective identity and social movements'. *Annual Review of Sociology* 27: 283–305.

Poloni-Staudinger, L. (2009). 'Why cooperate? Cooperation among environmental groups in the United Kingdon, France and Germany'. *Mobilization* 14(3): 375–96.

Porritt, J. (1996). 'The Aftermath'. In B. Bryant (ed.) *Twyford Down, Roads, Campaigning and Environmental Law*. London, E. and F.N. Spon: 297–309.

— (1997). 'Environmental politics: The old and the new'. *The Political Quarterly* 68(B): 62–73.

Princen, T. (1994). *Environmental NGOs in World Politics*. London, Routledge.

Purdue, D., J. Durrschmidt, et al. (1997). 'DiY culture and extended milieux: LETS, veggie boxes and festivals'. *Sociological Review* 45(4): 645–67.

Purkiss, J. (2000). Modern millenarians? Anti-consumerism, anarchism and the new urban environmentalism. In B. Seel, M. Paterson and B. Doherty (eds) *Direct Action in British Environmentalism*. London, Routledge: 93–111.

Pursey, T. (2009). 'The Tyranny of the most committed: Hegemony within a counter-Hegemonic Movement'. Unpublished BA thesis, University of Kent.

Randall, C. (2008). *Environment*. London, Office for National Statistics.

Rawcliffe, P. (1998). *Environmental Pressure Groups in Transition*. Manchester, Manchester University Press.

Ray, L. (1993). *Rethinking Critical Theory: Emancipation in the Age of Global Social Movements*. London, Sage.

Raymond, V. (2002). 'A taste of what's to come: Campaigners against airport's third runway turn up the volume'. *The Hounslow Chronicle* 31 October 2002.

Reimann, K. D. (2001). 'Building networks from the outside in: International movements, Japanese NGOs and the Kyoto climate change conference'. *Mobilization* 6(1): 69–82.

Reinelt, C. (1995). 'Moving onto the terrain of the state: The battered women's movement and the politics of engagement'. In M. Marx Feree and P. Yancey Martin (eds) *Feminist Organizations: Harvest of the New Women's Movement*. Philadelphia, Temple University Press: 84–103.

Rising Tide (2000a). *Den Haag 2000: Activist Information Book*. Oxford, Rising Tide.

— (2000b). 'UN Climate climate conference collapsed'. *Climate Update* COP6, Hague, November 2002.

— (2000c). *COP This! Rising Tide Information Sheet*. Oxford, Rising Tide.

Robinson, A. (1999). 'From NIMBY to NOPE: Building eco-bridges'. *Contemporary Politics* 5(4): 339–64.

Rochon, T. R. (1990). 'The West European peae movement and the theory of new social movements'. In R. J. Dalton and M. Kuechler (eds) *Challenging the Political Order*. Cambridge, Polity Press: 105–21.

Rohrschneider, R. (1990). 'The roots of public opinion toward new social movements: An empirical test of competing explanations'. *American Journal of Political Science* 34(1): 1–30.

Rootes, C. (1992). 'The new politics of new social movements: Accounting for British Exceptionalism'. *European Journal of Political Research* 22(2): 179–91.

— (1997a). 'Shaping collective action: Structure, contingency and knowledge'. In R. Edmondson (ed.) *The Political Context of Collective Action: Power, Argumentation and the State*. London, Routledge: 81–94.

— (1997b). 'Environmental movements and green parties in Western and Eastern Europe'. In M. Redclift and G. Woodgate (eds) *The International Handbook of Environmental Sociology*. Cheltenham, MA Edward Elgar: 319–47.

— (1998). 'Political opportunity structures: Promise, problems and prospects'. *La Lettre de la Maison Française* 10, Michaelmas-Hilary: 75–97.

— (1999). 'Acting globally, thinking locally? Propects for a global environmental movement'. *Environmental Politics* 8(1): 290–308.

— (2000). 'Environmental protest in Britain 1988–1997'. In B. Seel, M. Paterson and B. Doherty (eds) *Direct Action in British Environmentalism*. London, Routledge: 24–61.

— (2002). 'Britain'. *The Transformation of Environmental Activism: Final Report* EC Environment and Climate Research Programme (1994–1998): 9–50.

— (2003a). 'Why do some campaigns against waste facilities suceed where others fail?' In C. Ludwig, S. Hellweg and S. Stucki (eds) *Municipal Solid Waste Management: Strategies and Technologies for Sustainable Solutions*. Berlin, Heidelberg and New York: Springer: 425–45.

— (2003b). 'The resurgence of protest and the revitalisation of British democracy'. In P. Ibarra (ed.). *Social Movements and Democracy*. New York, Palgrave MacMillan: 137–68.

— (2006). 'Facing South: British environmental organizations and the challenge of globalization'. *Environmental Politics* 15(5): 768–86.

— (2007). 'Britain'. In C. Rootes (ed.) *Environmental protest in Western Europe*. Cambridge, Cambridge University Press.

— (ed.) (2007). *Environmental Protest in Western Europe*. Cambridge, Cambridge University Press.

Rootes, C., D. Adams and C. Saunders (2001). Local environmental activism in England: Environmental activism in Southeast London and East Kent Compared. *ECPR Joint Sessions*. Grenoble.

Rootes, C. and A. Miller (2000). The British environmental movement: Organisational field and network of organisations. *ECPR Joint Sessions*. Copenhagen.

Rootes, C. and C. Saunders (2007). 'The global justice movement in Great Britain'. In della Porta, Donatella (ed.) *The Global Justice Movement: Cross-national and Transnational Perspectives*. Boulder, US, Paradigm Press: 128–56.

Rose, F. (2000). *Coalitions across the Class Divide: Lessons from the Labor, Peace and Environmental Movements*. Ithaca, Cornell University Press.

Rosenthal, N., M, Fingrutd, M. Ethier, R. Karant and D. McDonald (1985). 'A case study of 19th Century women's reform in New York State: Social movements and network analysis'. *American Journal of Sociology* 90(5): 1022–54.

Roth, S. (2003). *Building Movement Bridges: The Coalition of Labor Union Women*. London, Praeger.

Rucht, D. (1988). 'Themes, logics and arenas of social movements: A structural approach'. In B. Klandermans, H. Kriesi and S. Tarrow (eds) *International Social Movement Research Volume 1: From Structure to Action: Comparing Social Movement Research Across Cultures*. Greenwich, CT and London, JAI Press.

Rucht, D. (1990). 'The strategies and action repertoires of new movements'. In R. J. Dalton and M. Kuechler (eds) *Challenging the Political Order*. London, Polity Press: 156–75.

— (1995). 'Ecological protest as calculated law-breaking: Greenpeace and Earth First! in comparative perspective'. In W. Rudig (ed.) *Green Politics Three*. Edinburgh, Edinburgh University Press: 66–89.

Rucht, D. and J. Roose (2007). 'Germany'. In C. Rootes (ed.) *Environmental Protest in Western Europe*. Cambridge, Cambridge University Press: 80–108.

Rupp, L. J. (1994). 'Constructing internationalism: The case of transnational women's organizations, 1888–1945'. *American Historical Review*, 99: 53–65.

— (2011). 'The persistence of transnational organizing: The case of the homophile movement'. *The American Historical Review* 116(4): 1014–39.

Sachs, W. (1991). 'Environment and development: The story of a dangerous liaison'. *The Ecologist* 21(6): 252–7.

Saunders, C. (2000). *Environmenatl Pressure Groups: Lessons Learned and Future Prospects*. Unpublished MSc thesis, University of Southampton.

— (2003). *A Clear Cut Case of Blurred Boundaries: The Problem of Delineating the British Environmental Movement*. The Ninth International Conference on Alternative Futures and Popular Protest, Manchester Metropolitan University.

— (2007a). 'Using social network analysis to explore social movements: A relational approach'. *Social Movement Studies* 6(3): 227–43.

—(2007b). 'The local and the national: relationships between national and local environmental organisations in London'. *Environmental Politics* 16(5): 742–64.

— (2007c). 'Comparing environmental movements in periods of latency and visibility'. *Graduate Journal of Social Science* 4(1): 109–39.

— (2008). 'Double-edged swords: Collective identity and solidarity in the environment movement'. *British Journal of Sociology* 59(2): 227–53.

— (2009a). 'It's not just structural: Social movements are not homogenous responses to structural features, but networks shaped by organisational strategy and status'. *Sociological Research Online* 14(1)4: www.socresonline.org.uk/14/1/4.html, last accessed 19 September 2012.

— (2009b). 'Organizational size and democratic practices: Can large be beautiful?' In D. della Porta (ed.) *Democracy in Social Movements*. Basingstoke, Palgrave McMillan.

— (2011). 'Unblocking the pathway to effective use of blockmodels in social movement research'. *Mobilization* 16(3): 283–302.

— (2012). 'Reformism and radicalism in the climate camp in Britain: Benign co-existence, tensions and prospects for bridging'. *Environmental Politics*, 21(5): 829–46.

Saunders, C. and M. Andretta (2009). The organizational dimension: The effect of formality, voice and influence on mobilization and participation in the global justice movement. In D. della. Porta (ed.) *Another Europe: Conceptions and Practices of Democracy in the European Social Forums*. Abingdon, Routledge: 128–48.

Saunders, C. and S. Price (2009). 'One person's eu-topia, another's hell: Climate Camp as a heterotopia'. *Environmental Politics* 16(5): 117–22.

Scarce, R. (1990). *Eco-Warriors: Understanding the Radical Environmental Movement*. Chicago: Noble.

Schattschneider, E. E. (1960). *The Semi-Sovereign People: A Realist's View of Democracy in America*. New York, Hold, Rinehart and Winston.

Scholsberg, D. (1999). 'Networks and mobile arrangements: Organisational innovation in the US environmental justice movement'. In C. Rootes (ed.) *Environmental Movements: Local, Global and National*. London, Frank Cass: 122–48.

Scott, A. (1990). *Ideology and New Social Movements*. London, Unwin Hyman.

Seel, B. (1997). 'Strategies of resistance at the Pollok free state road protest camp'. *Environmental Politics* 6(4): 108–39.

— (2000). 'Organisational Profile: Friends of the Earth England Wales and Northern Ireland'. Unpublished Transformation of Environmental Activism project material, University of Kent.

Seel, B., M. Paterson, et al. (2000). *Direct action in British Environmentalism*. London, Routledge.

Seel, B. and Plows. A. (2000). 'Coming live and direct: Strategies of Earth First!' In B. Seel, M. Paterson and B. Doherty (eds) *Direct Action in British Environmentalism*. London, Routledge: 112–32.

Sennett, R. (1998). *The Corrosion of Character: The Personal Consequences of Work in the New Capitalism*. London, Norton.

Shemtov, R. (2003). 'Social networks and sustained activism in local NIMBY campaigns'. *Sociological Forum* 18(2): 215–44.

Scholsberg, D. (199). 'Networks and mobile arrangements: Organizational innovation in the U.S. environmental justice movement'. *Environmental Politics*, 6(1): 122–48.

Sharp, P. (2003), T5 Court Support, *Hillingdon Times*, 23 October 2003.

Simon, H. A. (1991). 'Bounded rationality and organizational learning'. *Organization Science* 2(1): 124–34.

Smelser, N. J. (1962). *Theory of Collective Behaviour*. London, Routledge.

Snow, D. A. (2004). 'Framing processes, ideology and discursive fields'. In D. A. Snow, S. A. Soule and H. Kriesi (eds) *The Blackwell Companion to Social Movements*. Oxford, Blackwell: 380–412.

Snow, D. A. and R. D. Benford (1988). 'Master frames and cycles of protest'. In A. Morris and C. McClurg (eds) *Frontiers in Social Movement Theory*. New Haven, Yale University Press: 133–55.

Snow, D. A. and D. McAdam (2000). 'Identity work processes in the context of social movements: clarifying the identity/movement nexus'. In D. A. Snow, S. A. Soule and H. P. Kriesi (eds) *The Blackwell Companion to Social Movements*. Basingstoke, Wiley-Blackwell: 41–64.

Snow, D. A. and P. Oliver (1995). 'Social movements and collective behaviour: Social psychological dimensions'. In K. S. Cook, G. A. Fine and J. S. House (eds) *Sociological Perspectives in Social Psychology*. Boston, Allyn and Bacon: 571–600.

Snow, D. A., S. A. Soule and H. P. Kriesi (2007). *The Blackwell Companion to Social Movements*. Basingstoke, Wiley-Blackwell.

Snow, D.A. and S. A. Soule (2010). *A Primer on Social Movements*. London, W.W. Norton.

Spalter-Roth R. and R. Schreiber (1995). 'Outsider issues and insider tactics: Strategic tensions in the women's policy network during the 1980s'. In M. M. Ferree and P. Y. Martin (eds) *Feminist Organizations: Harvest of the New Women's Movement.* Philadelphia, Temple University Press: 105–27.

Staggenborg, Suzanne (2010). *Social Movements*. Oxford, Oxford University Press.

Starr, A. (2000) Naming the Enemy: Anti-Corporate Movements Confront Globalization. New York, St Martin's Press.

Stewart, J. (2004). Campaign Opportunities Post White Paper. *Airport Watch post White Paper conference*. London.

Stewart J. D. (1958). *British Pressure Groups*. Oxford, Clarendon Press.

Stop Esso (2001). *The Case against Esso: Stop Esso Briefing*. London, Stop Esso.

Storr, M. (2002). 'Sociology and social movements: Theories analyses and ethical dilemmas'. In P. Hamilton and K. Thompson (eds) *The Uses of Sociology*. Buckingham, Open University Press: 156–69.

Strobel, M. (1995). 'Organizational learning in the Chicago Women's Liberation Union'. In M. M. Ferree and P. Y. Martin (eds) *Feminist Organizations: Harvest of the New Women's Movement*. Philadelphia, Temple University Press: 145–64.

Suh, D. (2001). 'How do political opportunities matter for social movements?' *Sociological Quarterly* 42(3): 437–60.

Szerszynsky, B. (2002). 'Ecological rites: Ritual action in environmental protest events'. *Theory, Culture and Society* 19(3): 51–69.

Tarrow, S. (1998). *Power in Movement: Social Movements and Contentious Politics*. Cambridge, Cambridge University Press.

Taylor, V. (1989). 'Social movement continuity: The women's movement in abeyance'. *American Sociological Review* 54: 761–75.

— (1995). 'Watching for the vibes: Bringing emotions into the study of feminist organizations'. In M. M. Ferree and P. Y. Martin (eds) *Feminist Organizations: Harvest of the New Women's Movement*. Philadelphia, Temple University Press: 223–33.

Taylor, V. and Whittier, N. W. (1992). 'Collective identity in social movement communities: Lesbian and feminist mobilizations'. In A. D. Morris and C. McClurg Muller (eds) *Frontiers in Social Movement Theory*. New Haven CT, Yale University Press: 104–29.

Thornton, S. (1995). Club Cultures: Music, Media and Subcultural Capital. Cambridge, Polity Press.

Tilly, C. (1985). 'Models and realities of popular collective action'. *Social Research* 52(4): 717–47.

— (2001). 'Mechanisms in political processes'. *Annual Review of Political Science* 2001(4): 21–41.

Tilly, C. and S. G. Tarrow (2007). *Contentious Politics*. Boulder, Paradigm.

Todeva, E. and D. Knoke (2002). 'Strategic alliances and corporate social capital'. In J. Allmendinger and J. Hinz (eds) *Sociology of Organizations*. Westdeutscher, Verlag: 345–80.

Touraine, A. (1981). *The Voice and the Eye: An Analysis of Social Movements*. Cambridge, Cambridge University Press.

— (1984). *Return of the Actor: Social Theory in Post-Industrial Society*. Minneapolis, University of Minnesota Press.

Traugott, M. (1978). 'Reconceiving social movements'. *Social Problems* 26(1): 38–49.

Tucker, K. H. Jr. (1989). 'Ideology and social movements: The contributions of Habermas'. *Sociological Inquiry* 59(1): 30–47.

— (1981). 'How new are the new social movements?' *Theory Culture and Society* 8(2): 75–98.

Turner, R. H. (1981). 'Collective behaviour and resource mobilization as approaches to social movements: Issues and continuities'. *Research in Social Movements Conflict and Change* 4: 1–26.

Turner, R. H. and L. M. Killian (1957). *Collective Behaviour*. New York, Prentice Hall.

Van Der Heijden, H. (1999). 'Environmental movements, ecological modernisation and political opportunity structures'. *Environmental Politics* 8(1): 199–221.

— (2006). 'Globalization, environmental movements, and international political opportunity structures'. *Organization and Environment* 19(1): 28–45.

Van Dyke, N. and H. J. McCammon (2010). *Strategic Alliances: Coalition Building and Social Movements*. Minnesota, University of Minnesota.

Wall, D. (1999a). *Earth First! and the Anti-roads Movement: Radical Environmentalism and Compartative Social Movements*. London, Routledge.

— (1999b). 'Mobilising EF! in Britain'. *Environmental Politics* 8(1): 81–100.

Wall, D. (2000). 'Snowballs, elves and skimmingtons? Genealogies of environmental direct action'. In B. Seel, M. Paterson and B. Doherty (eds) *Direct Action in British Environmentalism*. London, Routledge: 79–92.

Walls, J. (2002). 'The Campaign Against "Live Exports" In the UK: Animal protectionism, the stigmatisation of place and the language of moral outrage'. *Sociological Research Online* 7(1) <www.socresonline.org.uk/7/1/walls.html>.

Walter, N. (1998). *The New Feminism*. London, Little, Brown and Company.

Waterman, P. (2001). *Globalisation, Social Movements and the New Internationalisms*. London, Continuum.

Weber, K. (2006). 'From nuts and bolts to toolkits: Theorizing with mechanisms'. *Journal of Management Inquiry* 15(2): 119–23.

Weber, M. (1971 [1926]). *The Theory of Social and Economic Organisation*. New York, Free Press.

Weller, J. M. and E. L. Quarantelli (1973). 'Neglected characteristics of collective behaviour'. *American Journal of Sociology* 79(3): 665–85.

Welsh, I. (2001). 'Anti-nuclear movements: Failed projects or heralds of a direct action milieu?' *Sociological Research Online* 6(3): www.socresonline.org.uk/6/3/welsh.html>, last accessed 17 September 2012.

Welskopp, T. (2004). 'Crossing the boundaries? *Dynamics of Contention* viewed from the angle of a comparative historian'. *International Review of Social History* 49: 122–31.

Weston, J. (1989). *The Friends of the Earth Experience: The Development of an Environmental Pressure Group*. Oxford, Oxford Polytechnic, School of Planning.

Whitelegg, J. (2000). *Aviation: The Social, Economic and Environmental Impact of Flying*. London, Ashden Trust.

Whiteley, P. and S. J. Winyard (1987). *Pressure for the Poor: The Poverty Lobby and Policy Making*. New York, Methuen and Co Ltd.

Williams, R. H. (2004). 'The cultural context of collective action: Constraints, opportunities and the symbolic life of social movements'. In D. A. Snow, S. Soule and H. P Kriesi (eds) *The Blackwell Companion to Social Movements*. Basingstoke, Wiley Blackwell: 91–115,

Williams Ellis, C. (1996 [1928]). *England and the Octopus*. London, The Beacon Press.

Wilson, G. K. (1990). *Interest Groups*. London, Blackwell.

Wolsink, M. (1994). 'Entanglement of interests and motives: Assumptions behind the NIMBY-theory on facility siting'. *Urban Studies* 31(6): 851–66.

— (2006). 'Invalid theory impededs our understanding: A critique of the persistence of the language of NIMBY'. *Transactions of the Institute of British Geographers* 31(1): 85–91.

Woodsworth, A. (2008). Growth in the UK Climate Direct Action Movement: Experience, Politics and Practice. Unpublished PhD thesis, University of East Anglia.

Worthington, B. (2003). 'The heat is on'. *Change Your World* 43 (October/November): 16–17.

Van Dyke, N. and H. J. McCammon (2010) *Strategic Alliances: Coalition Building and Social Movements*, Minneapolis: University of Minnesota Press.

Xie, L. and H. A. Van Der Heijden (2010) 'Environmental movements and political opportunities: The case of China'. *Social Movement Studies* 9(1): 51–68.

Young, R. C. (1988). 'Is population ecology a useful paradigm for the study of organizations?' *American Journal of Sociology* 94(1): 1–24.

Young, S. (1993). *The Politics of the Environment*. Manchester, Baseline Books.

Zald, M. (1992). 'Looking backward to look forward: Reflections on the past and future of the resource mobilization research programme'. In A. Morris and C. McClurg Mueller (eds) *Frontiers in Social Movement Theory*. New Haven, CT, Yale University Press, Chapter 14.

— (ed.) (1976). *Organizing for Community*. New York, Quadrangle.

Zald, M. and R. Ash (1966). 'Social movement organisations, growth, decay and change'. *Social Forces* 44: 327–40.

Zald, M. and J. McCarthy (1987). *Social Movements in an Organizational Society*, New Brunswick, Transaction Publishers.

Index